How Information Systems Can
Help in Alarm/Alert Detection

How Information Systems Can Help in Alarm/Alert Detection

Edited by

Florence Sèdes

ELSEVIER

First published 2018 in Great Britain and the United States by ISTE Press Ltd and Elsevier Ltd

ISTE Press Ltd
27-37 St George's Road
London SW19 4EU
UK

www.iste.co.uk

Elsevier Ltd
The Boulevard, Langford Lane
Kidlington, Oxford, OX5 1GB
UK

www.elsevier.com

Notices

For information on all our publications visit our website at http://store.elsevier.com/

British Library Cataloguing-in-Publication Data
A CIP record for this book is available from the British Library
Library of Congress Cataloging in Publication Data
A catalog record for this book is available from the Library of Congress
ISBN 978-1-78548-302-8

Printed and bound in the UK and US

Contents

Chapter 5. Information Systems for Supporting Strategic Decisions and Alerts in Pharmacovigilance   133

Yannick BARDIE, Thérèse LIBOUREL

Chapter 6. An Ontologically-based Trajectory Modeling Approach for an Early Warning System.   165

Jamal MALKI, Alain BOUJU

Chapter 9. How Can Computer Tools Improve Early Warnings for Wildlife Diseases? 241
Pierpaolo BRENA, Dominique GAUTHIER, Antoine HUMEAU, Florence BAURIER, Frédéric DEJ, Karin LEMBERGER, Jean-Yves CHOLLET, Anouk DECORS

Introduction

Predicting natural disasters (floods, avalanches, earthquakes, etc.), health monitoring (foot and mouth disease, pesticide pollution, monitoring of marine mammals, etc.), air, sea or land transport, and even space surveillance for preventing the collision of orbital objects involves more and more people within Information Systems, whose aim is to disseminate alerts. By expanding the capabilities and functionalities of such national or international systems, social networks are playing an increasing role in dissemination and sharing actions, for example with the support of systems such as Google Alerts https://www.google.co.uk/alerts which concerns the publication of online content. The micro-blogging platform Twitter also offers a dissemination service, designed to assist government organizations in the dissemination of alerts to the general public. The proper functioning of such systems depends on fundamental attributes such as resilience, rapidity, and responsiveness: any alert must reach the right recipient at the right time and in the right place, while remaining relevant despite the various constraints. These constraints can be linked on the one hand to external influences such as hardware failures, connection issues, a breakdown in communication channels, and on the other hand to confidentiality; for example the collection and use of personal data (with or without the user's consent) or the disparity of access policies (generation according to industrial, technological or security constraints, the management of internal/external policies and so on) between actors. This book opens the discussion on the "delay", dynamics and reactivity of alert systems, integrating problems concerning confidentiality, information filtering, security and citizens' potential usage of new devices and social networks.

Crisis management is one area of application of decision-support systems that is becoming increasingly popular and more widespread with the use of mobile devices. Many works related to the dissemination of alerts and alarms focus on such systems, requiring designers to deal with issues related to the paradigm shift between normal usage modes and crisis usage modes. This requires thinking about how this usage change takes place, for example with feedback or warning measures, decisions or changes in the type of governance. Therefore, the monitoring of information within the information system, its interfaces, and in decision-making and monitoring processes imposes new constraints or rather, on the contrary, the relaxing of some of them (privacy vs. security) such as in the fight against the dissemination of false information (hoaxes, fake news, spam, etc.). Numerous works are emerging in the field of false alarm detection with distorted alerts, those that arrive too late or those that never arrive due to not having filtered through access policies, and these are current software architecture obstacles. At the same time "alerters" scream and try to be heard among the crowded social media sphere: they are identified, but sometimes too late. This phenomenon of criticality can be identified in other areas such as ecology (extinction of species), meteorology (floods, natural hazards) or pharmacovigilance, as illustrated in the chapters of this book.

Detecting the event leading to the triggering of an alarm or alert remains an issue in various areas from nature, i.e. flooding, animals or earthquakes, to software systems. In order to maintain the liveness, dynamicity and reactivity of alarm systems, the warning information must reach the right destination at the right moment and in the right location, and remain relevant for the recipient, in spite of the various and successive filters of confidentiality, privacy, firewall policies, etc. Also relevant in this context are technical contingency issues: material failure, energy or connection defects, the break of channels, independence of information routes and sources etc. The problem is similar with alarms in crowd media, (mis)information vs. rumours: how to make the distinction and to ensure the accuracy of social information?

The aim of this book is to allow collaborating researchers and practitioners working in various areas to give different and complementary points of view on this multidisciplinary domain, gathering and eliciting generic notions, models and processes. Such an original interdisciplinary approach is illustrated by applications in various domains centered on a common concern about data management: information systems, social networks, pharmacy, climate, ecology, etc. Many systems today are based on smartphone technology and mobility, common denominators of citizen alarm management, as well as processes such as crowdsourcing and collaborative annotation, e.g. in natural diseases and medical contexts.

Predicting Alarms through Big Data Analytics: Feedback from Industry Pilots

Christophe PONSARD, Annick MAJCHROWSKI and Mathieu GOEMINNE

This chapter shows how Information Systems can better reach and maintain system-wide strategic goals by enabling the system to achieve predictive reasoning. In the challenging context of big data, such reasoning makes it possible to raise alarms before any negatively impacting consequences have occurred. The chapter concretely details the use of different techniques from big data analytics and presents operational research on real-world examples in two different domains: IT maintenance and clinical pathways. This first chapter gives a relevant introduction to the book by combining software and health contexts. This real-world industrial background is highly valuable in demonstrating the accuracy of the issues we intend to fix in this publication.

Mobility and Prediction: an Asset for Crisis Management

Nicolas GUTOWSKI, Tassadit AMGHAR, Olivier CAMP and Slimane HAMMOUDI

Recommendations have long been a means of helping users select services. In a smart city environment, recommendation algorithms should take into account the user's context in order to improve accuracy. What is the context of a smart city user and how can it be captured? These are the two questions the authors answer in this chapter. After specifying what they understand by context information, they show how the city's mobility pattern can be used to infer rich contextual information. The main objective is to recommend services according to an estimated trajectory of a user in the smart city. Emergency situation and crisis management are among the most crucial dimensions in the design of smart and future cities.

Smartphone Applications: a Means to Promote Emergency Management in France?

Johnny DOUVINET

When signaling an alarm regarding a current danger, real-time information and its diffusion to a large audience are crucial elements in avoiding risk behaviors (traffic jams, panic), indicating dangerous areas, and preparing the responsible actors to manage emergencies. Given the gravity of the situations it announces and the associated responsibility, the services offered by the State and its representatives at local level are the only services in France allowed to monitor, administer, perform and spread alerts throughout the population. Institutional means will not suffice so long as the timeframes necessary for their implementation are restricted by the administrative apparatus. Faced with this need, the fact that individuals are likely to have their smartphones with them and are capable of receiving or sending emergency messages through an application in an environment undergoing a disaster provides an opportunity that the operational actors are aware of and that should be taken advantage of. However, the authorities seem little inclined to change their practices and citizens push the question of risk far from their daily concerns. This chapter deals with the conditions for success and the factors blocking it, and how their use can be promoted in such a context. These challenges become more and more important with the general use of social networks and the potential application of crowdsourcing, having to cope with the quality, veracity, consistency and reliability of people, devices and information.

Mobiquitous Systems Applied to Earthquake Monitoring: the SISMAPP project

Anne-Marie LESAS

Modern smartphones embed sophisticated technologies and could become de facto mobile seismic stations capable of being easily deployed on a large scale at a low cost. The SISMAPP project studies the use of mobiquitous technologies applied to earthquake management. In this chapter, the author presents the prototype of a mobiquitous platform to monitor before, during and after earthquakes based on the use of smartphones and the exploitation of their features: among other things, their inertial sensors are used to detect potentially seismic events and collect motion measurements that could be useful for seismology research and the discovery of new models, their connectivity applied to the establishment of a peer-to-peer mesh to broadcast alerts and make local instant messaging available even when cellular networks are down, and the use of its last known GPS data for victim geolocation. The ubiquity of the Internet combined with the mobility of the smartphone leads to the concept of ATAWAD (AnyTime, AnyWhere, AnyDevice) which allows the individual to access digital services anytime, from anywhere and with any device: the user equipped with a smartphone has become the provider and source of valuable information which can be collected in real time or retrospectively, making this device a powerful tool that can be applied to the field of seismology. The pertinence of their use in the framework of crowdsourced seismic surveillance, with the use of their connectivity and their on-board sensors, relies on the original algorithm the author developed for motion detection of potentially seismic origin and the collection of acceleration measurements captured on the cellphone's triaxial accelerometer designed to monitor and scientifically analyze real-time or postevent data.

Information Systems for Supporting Strategic Decisions and Alerts in Pharmacovigilance

Yannick BARDIE and Thérèse LIBOUREL

This chapter focuses on a current societal issue: how can the quality and the safety of health products available on the market be guaranteed to every citizen? This topic is directly related to the notion of pharmacovigilance and in the broader sense to that of surveillance and strategic foresight (SF). Pharmaceutical accidents of the industrial era bring about issues related to the implementation of a security system in this area, similar to what already exists in the areas of civil nuclear, space and aerospace. The main topic of pharmacovigilance concerns the surveillance of drugs and prevention against the risk of adverse effects resulting from their use, whether this risk is potential or supported by proof. It constitutes a guarantee that remains valid throughout the lifetime of a drug. It thus comes under the umbrella of the science concerned with the detection, assessment, understanding and prevention of adverse effects or any other problem related to drugs.

More specifically, the authors focus on pharmacovigilance implemented by national and international health institutions and pharmaceutical industries during trials and clinical studies.

An Ontologically-based Trajectory Modeling Approach for an Early Warning System

Jamal MALKI and Alain BOUJU

This chapter presents an approach for integrating trajectories of marine mammals, namely seals, in an early warning tracking system. The raw data captured, commonly called trajectories, traces animals from a departure point to a destination as data sequences (sample points captured, time of the capture). Trajectory data are captured by sensors included in a tag glued to the fur of the animal, behind the head. Captured trajectories consist of spatial, temporal and spatio-temporal data. These datasets are organized into sequences. Every sequence, mapped to a temporal interval, characterizes a defined state of the animal. In our application, we consider three main states of a seal: hauling out, diving and cruising. Every state is related to a seal's activity. The authors study the ontological inference complexity, especially in terms of inference space storage complexity, proposing two-tier inference filters on trajectory data. The chapter summarizes works related to early warning and monitoring systems with a focus on those based on trajectory data, and those that define data models taking into account low level and semantic aspects. The domain is modeled from a "trajectory ontology" and a "domain trajectory model".

Toward a Modeling of Population Behaviors in Crisis Situations

Elsa NEGRE, Maude ARRU and Camille ROSENTHAL-SABROUX

Many indicators and sensor systems are designed to produce alerts and reduce disaster risks. Following the development of Information and Communication Technologies (ICTs), it is now faster and more efficient to manage real time data, make maps from geolocalized data and to make assessments based on scenarios that integrate data from different sources. These evolutions have made it possible to improve crisis management systems, developed to support those who respond to disasters (humanitarian, economic, ecological or social for example), and are becoming more and more complex. These crisis management systems help in particular to predict, as soon as possible, the consequences of a crisis and its evolution in a given territory. Despite knowledge and techniques developed in order to minimize or avoid disastrous consequences that crises can produce, they remain, by definition, determined by uncertain phenomena, which are not always considered in these crisis management systems. The vulnerability of territories, the need for coordination among services and the probable behaviors of populations in danger, for example, are sometimes neglected. The authors present their definition of the general concept of behavior based on the state of the art, specifying the stakes of behavior in crisis situations and the most commonly observed reactions. A list of factors is identified as having an impact on behavior in a crisis situation, and each factor is detailed and associated with a list of indicators.

Online Social Network Phenomena: Rumor, Buzz and Spam

Manel MEZGHANI, Mahdi WASHHA and Florence SÈDES

In order to gain insight into information quality problems, the authors discuss in detail three common negative phenomena appearing in Online Social Networks (OSN) with their main strengths and drawbacks. An overview of the concept of buzz, its definition and its detection method is given, and a precise definition for the rumor concept is provided with an overview of current methods. The most common type of noisy information appearing on OSNs with its levels of detection is the third negative phenomenon. Detection and filtering methods intend to cope with these three common negative phenomena appearing in OSNs, i.e. buzz, rumor and spam.

These phenomena remain major problems, decreasing the performance of systems based on social data. The research problems addressed to improve information quality are challenging and a deeper understanding of the motivations of the people who diffuse information on the Internet is needed. Treating noisy data in a big data context is considered as a very important challenge that may be useful in several applications such as recommendations (for example viral marketing), social media, the Internet of Things (IoT), etc.

How Can Computer Tools Improve Early Warnings for Wildlife Diseases?

Pierpaolo BRENA, Dominique GAUTHIER, Antoine HUMEAU, Florence BAURIER, Frédéric DEJ, Karin LEMBERGER, Jean-Yves CHOLLET and Anouk DECORS

This chapter illustrates the contribution of computer tools to enhance the early warning of wildlife diseases by a surveillance network composed of people and organizations operating at a national scale.

First, it describes the current functioning of the SAGIR network and presents the aspects of wildlife disease early warning that are critical to ensure the early detection of epidemiological events. Then, it presents the contribution of the Epifaune database and computing interface in the optimization of real-time data production and management by providing a unified data structure and standardized terminology. Finally, it describes the statistical tools that are currently being investigated to enhance the sensitivity and the specificity of automated alarms for the detection of both disease outbreaks and spatiotemporal disease clusters.

Wildlife diseases are still poorly referenced and environmental factors specific to wildlife disease surveillance constitute a great limiting factor for the filling of these knowledge gaps. The Epifaune database aims to enhance the rapid production and centralization of data that is both reliable and based on standardized structure and terminology.

Moreover, statistical algorithms are currently being developed to enhance the specificity and sensitivity of human detections of epidemiological events. The expertise of local field observers allows for the analysis of mortality and morbidity events across time and space. These tools will hopefully improve the detection of wildlife diseases and allow management measures to be triggered early enough to limit the impact of wildlife pathogens on biodiversity, livestock and humans.

1

Predicting Alarms through Big Data Analytics: Feedback from Industry Pilots

The information explosion our world is currently facing is both a challenge and opportunity for the design of information systems (IS). This chapter shows how ISs can better reach and maintain system-wide strategic goals by enabling the system to achieve predictive reasoning, which enables alarms to be raised before any negative consequences have occurred. This chapter details the use of different practical techniques from big data analytics as well as operational research on real-world examples in two different domains: IT maintenance and clinical pathways.

1.1. Introduction

An IS is an organized system for the collection, organization, processing, storage and communication of information. It groups all of the functions (input, output, transport, processing and storage) of an application as well as databases, technical facilities and manual procedures, which support business processes [ISO 15]. Today's information systems are present everywhere and control many personal and professional aspects of our daily lives. They are also becoming increasingly connected with the physical world due to the development of mobile devices, the emergence of the Internet of Things and cyber-physical systems.

Chapter written by Christophe PONSARD, Annick MAJCHROWSKI and Mathieu GOEMINNE.

A consequence of this increasing connectivity is the information explosion depicted in Figure 1.1. This exponential rate is widely reported as the big data area. To cite a few statistics, it is estimated that 90% of the world's data have been produced in just the last 2 years and the amount of data created by businesses doubles every 1–2 years [ROT 15]. The zettabyte (10^{21} bytes) was reached around 2010 and by 2020, more than 40 zettabytes will be available. An important change also illustrated in the figure is that nowadays most of the data are being generated by devices rather than people.

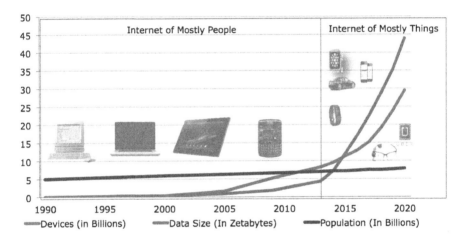

Figure 1.1. *Boom in data collection devices (from [MAS 16]).*
For a color version of the figure, please see
www.iste.co.uk/sedes/information.zip

The main challenges an IS has to face with big data are often summarized by a series of "V" words. In addition to the *Volume* (i.e. the risk of information overload) already mentioned, other data dimensions are the *Variety* (i.e. the diversity of structured and non-structured formats), the required *Velocity* (i.e. highly reactive, possibly real time, data processing), the need for *Visualization* (in order to interpret them easily) and the related *Value* (in order to derive an income) [MAU 16].

An interesting opportunity raised by the volume and quality of data available is that it provides the grounds for reaching a deeper understanding of how the system actually works as well as the extent to which it fails. In this chapter, we will move away from a specific domain and use a system-level approach as defined by goal-oriented requirements engineering frameworks [VAN 01]. Figure 1.2 gives a general overview of the different types of alarms that can be raised through the combined use of monitoring of known threats identified using standard designed time techniques and runtime data analytics that are able to learn from the actual behavior.

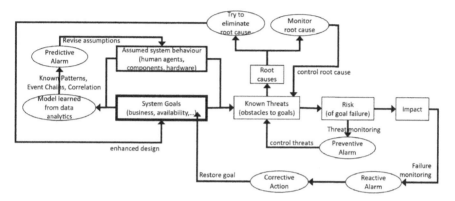

Figure 1.2. *Overview of alarm strategies based on design time analysis and runtime data analytics*

Of course, reaching a higher level of anticipation of all possible problems also requires more information to be collected and the deployment of more powerful data analysis capabilities. Selecting an adequate strategy depends on many factors like cost, technical complexity and efficiency in risk reduction. It usually leads to a mixed solution where simple reactive alarms are raised for goals with limited impact while preventive alarms are generated when some known risk factors are materializing. In addition, certain predictive or even proactive analyses can be carried out to protect against the unknown, especially in systems that have less history or are very open.

This chapter aims to provide practical guidelines to make the best compromise in the design of such a strategy. Our approach will be structured as follows. As a first step, section 1.2 will give some background on the terminology, the goal level system analysis and relevant types of data analytics. It will also present the different technical options available (such as different classes of machine learning, complex event processing approaches, operation research, etc.) but without going into the implementation details. In order to provide more practical insight, section 1.3 gives an overview of our methodology and the case studies that are described in sections 1.4 and 1.5. The first study is on the maintenance of a data center in the IT domain while the second covers the management of a large set of patients engaged in chemotherapy clinical pathways in the health domain. Finally, section 1.6 provides discussions in relation to related work before we draw conclusions in section 1.7.

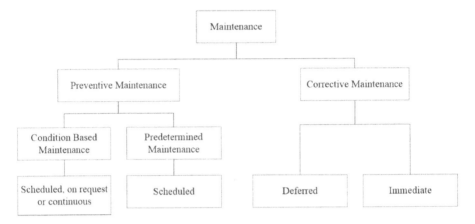

Figure 1.3. *Overview of ISO16350 standard for IT maintenance*

1.2. Background: alarm terminology, system analysis and data analytics

1.2.1. *Terminology for alarm types and processing strategies*

Different domains have defined their own classification of how a system can trigger alarms and react in order to ensure the continuity of system operation, for example:

– for system maintenance, the standard ISO/IEC 16350 defines different maintenance types (illustrated in Figure 1.3) [ISO 15];

– for IT services, the Information Technology Infrastructure Library (ITIL) is widely used [OFF 11];

– in the broader area of business continuity management, many reference frameworks have been published [HIL 10] and standardized [ISO 12], including for SMEs [ENI 10].

Unfortunately, different domains use different terms and sometimes use the same term with different meaning. In order to cope with this, we abstract away from a specific domain. Table 1.1 defines common high level terminology (along with its meaning) related to the main strategies a system can deploy in order to ensure continuity. For each strategy, the table details the kind of alarm that is raised, the typical impact, deployment consideration and a representative example.

Strategy	Reactive	Preventive	Predictive	Proactive
Alarm triggering and processing	The IS detects a goal failure and triggers an alarm that is managed manually or by another system in order to take corrective actions that will restore the goal.	The IS periodically checks for conditions well known for triggering a failure and takes adequate actions in such a case.	The IS learns about past failures and monitors data in order to be able to warn about situations that could degrade and lead to a failure.	The IS provides deeper analysis about possible root causes that should be addressed in order to make the system intrinsically more reliable.
Impact	High: a failure state is reached that possibly impacts the clients in terms of service availability and degrades the confidence in the system.	Controlled: The system is robust to the known class of failures.	Low: The system is able to gain experience from its past behavior to better anticipate a larger class of problems.	Lowest: The system design is progressively improved.
Deployment	Easy: Usually goals are monitored by the system, in the most basic case, the end-user will raise the alarm.	Medium: Threats must be known from an adequate risk analysis (to avoid unnecessary controls resulting in extra costs) and be monitorable.	More difficult: Requires the deployment of data analytics and that the right information is collected.	Hard: Requires in-depth system analysis, design changes and some redeployments.
Example of alarms (IT case study)	Watchdog or customer reporting an application has crashed.	Loss of redundant disk drive on a file server, service operating at 95% of its capacity.	Detection of the application of an OS patch that is correlated with application failure.	Elimination of unreliable components by switching to a more reliable version or implementation.

Table 1.1. *Main continuity strategies and alarm types raised in IS systems*

1.2.2. *Goal-oriented requirements engineering*

Goals encompass, at different levels of abstraction, the various objectives the system under consideration should achieve. Goal-oriented requirements engineering (GORE) is concerned with the use of goals for eliciting, elaborating, structuring, specifying, analyzing, negotiating, documenting and modifying requirements [VAN 01]. We will rely on the KAOS GORE framework, which is fully described in [VAN 09]. In short, the KAOS meta-model is structured around the following four submodels:

– the *object model* defines and interrelates all concepts involved in the goal specifications. Its representation is aligned with UML class diagrams and allows entities, relations, events and agents to be structured;

– the *goal model* structures functional and non-functional goals of the considered system. It also helps identify potential conflicts and obstacles related to goals and reasons about their resolution. It is graphically represented as a goal tree;

– the *agent model* identifies the agents of both the system and the environment as well as their interface and responsibilities. They can be shown as parts of goal trees or in more specific diagrams;

– the *operations model* describes how agents functionally co-operate to ensure the fulfillment of the requirements assigned to them and hence the system goals. Functional flow diagrams are used in Figure 1.4.

We will focus here on the most important part: the goal model. We will illustrate it on the simple introductory example of a repair service. The different levels of abstraction to express goals can range from strategic, high-level goals, like "Maintain[AllServicesAvailable]" down to operational goals such as "Achieve[Normal Equipment Repaired Within One Day]" as depicted in Figure 1.5. High-level goals can be progressively refined into more concrete and operational goals through relationships linking a parent goal to several subgoals, with different conditions of satisfaction either "AND-refinement" (all subgoals need to be satisfied) or "OR-refinement" (a single subgoal is enough, i.e. acceptable alternatives exist). The "WHY" and "HOW" questions can be used to conveniently navigate, respectively, parent and subgoals. The goal decomposition stops when reaching a goal controllable by an agent, i.e. answering the "WHO" question about responsibility assignment. These goals are either requirements on the software or expectations of the behavior of agents in the environment. Domain properties can also be taken into account to justify a refinement, e.g. "a disk drive cannot store more information than its stated capacity".

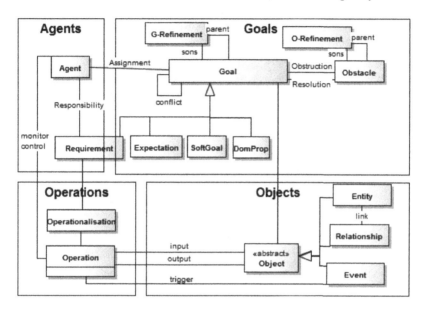

Figure 1.4. *Overview of the KAOS meta-model*

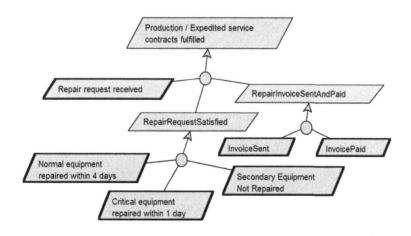

Figure 1.5. *Example of goal refinement in a repair service*

Two key concepts present in the meta-model are important to detail in order to reason about possible goal failure: *Obstacles* and *Conflicts*.

Obstacles represent what could go wrong with the system design [VAN 00]. An obstacle is a precondition for the non-satisfaction of a goal. Just like goals, obstacles can be refined into sub-obstacles using an AND-OR refinement tree. An obstacle diagram for a given goal is a tree that shows how a root obstacle is refined into subobstacles, mainly using OR-refinements. An example of an obstacle refinement to "repair within one day" is depicted in Figure 1.6. Possible reasons for failure could be the lack of spare parts in storage or the lack of resources. In order to avoid goal failure, more elementary obstacles must be addressed.

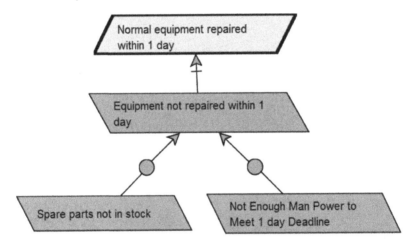

Figure 1.6. *Example of obstacle analysis*

A whole set of strategies are available for this and are fully described in [VAN 00]. These can be grouped in a consistent way with the terminology defined in the previous section:

– *reactive strategies*: goal restoration (e.g. make urgent order to get spare part within the day or send a new piece rather than trying to repair), obstacle mitigation (e.g. call a customer to see if she can tolerate a time period exceeding one day), do nothing (e.g. if impact is expected to be very low);

– *preventive strategies*: obstacle anticipation (when some condition is known to lead to an obstacle, e.g. very few spare parts left), obstacle prevention (i.e. removing it by design, for instance by making sure spare parts or manpower will always be available), goal deidealization (i.e. making a goal less strict, for instance by revising deadline to 4 days for more orders);

– *predictive strategies*: such strategies enable the identification of obstacles by learning from observation of the running system. The result can be analyzed to explicitly enrich the initial model (missed obstacles) or can be kept implicit but nevertheless initiates specific alarms;

– *proactive strategies*: focus on root causes, this is typically achieved by repeating the previous steps multiple times on goals that are progressively introduced to make the system more resilient.

Conflicts correspond to situations where a set of goals cannot be achieved simultaneously. The more general and usual case is that these goals are actually only really conflicting when some specific boundary condition occurs. The correct term as defined is actually a divergence [VAN 98]. An obstacle can be seen as the boundary condition in the degraded case of a divergence involving a single goal. As a generalization of the notion of obstacle, the boundary condition is a key property to monitor and similar strategies to detect and resolve conflicts are also available.

1.2.3. *Overview of data analytics*

Analytics is a multidisciplinary concept and can be defined as the means to acquire data from diverse sources, process them to elicit meaningful patterns and insights, and distribute the results to proper stakeholders [CHE 12, POW 14]. Business Analytics is the application of such techniques by companies and organizations in order to get a better understanding of the level of performance of their business and drive improvements. Three complementary categories of analytics can be distinguished and combined in order to reach the goal of creating insights and helping to make better decisions. These analytics consider different time focus, questions and techniques, as illustrated in Figure 1.7 [MIN 13, SOL 16].

– *Descriptive analytics* looks to the past and the present, and attempts to answer questions such as "What has happened?" and "What is the current state of my system?". It is based on a set of techniques for reviewing the data set(s) in order to understand the data and analyze business performance, such as statistics analysis, classification and categorization methods. It also includes diagnotics analytics that aims to answer questions such as "Why did it happen?", i.e. understanding the reasons for events that happened in the past.

– *Predictive analytics* looks to the future and aims to answer questions such as "What will happen?" and "Why will it happen?" through a set of techniques that analyze current and past data to find out what is most likely to happen (or not). Relevant approaches are based on data mining and machine learning techniques.

– *Prescriptive analytics* also looks at the future but with a focus on providing recommendations and guidance, i.e. answering the questions "What should I do?" and "Why should I do it?". A set of specific techniques such as optimization, simulation and business rules/expert systems are used to propose possible courses of action that can address the risks that are raised by predictive analytics.

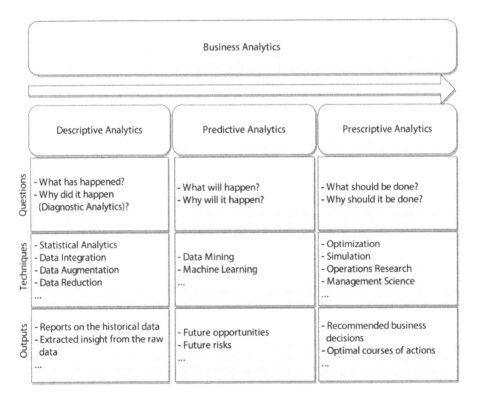

Figure 1.7. *Overview of analytics in terms of questions, techniques and outputs [SOL 16]*

Considering the relation between business intelligence, data mining and big data analytics, business intelligence essentially focuses on structured data and on the production of key performance indicators and dashboards. It therefore mainly focuses on the descriptive dimension. Data mining was developed in the 1990s with the aim of extracting data patterns in structured information (databases) to discover business factors on a relatively small scale. In contrast, big data considers unstructured data and operates on a larger scale [GAN 15]. However, a similarity between business intelligence and big data analytics, from a processing point of view, is that both require the close co-operation of data scientists and management in order to be successful [HOP 15]. Many methodologies and process models developed for data mining and knowledge discovery can actually be applied for big data analytics [MAR 10].

1.3. Overview of the case studies and methodology

The two case studies presented in this section are kept confidential. However, their main characteristics are detailed in Table 1.2 using the three main "*Vs*" and the main challenge they present are highlighted. These case studies are actually part of a larger set of eight case studies conducted according to a common methodology mainly based on CRIS-DM (Cross Industry Standard Process for Data Mining) [SHE 00]. The methodology followed is fully described in [PON 17]. The case studies presented were selected for their variety of alarm triggering and processing strategies, including their use of predictive analytics.

No.	Domain	Volume	Velocity	Variety	Main challenge
1	IT maintenance	About 3,000 servers	High (databases, events, logs, etc.)	Real time	Predictive maintenance, cost optimization
2	Health	900 beds on three sites	Real time	Several sources and formats	Reduce morbidity and mortality, and guarantee confidentiality

Table 1.2. *Main characteristics of our case studies*

Both case studies will be detailed using the following structure:

– domain and problem description;

– high-level objectives, including specific key performance indicators (KPIs);

– global solution architecture;

– illustration on relevant alarm processing of the categories presented in section 1.2.

1.4. Case Study 1: improving IT availability using predictive maintenance

1.4.1. *Domain description*

We consider here the case of a large IT provider managing more than 3,000 servers that are hosting many websites, running applications and storing large amount of related customer data. No matter what efforts are taken, servers are still likely to go offline, networks to become unavailable or disks to crash (generally at unexpected times that are less convenient and more costly to manage like night or weekends). The company considered is currently applying standard incident management and preventive maintenance procedures based on a complete monitoring infrastructure covering both the hardware (network appliances, servers, disks) and the application level (service monitoring).

On the reactive side: incident management tickets can be triggered internally based on a detected failure event and by tracing its impacts on applications and the related client Service Level Agreement (SLA), making it possible to react as quickly as possible. It also provides a helpdesk so clients can initiate tickets from their side. It can then be traced down to the infrastructure level and generally be related to an ongoing operation.

On the preventive side: in order to reduce reactive failures that impact service availability and client satisfaction, scheduled preventive maintenance activities (such as backup of critical data, critical software updates and hardware component cleaning) are regularly applied.

1.4.2. *High-level goals and KPI*

In order to further reduce the number of reactive events and optimize preventive maintenance, the company is willing to develop more predictive maintenance by trying to anticipate the unavailability of the servers in such a way that they can react preventively and, ultimately, prevent such unavailability. In the process, the client wants to diagnose the root causes of incidents and resolve them in order to avoid further possible incidents which could have catastrophic consequences when occurring in a reactive mode.

The ultimate goal is to increase the service availability, the customer satisfaction and also reduce the operating costs. We can consider the following costs:

– maintenance on hardware and software that could be reduced if predictions reduce the intervention time due to better prediction;

– personnel working on these incidents;

– any penalties related to customer SLAs;

– indirect effects on the client's business and its brand image.

1.4.3. *Architecture*

Figure 1.8 shows the high-level architecture with the flow of monitoring events and possible tickets from the helpdesk that are correlated with failure alarms. Reactive and preventive processes are also represented. The proposed extension to this architecture is a predictive component analyzing the flow of monitored events without focusing only on immediate or short-term failure indicators. Instead it can predict punctual events such as unavailability or disk or database down alerts based on other data that seem uncorrelated at first glance but from which actual failure and maintenance-related knowledge can be learned based on innovative techniques such as pattern discovery and machine learning (see section 1.2.3).

1.4.4. *Alarm management*

This section reports on the main benefits of using the predictive component. For confidentiality reasons, the figures in this section are adapted from [DEP 15].

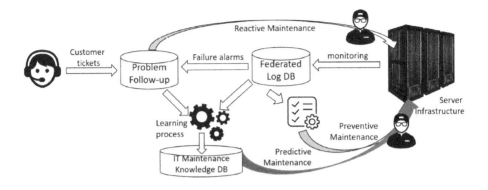

Figure 1.8. *Extended architecture for predictive maintenance*

Lowering reactive alarms

With advanced monitoring capabilities, reactive alarms are rarely related to a completely unforeseen failure. As shown in Figure 1.9, postmortem analysis generally shows a number of anomalies can be observed before the failure actually occurs.

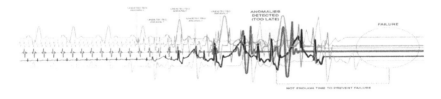

Figure 1.9. *Anomalies detected too late to avoid a reactive behavior.
For a color version of the figure, please see
www.iste.co.uk/sedes/information.zip*

The problem is more about relating the event to the possible failure, knowing what to do to prevent it and having enough time to implement such actions. Such a failure scenario is depicted in Figure 1.9 and calls for using better predictive techniques that can provide better and faster diagnostics, enabling a quicker reaction time.

Better preventive alarms

Preventive alarms can be based on periodic checks, usually based on a threshold (e.g. disk filled at X%) but this does not take the system dynamics into account and therefore could trigger false positives (which imply maintenance costs that could be avoided) or could miss certain events (e.g. disk filling too quickly so no time to react). Better results are achieved using techniques to learn "safe zones" for specific indicators (see Figure 1.10).

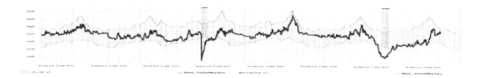

Figure 1.10. *Analysis of historical data. For a color version of the figure, please see www.iste.co.uk/sedes/information.zip*

Another case that requires smarter processing capabilities concerns the need to raise alarms related to the absence of some expected event (e.g. some predicable load not observed, see Figure 1.11).

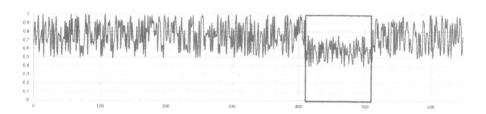

Figure 1.11. *Analytics for a crash detection. For a color version of the figure, please see www.iste.co.uk/sedes/information.zip*

Root cause analysis

A typical indirect cause of failure is a recent modification applied to the system configuration. For example, Figure 1.12 shows a disk thrashing whose cause can be traced to the application of a software patch.

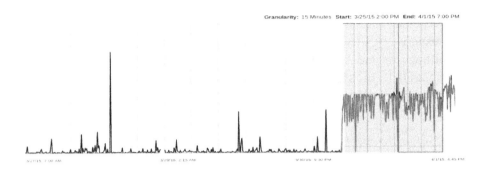

Granularity: 15 Minutes Start: 3/25/15 2:00 PM End: 4/1/15 7:00 PM

Figure 1.12. *Analytics for a process thrashing on disk. For a color version of the figure, please see www.iste.co.uk/sedes/information.zip*

1.5. Case study 2: better care quality through clinical pathways

1.5.1. *Domain description*

In Western countries, due to progress in medical care and ageing of the population, hospitals have to manage increasingly complex and multidisciplinary medical procedures over a growing pool of patients. In the worst case, this results in a decrease in the quality of care received by patients, which does not always match the recommended care process prescribed. A survey of 30 pathologies ranging from osteoarthritis to breast cancer observed that, on average, half of the patients received the recommended medical care [MCG 03].

In order to reduce the variability in clinical processes and improve the quality of care, a level of standardization was proposed through clinical pathways (or care pathways). A clinical pathway is defined as a multidisciplinary specification of the treatment process required by a group of patients presenting the same medical condition with a predictable clinical course [CAM 98]. It describes concrete treatment activities for patients having identical diagnoses or receiving the same therapy.

This standardization usually results in fewer delays, higher quality assurance and reduced costs. As they are strongly oriented on the process description, clinical pathways also maintain a global view on the patient's overall journey, instead of individual doctors having a view exclusively limited to their medical speciality [VAN 13]. The use of clinical pathways has been reported as successful in many therapies, such as arthroplasty [WAL 07] and breast cancer [VAN 13]. Clinical pathways in oncology involve a precise description of the therapeutic workflow and all its ancillary activities as illustrated in Figure 1.13.

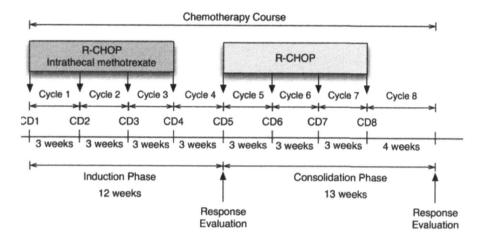

Figure 1.13. *A typical chemotherapy workflow*

The typical workflow for chemotherapy is a sequence of drug deliveries or cycles, typically administered in day hospital. Each cycle is followed by a resting period at home that lasts for a few days to a few weeks. A minimum interval between cycles is required because chemotherapy drugs are toxic and the body needs some time to recover between two drugs deliveries. When following the ideal treatment protocol, the number of cancerous cells is progressively reduced, hopefully to reach a full recovery or cancer remission as shown in Figure 1.14(a). If for some reason, chemotherapy cycles do not closely follow the intended periodicity or if doses are significantly reduced, the treatment efficiency may be suboptimal. In such conditions, cancerous cells may multiply again, which can result in a cancer relapse as shown in Figure 1.14(b).

The more specific case we consider here is a chemotherapy pathway for breast cancer. It involves about 200 patients simultaneously over a period of several months. The typical rest period is 3–4 weeks with up to eight cycles.

This represents thousands of appointments to schedule/reschedule depending on the actual deliveries. Large amounts of medical data are also recorded about the patient's condition (blood analysis, actual delivery, observed reactions). Many process KPIs are defined in relation to key goals, detailed in section 1.5.2. These are recorded to check the quality of the process such as workflow compliance, patient waiting time, staff load and service occupancy ratio. Applying analytics techniques to these data can help to improve these KPI, especially those impacting the treatment effectiveness.

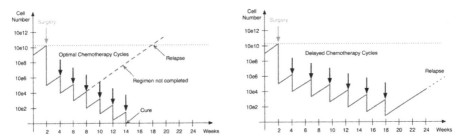

Figure 1.14. *Optimal chemotherapy cycles. For a color version of the figure, please see www.iste.co.uk/sedes/information.zip*

1.5.2. *High-level goals and KPI*

Figure 1.15 shows the high-level goals for the optimal organization of care pathways. The adequate workflow should be enforced for all patients within the recommended deadlines. Ethical principles also require a fair allocation of resources, i.e. every patient deserves optimal care regardless of his/her medical condition or prognosis. The workload should also be balanced to avoid staff having to manage unnecessary peak periods.

Reaching these goals together, of course, requires enough resources to be available and a number of related obstacles (in red) must be addressed. Monitoring the flow of patients joining and leaving the pathway is important. The available workforce is influenced by the staffing level and public holidays, which reduce the slots available for patient treatment. A number of mitigation actions are also identified to better ensure that the workforce is well-adapted. A key agent with a key responsibility in the system is the scheduler that must manage all the appointments. Human agents are not appropriate for this task because the problem is very large and it is difficult to find a solution that simultaneously meets all patients and service constraints. Moreover, planning must constantly be reconsidered to deal with unexpected events and the flow of incoming/outgoing patients. In contrast, a *combined predictive and prescriptive solution is very interesting because it has the capability to ensure optimal care and service operation by also taking into account risks that some patient(s) could be delayed.*

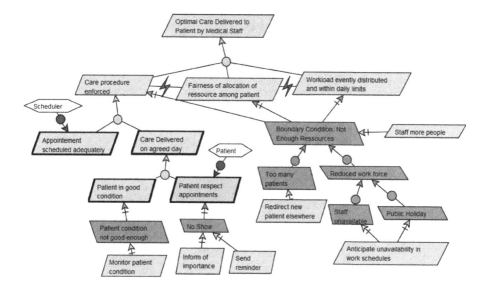

Figure 1.15. *Goal analysis for clinical pathways: strategic goals and main obstacles. For a color version of the figure, please see www.iste.co.uk/sedes/information.zip*

In order to measure the quality of chemotherapeutic cycles, a quantifiable indicator called the "relative dose intensity" (RDI) [LYM 09] was defined. It captures both the fact that the required dose is administered and the timing of the delivery, on a scale from 0% (no treatment) to 100 % (total conformance).

$$\mathrm{RDI} = \frac{\mathrm{Planned\_dose}}{\mathrm{delivered\_dose}} \times \frac{\mathrm{real\_duration}}{\mathrm{planned\_duration}}$$

Medical literature has shown, for a number of cancers, that relapse-free survival is strongly correlated with the RDI. For instance, for breast cancer, a key threshold value is 85 % [PIC 00]. Hence, this indicator has a gauge that should be carefully managed across the whole clinical pathway.

1.5.3. *Architecture*

The architecture of our solution is modular and agent based as depicted in Figure 1.16. It involves many technologies enabling prescriptive analytics such as an optimization solver and a simulator. A complete recording of all events is also ensured by a persister that enables a central orchestrator to also use some predictive analytics.

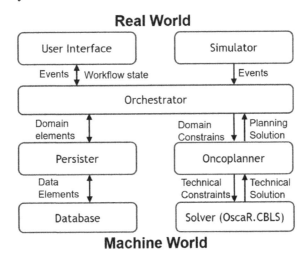

Figure 1.16. *Architecture of the clinical pathway system*

– The *orchestrator* is the central agent. It ensures that the system behavior is consistent with the input received and that the information generated by the system is dispatched to the end user. This component will initiate new scheduling based on incoming events or even anticipated risks.

– The *user interface* captures relevant patient information and gives comprehensive views over the pathways at different levels of detail.

– The *simulator* is used to validate specific what-if scenarios, like the impact of the planned RDI of postponing a patient. It can also be used for running the whole system in a simulation mode.

– The *persister* is in charge of recording all the events and state information about the patients involved in the clinical pathways. It provides a domain representation to the orchestrator and relies on a relational database for persistent storage.

– The *oncoplanner* is responsible for proposing solutions matching the domain constraints sent by the orchestrator when a change requires that an updated solution is computed. It relies on the OscaR.cbls framework. The oncoplanner is an online scheduler, which means that it constantly tries to find a better solution, matching all the constraints and minimizing known risks. It works on the full set of patients, their full planned treatment and the service availability, while appointments are only confirmed for the next cycle. This gives the planner freedom to reschedule the future, preferably beyond the confirmed appointments, as shorter-term replanning would require that patients are contacted and should be done with care and only if absolutely necessary.

1.5.4. *Alarm management*

The operation of clinical pathways is characterized by the occurrence of many events that may be expected or not and thus impact the scheduled behavior. We present here some representative alarms that are generated to deal with the management of possible deviations.

Raising alarms related to patient scheduling problems

A key activity is to confirm the future drug delivery date. This process takes into account both patient and service availabilities. In the normal case, each delivery should be planned as soon as possible, i.e. with a minimal rest period because delays will degrade the RDI. In the case of degradation, an alarm can be raised directly at the planning phase. The agenda user interface can also materialize this constraint by displaying a time window between the earliest possible date (for enough recovery) and the latest date (i.e. with a controlled degradation of the RDI depending on the overall progress of the treatment). Such an alarm and time window is depicted in Figure 1.17.

Raising alarms on anticipated degradation of service operation

Figure 1.18 shows the service workload combining both monitored data (before the red line representing current time) and the anticipated workload (after the red line). Two operational thresholds can be defined: one at 90% means that the service is operating in high load with low margins in case of staff unavailability and another one at 50% means that the service is not filled enough and thus is costly to run. Different scenarios can be identified and simulated, for example enforcing a maximal load and checking the impact on

RDI, redirecting new patients (based on known incoming rate) and increasing the staffing (e.g. if high load becomes frequent).

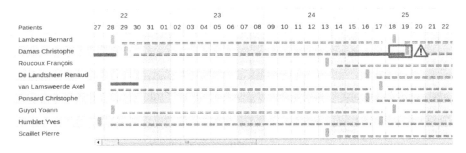

Figure 1.17. *Schedule showing a warning time window for a patient due to availability problems. For a color version of the figure, please see www.iste.co.uk/sedes/information.zip*

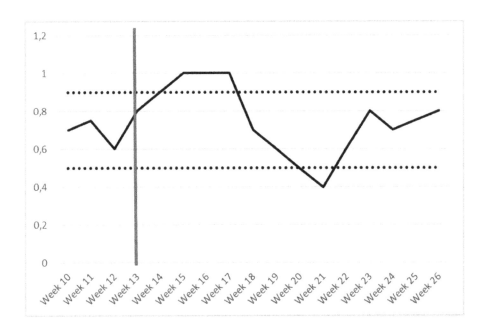

Figure 1.18. *Global monitored and anticipated workload for service operation*

In order to guide the decision-making process, the actual and anticipated RDI curves can be jointly analyzed as shown in Figure 1.19. These curves typically show some degradation of RDI over time but which should stay beyond the target 0.85% limit.

Using predictive analytics

Known adverse events to the normal operation of the system comprise everthing that can impact RDI such as patient no show, medical no go (e.g. due to an immune system being too weak) or patient intolerance resulting in a partial dose delivery. Such events can be correlated with available medical and patient profile data in order to build a predictive model that can empower the system with new capabilities. For example, possible intolerance or interaction with another pathology could be anticipated and solved by selecting an alternative drug cocktail.

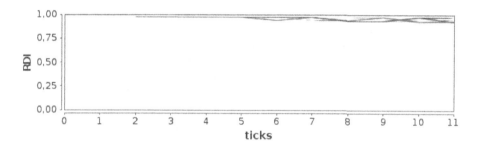

Figure 1.19. *Global monitored RDI for the pool of patients. For a color version of the figure, please see www.iste.co.uk/sedes/information.zip*

1.6. Discussion and related work

This section discusses the outcome of our cases studies in light of some related work. It also takes a step away from the specific case studies to formulate more general guidelines that can be helpful for companies considering the use of big data analytics for better predicting and/or preventing alarms.

Analytics techniques provide a gradual support to strategies for alarm management. This fact is presented in Table 1.1 from the background material and is confirmed by our pilots. Efficient *reactive alarm management* requires a prompt understanding of what is happening and identification possible casual links, such as the fact that the interruption of a service will quickly lead to verification of all the paths a request can follow between the endpoints at the firewall level to the involved application servers and (possibly involved) databases or third-party services. This only requires descriptive analytics. *Preventive alarm management* relies on known statistics that can also be achieved through descriptive analytics, while *preventive alarm management* can naturally benefit from preventive analytics. The most advanced strategy is a *proactive alarm management*, which requires us to go beyond event anticipation and also uses prescriptive techniques to enhance the system on the go.

Descriptive analytics is a prerequisite in all cases because it is about understanding what is happening and identifying the underlying causes of the observed events. In our case, this kind of analytics consists of associating alarms with specific component failures or unexpected events. Without good descriptive analytics, trying to predict or prevent these alarms is useless. Good performance in descriptive analytics requires verification that the system is achieving a good level of monitoring and accuracy: if the observability of some parts of the system is too limited, this part will be a "black box" for which it is impossible to provide precise diagnostics. For example, without precise disk monitoring capabilities, one could say if the network seems fine but some files cannot be accessed "there is a storage problem", without being able to tell precisely which NAS is offline.

From there, it is also hard to accurately predict possible failures like relating a file access retry to a precise disk in prefail phase. The same yields for our second case: the system should have a very accurate picture of the real world from the available resources, as well as the exact status of each patient, to drive the whole clinical pathway in a way that is both predictable and prevents patient RDI degradation. With poor descriptive analytics, the system is only likely to provide poor predictive and prescriptive performances according to the "garbage in – garbage out" principle.

A good alarm management solution is a balanced mixture of different strategies. The simple strategy is the *reactive strategy which only requires descriptive analytics* in order to guide understanding of the problem. As mentioned in Table 1.1, this is easy to achieve but could result in high impact due to the potentially "irreversible" damage caused to the users of the system (e.g. missed deadline, loss of treatment efficiency). It is therefore interesting to start reasoning on such impacts using the obstacle analysis techniques proposed in section 1.2.2 and to *deploy preventive and predictive strategies, typically relying on predictive analytics*, i.e. to analyze each event to assess whether it can impact the strategic goals that are expected to be ensured with a high level of satisfaction and reliability. The ultimate step is to *reach proactive maintenance using prescriptive techniques*, with which the system is constantly trying to improve itself based on proposed action plans that will reduce the margin of possible failures in the future. Of course, the cost of using more advance techniques must be worth the resulting improvement, and in the end it comes down to measuring the risk in terms of impact and likelihood. Issues associated with a small impact can be taken into account in a reactive way, while issues associated with a higher impact should be managed in a predictive way. Mission or safety critical services may require us to deploy highly proactive techniques. In our second pilot, for example, the system is constantly trying to improve itself using an online optimization engine.

Managing the rise in maturity is also important because a company cannot immediately become an expert in advanced analytic techniques. Furthermore, finding the right balance in terms of technical solutions requires a progressive technique deployment to be followed. A logical path consists of following the descriptive to preventive level, and finally prescriptive levels. In fact, different maturity models have been defined for scientific data management practices. They are inspired by the capability maturity model (CMM) and aim to support both assessment and improvement activities [CRO 10, NOT 14]. Such models describe the key process areas and practices necessary for effective management. They are typically organized on a five-level scale, from the lowest "defined" or "ad hoc" level to the highest "optimized" or "breakaway" level. In such a model:

– at level 1, descriptive analytics is used in a very limited and ad hoc way to describe what has happened. Only a few people use it;

– at level 2, descriptive analytics is deployed and used by decision makers to understand what has happened;

– at level 3, predictive analytics helps to make forecasts about what could happen in the system;

– at level 4, predictive analytics is used with some prescriptive analytics to support the optimization of an organization's decision making;

– at level 5, all forms of analytics are deployed to optimize the system processes and are automated where possible.

Defining measurable and progressive objectives

A key driver in deploying a solution that will reach the right balance mentioned is to take into account the value that is obtained by data collection and processing. The right way to measure this value should be defined directly in connection with the business understanding phase and will typically rely on KPIs. Such KPIs are generally already defined and measured in business intelligence solutions, which are often already deployed in companies to achieve a business understanding. Such a solution can naturally be connected with more advanced forms of analytics based on data collection at larger scale and using both structured and semistructured datasets [HOP 15].

Based on such KPI, different improvement strategies can be identified, compared and lead to the definition of a specific business goal. In the case of our first pilot, a highly rewarding goal is to reduce costly emergency repairs performed overnight or during weekends. In our second pilot, a key goal that contributes to increasing both care quality and service performance is to reduce unanticipated no shows. Reasoning on such goals using the proposed techniques will first help to make sure the right kind of data is being monitored. On this basis, analytics will help in consolidating the obstacle analysis and mitigation processes presented in section 1.2.2 by establishing the real risk posed by known obstacles and help in the discovery of unanticipated ones that might, for example, be related to specific patient characteristics or interaction between different pathologies.

The availability of the KPI measurement infrastructure will also make it possible to directly measure the extent to which the targeted goal is met and assess whether it is relevant to invest in more powerful analytics to reach higher levels of satisfaction.

Project management aspects

Last but not least, the successful deployment of big data analytics is not only a matter of technological expertise. While organizations typically view big data technologies as holding a lot of potential to improve their performance and create competitive advantages, many actually fail to achieve these promises. A 2013 report surveying 300 companies about big data revealed that "55% of big data projects don't get completed, and many others fall short of their objectives" [KEL 13]. A Gartner survey conducted online in 2016 reported that many companies remain stuck at the pilot stage: only 15% actually deployed their big data project to production [GAR 16]. Overall these numbers are far worse than the average failure rate of IT projects (about 50% projects challenged and 20% failing according to [STA 15, LAU 15]).

Looking at the cause of such failures, it appears that the main factor is actually not the technical dimension but rather the process and people dimensions, which are thus equally important [GAO 15]. However, looking at the literature, the technical dimension is often emphasized, especially the use of algorithms that produce a sharp analysis. In contrast, much less effort seems to be devoted to methods and tools that can help teams to achieve big data projects more effectively and efficiently [SAL 16]. There is, however, some recent work in that area, identifying key factors for a project's success [SAL 15], stressing management issues [COR 16], insisting on the need for team process methodologies and making a critical analysis of analytical methods [SAL 16]. Based on this observation, we have also described how to address the challenges and the risks of deploying a big data solution within companies to support their business development [PON 17]. In this work, we report on different methods from the literature and show our experience on a series of case studies (including some reported here) in order to reach a successful deployment.

1.7. Conclusion and perspectives

In this chapter, we looked at different strategies for alarm management in software-controlled systems, which means the vast majority of systems in almost all business domains. On the one hand, we have shown how such strategies can be analyzed from a system goal and risk perspective, and, on the other hand, how analytics techniques match different kinds of strategies. In the end, we came up with an interesting unified approach that can be deployed in a stepwise way. It can be controlled by business-level KPIs making sure that deploying the alarm management and related maintenance system will generate value for the company, reduce risk and keep the incurred cost under control. The incremental approach suggested also allows companies to better cope with the technical complexity of mastering advanced analytics which is introduced in later phases, when more complex and combined alarm management strategies are introduced. An informal CCM-like approach was also presented to support this process. We also illustrated our approach on two complementary case studies in two different domains: IT and healthcare. Finally, we came up with a series of practical guidelines that could be useful for any company engaged in the deployment of analytics to better manage how its system is meeting its business goal based on the detection, prevention and reduction of possible alarms, which in the broad sense can be any kind of deviation from the business target.

Our work is still open to different improvements driven by the feedback gained from deployment in other business sectors and by methodological refinements. The presented case studies are parts of a larger deployment experiment covering eight complex pilots, which will cover systems in other sectors, such as space communication systems and pharmaceutical traceability. We expect to gain more insight and also identify new strategies from these sectors that could be generalized to other domains.

1.8. Acknowledgments

We warmly thank CETIC partners from the IT and health domains for sharing their case studies and providing feedback on how to best develop information systems with built-in predictive capabilities, especially in the scope of the PIPAS and PIT Big Data projects from the Walloon Region.

1.9. References

[CAM 98] CAMPBELL H., HOTCHKISS R., BRADSHAW N. *et al.*, "Integrated care pathways", *British Medical Journal*, vol. 316, no. 7125, pp. 133–137, 1998.

[CHE 12] CHEN H., CHIANG R.H.L., STOREY V.C., "Business Intelligence and Analytics: From Big Data to Big Impact", *MIS Q.*, vol. 36, no. 4, pp. 1165–1188, available at: http://dl.acm.org/citation.cfm?id=2481674.2481683, 2012.

[COR 16] COREA F., *Big Data Analytics: A Management Perspective*, Springer International, Basel, 2016.

[CRO 10] CROWSTON K., QIN J., "A Capability Maturity Model for Scientific Data Management: Evidence from the Literature Proceedings of the American Society for Information Science and Technology", vol. 48, no. 1, January 2011, 2010.

[DEP 15] DEPREN M.Ö., *Operational Excellence in IT Service Management*, IBM Business Connect, Istanbul, 2015.

[ENI 10] ENISA, IT business continuity management. An approach for small medium sized organizations, European Network and Information Security Agency, ENISA Report, 2010.

[GAN 15] GANDOMI A., MURTAZA H., "Beyond the hype: Big data concepts, methods, and analytics", *International Journal of Information Management*, vol. 35, no. 2, pp.137–144, available at: http://www.sciencedirect.com/science/article/pii/ S0268401214001066, 2015.

[GAO 15] GAO J., KORONIOS A., SELLE S., "Towards a process view on critical success factors in big data analytics projects", *AMCIS*, 2015.

[GAR 16] GARTNER, "Investment in big data is up but fewer organizations plan to invest", available at: http://www.gartner.com, 2016.

[GOO 11] GOOCH P., ROUDSARI A., "Computerization of workflows, guidelines, and care pathways: a review of implementation challenges for process-oriented health information systems", *Journal of the American Medical Informatics Association*, vol. 18, no. 6, pp. 738–748, November 2011.

[HIL 10] HILES A., *The Definitive Handbook of Business Continuity Management*, John Wiley & Sons, Hoboken, 2010.

[HOP 15] HOPPEN D., "7 characteristics to differentiate BI, Data Mining and Big Data", available at: https://aquare.la/articles/2015/05/01/7-characteristics-differentiate-bi-data-mining-big-data, 2015.

[HUG 15] HUGHES L.D., OWIVEDI Y.K., SIMINTIRAS A.C. *et al.*, *Success and failure of IS/IT projects: a state of the art analysis and future directions*, Springer Int. Publishing, 2015.

[ISO 12] ISO 22301. Societal Security. Business Continuity Management Systems. Requirements, British Standards Institute, London, 2012.

[ISO 15] ISO/IEC 16350-201. Information technology–systems and software engineering–application management, available at: https://www.iso.org/standard/ 57922.html, 2015.

[KAI 15] KAISLER S., ESPINOSA J.A., ARMOUR F. *et al.*, "Advanced analytics for big data", *Encyclopedia of Information Science and Technology, 3rd ed.*, Information Resources Management Association (IRMA), Hershey, 2015.

[KEL 13] KELLY J., KASKADE J., "CIOs & big data: what your IT team wants you to know", available at: http://blog.infochimps.com/2013/01/24/cios-big-data, 2013.

[LYM 09] LYMAN G., "Impact of chemotherapy dose intensity on cancer patient outcomes", *Journal of the National Comprehensive Cancer Network*, vol. 7, no. 1, pp. 99–108, 2009.

[MAR 10] MARISCAL G., MARBAN O., FERNANDEZ C. *et al.*, "A survey of data mining and knowledge discovery process models and methodologies", *Knowledge Eng. Review*, vol. 25, no. 2, pp. 137–166, available at: https://www.bibsonomy.org/bibtex/2b56fb44a3df47f9452f89 e9dd39baf21/dblp, 2010.

[MAR 16] MARYNISSEN J., DEMEULEMEESTER E., Literature review on integrated hospital scheduling problems, Working Papers Department of Decision Sciences and Information Management no. 555258, KU Leuven, Faculty of Economics and Business, 2016.

[MAS 16] MASSON R., "Breakfast with ECS: from toasters to tablets: the technology of IoT", available at: http://emergingtechblog.emc.com/author/robert-bobski-masson, 2016.

[MAU 10] MAURO C., HAPPLE T., SUNYAEV A. *et al.*, "From medical processes to workflows: modeling of clinical pathways with the unified modeling language", *International Conference on Health Informatics (HealthInf)*, Valencia, Spain, 2010.

[MAU 16] MAURO A.D., GRECO M., GRIMALDI M., "A formal definition of big data based on its essential features", *Library Review*, vol. 65, no. 3, pp. 122–135, 2016.

[MCG 03] MCGLYNN E.A., ASCH S.M., ADAMS D. *et al.*, "The quality of health care delivered to adults in the United States", *New England Journal of Medicine*, vol. 348, no. 26, pp. 2635–2645, 2003.

[MIN 13] MINELLI M., CHAMBERS M., DHIRAJ A., *Big data, big analytics: emerging business intelligence and analytic trends for today's businesses*, John Wiley & Sons, Hoboken, 2013.

[NOT 14] NOTT C., "Big data & analytics maturity model", http://www. ibmbigdatahub.com/blog/big-data-analytics-maturity-model, 2014.

[OFF 11] OFFICE C., *ITIL Service Operation 2011 Edition*, The Stationery Office, Norwich, 2011.

[PIC 00] PICCART M., BIGANZOLI L., DI LEO A., "The impact of chemotherapy dose density and dose intensity on breast cancer outcome: what have we learned?", *European Journal of Cancer*, vol. 36, suppl. 1, pp. 4–10, 2000.

[PON 17] PONSARD C., MAJCHROWSKI A., MOUTON S., "Process guidance for the successful deployment of a big data project: lessons learned from industrial cases", *Proceedings of 2nd International Conference on Internet of Things, Big Data and Security*, Porto, Portugal, 2017.

[POW 14] POWER D.J., "Using 'Big Data' for analytics and decision support", *Journal of Decision Systems*, vol. 23, no. 2, pp. 222–228, 2014.

[ROT 15] ROT E., "How much data will you have in 3 years?", available at: http://www.sisense. com/blog/much-data-will-3-years, 2015.

[SAL 15] SALTZ J.S., "The need for new processes, methodologies and tools to support big data teams and improve big data project effectiveness", *IEEE International Conference on Big Data*, Santa Clara, USA, 2015.

[SAL 16] SALTZ J., SHAMSHURIN I., "Big data team process methodologies: a literature review and the identification of key factors for a project's success", *Proceedings of IEEE International Conference on Big Data*, Washington D.C, USA, 2016.

[SHE 00] SHEARER C., "The CRISP-DM model: the new blueprint for data mining", *Journal of Data Warehousing*, vol. 5, no. 4, pp. 13–22, 2000.

[SOL 16] SOLTANPOOR R., SELLIS T., "Databases theory and applications: 27th australasian database conference", CHEEMA M.A. ZHANG W., CHANG L. (eds), *Prescriptive Analytics for Big Data*, Springer International Publishing, Sydney, pp. 245–256, 2016.

[STA 15] STANDISH GROUP, 2015 CHAOS Report, Boston, available at http://www.standishgroup.com, 2015.

[VAN 98] VAN LAMSWEERDE A., LETIER E., DARIMONT R., "Managing conflicts in goal-driven requirements engineering", *IEEE Trans. Softw. Eng.*, vol. 24, no. 11, pp. 908–926, November 1998.

[VAN 00] VAN LAMSWEERDE A., LETIER E., "Handling obstacles in goal-oriented requirements engineering", *IEEE Transactions on Software Engineering,* vol. 26, no. 10, pp. 978–1005, 2000.

[VAN 01] VAN LAMSWEERDE A., "Goal-oriented requirements engineering: a guided tour", *Proceedings of the Fifth IEEE International Symposium on Requirements Engineering,* pp. 249–262, 2001.

[VAN 09] VAN LAMSWEERDE A., *Requirements Engineering – From System Goals to UML Models to Software Specifications*, John Wiley & Sons, Hoboken, 2009.

[VAN 13] VAN DAM P.A. *et al.*, "A dynamic clinical pathway for the treatment of patients with early breast cancer is a tool for better cancer care: implementation and prospective analysis between 2002–2010", *World Journal of Surgical Oncology*, vol. 11, no. 1, p. 70, 2013.

[WAL 07] WALTER F., BASS N., BOCK G. *et al.*, "Success of clinical pathways for total joint arthroplasty in a community hospital", *Clinical Orthopaedics and Related Research*, vol. 457, pp. 133–137, 2007.

2

Mobility and Prediction: an Asset for Crisis Management

Recommendations have long been a means of helping users select services. In a smart city environment, recommendation algorithms should take into account the user's context in order to gain in accuracy. What is the context of a smart city user and how can it be captured? In this chapter, we answer these two questions. After specifying what we understand by context information, we show how the city's mobility pattern can be used to infer rich contextual information. The main objective of our project will be finally to recommend services according to an estimated trajectory of a user in the smart city. For the application domains that we wish to consider in the future, we have emergency situation and crisis management which are among the most crucial dimensions of smart and future city design.

2.1. Introduction

Advances in sensors, Internet of Things (IoT), wireless communication and information infrastructures such as GPS, WiFi and mobile phone technology expose users to an enormous number of mobile services available anytime and anywhere [GEO 16]. Nevertheless, considering the large number of services, it is very difficult for a user to find, among them, those that are the most adapted to his or her current situation. Even worse, the user could, in a given situation,

Chapter written by Nicolas GUTOWSKI, Tassadit AMGHAR, Olivier CAMP and Slimane HAMMOUDI.

be unable to find a relevant service. To overcome these limitations, the smart city, through its communication infrastructure and information system, has the capacity to recommend to the user the most appropriate services at a given moment by considering people, services, providers and locations together. In the same way as recommendation systems have been used in various fields to pick the most adapted service according to a user's previous behaviors and actions, it seems natural to develop mobile recommendation systems to suggest the right services or information to the right mobile users at a given time and place.

Considering such possibilities, the smart city would thus become a real-time information system staging users, contexts and services, and hence contributing to its users' decision-making process. As such, the smart city tends to reduce the gap between the physical and digital worlds. According to the Smart City Council, a smart city can be considered as a city that uses information and communication technologies to enhance its livability, workability and sustainability. Mobile crowd sensing and computing (MCSC) [HAD 14, GUO 15] is a recent paradigm that encompasses the major smart city issues for cross-space and large-scale sensing. It has resulted in the development of various sensing and computing applications in the field of smart cities (e.g. transportation, health care, environment, urban mobility, service providing).

A consequence of the recent development of smart city applications is a growing research activity in several topics such as mobile contextual recommendation systems [LEV 12, ALA 14, BAO 15], urban mobility [MUS 12], context-aware modeling [BOU 09] or big (geo) data processing and analytics [CRA 12]. These studies use various methods including reinforcement learning, filtering and clustering or hidden Markov model, to partially meet the requirements of smart city projects. Moreover, those methods are enhanced by the rise of big data, which constitutes a new approach considered to be the fourth scientific paradigm known as the "big e-science" [HEY 09]. It seems important to take big data into account as smart city projects are generally in line with the first three Vs of big data: volume, velocity and variety of data.

In the context of smart cities, personalization is a real challenge that focuses on bringing the services of a city closer to its citizens. The aim of our project is to design and implement a context-aware service recommendation system for mobile users in a smart city. Our system should be able to deliver the most appropriate service to a given user according to his or her geolocation and surrounding context at a given instant. Considering the fact that the choice of the right service is a time-consuming operation, it may be relevant in some cases to predict where the user will be in the near future in order to deliver a service depending on his or her future location and surrounding context. Thus, an important aspect of our work is to predict the location of mobile users in the smart city [MUS 12]. In addition to real-time processing and its required scalability [WAN 16], we will need to take into consideration other known issues such as the cold start problem [NGU 14], the short lifespan of services [WEI 17] and context awareness [GAL 15].

The contributions of this chapter are threefold:

1) context modeling and sensing, which should allow us to capture and model information that characterizes the situation of users [HAM 15]. Actually, the context model is a centerpiece for the design of a context-aware service recommendation system [LI 10];

2) study and prediction of urban mobility [MUS 12]: The geolocation of the system's users is, of course, a key element in the recommendation of geolocated services. The study of urban mobility patterns in the city should allow us to define a realistic mobility model capable of providing the necessary elements for the prediction of user routes, and thus, their future geolocation;

3) implementation of a prototype: in our case study, we evaluate our approach through the implementation of a proof of concept framework that uses Wifilib, a citywide free WiFi network deployed in Angers. We have developed a prototype (*Ur-MoVe*: Urban Mobility and Visualizer) that used Wifilib connection traces to allow the visualization and prediction of urban geolocation in a city. In this chapter, we discuss and focus on mobility data in the city of Angers.

Among the application domains that we wish to consider in the future, emergency situation and crisis management will be privileged. In fact, emergency response system and resilience are among the most crucial dimensions of smart and future city design due to the increase in various disruptions caused by either natural disasters or conflicts. In this context, the localization and tracking of users would play a vital role, for example in finding a shorter route in an unknown area when rescuing people.

The chapter is organized as follows. Section 2.2 presents the related works concerning research on MCSC applications and focuses more specifically on two aspects: recommendation systems and human mobility analysis. Section 2.3 describes our proposed framework along two dimensions: context and context-aware services, and context-aware recommendation systems. In section 2.4, we detail the analysis of urban mobility by presenting *Ur-MoVe*, the application we have developed and its results about mobility and prediction. Finally, section 2.5 presents our conclusion and perspectives.

2.2. Related works on MCSC

MCSC is a promising new paradigm for cross-space and large-scale sensing [GUO 15]. MCSC is also useful from a computing point of view for recommendation systems. This paradigm encompasses a wide range of applications in very different domains: urban traffic monitoring, environment monitoring, transportation and traffic planning, urban dynamics sensing, location services, mobile recommendation, health care, public safety, etc. In relation to emergency situation and crisis management, as discussed in [GUO 15], a powerful demonstration of MCSC came after the January 2010 earthquake in Haiti [BEN 11]. By analyzing large-scale mobile phone user data on pre- and post-earthquake movement behaviors, they built a model that could predict community responses to future disasters. Similarly, it was reported in [SAK 10] that Twitter could give near real-time reports of earthquakes for a region by analyzing geotagged user posts. Our work focuses on mobile context-aware recommendation and relies on urban dynamics sensing for context capture. It thus focuses on the following two main fields of research:

– *service recommendation*: the main aim of our framework is to recommend services to users in a smart city using their profiles and surrounding environment according to their predicted location;

– *human urban mobility/behavior patterns*: a user's context is closely linked to his or her mobility and to the global mobility in his or her surroundings. Therefore, in order to define context precisely, it seems important to analyze and study the city's urban dynamics in order to extract mobility patterns. For this reason, our framework provides an urban mobility visualization tool. This tool also aims to estimate the next location of a given user. This estimated location of users will serve to enrich their context.

2.2.1. *Service/activity recommendation*

Service/activity recommendation is a wide field of research aimed at providing suggestions of personalized and adaptive services and activities to mobile users. For example, Levandoski *et al.* [LEV 12] proposed a Location-Aware Recommender System (LARS), using location-based ratings to produce recommendations, which are computed using a global item-based collaborative filtering (CF) method. Other works tend to use combined inputs for their recommendation system. For example, Zhang *et al.* [ZHA 13] proposed a unified recommendation model for offline social events group recommendations. They consider location features, social features and implicit patterns simultaneously. CF is considered as the most popular approach used for recommendation systems [WEI 17]. A parallel field of research focuses on learning methods such as reinforcement learning or deep learning. It tends to advocate the use of hybrid methods in recommendation systems. For instance, Wei *et al.* [WEI 17] proposed a hybrid method using CF and deep neural network to find a solution to the cold start problem of items newly added to a preexisting pool of available items. Another approach is to use a reinforcement learning method to solve the historical multi-armed bandit problem coined by Robbins [ROB 52]. For example, this is used for online or mobile user recommendation systems such as those described in [BOU 14]. It uses different algorithms such as ϵ-Greedy and UCB [AUE 02] or contextual bandit problem-solving algorithms such as LinUCB [LI 10], OFUL and CL-BESA [GAL 15]. The use of those methods allows the system to learn from the users and their interests from a pool of information. They rapidly allow the selection of a strategy that discriminates the non-relevant items and selects the items which best match the users. After a sufficient number of rounds, this method tends to the best hidden probability convergence of matches between users and the service that is recommended. Such methods have high computation needs and must perform numerous rounds to reach an acceptable level of precision. For this reason, they seem relevant to be used in a context such as smart cities in which large amounts of data produced by a large number of mobile users provide a sufficient quantity of information in a short time.

2.2.2. *Human mobility*

Human mobility is the subject of many studies that examine the mobility and behavioral patterns in urban areas. Different methods are investigated and used to carry out such studies. For instance, Noulas *et al.* [NOU 12] highlights mobility patterns using the check-in histories of location-based social network (LBSN) users. An LBSN is defined as: *"a type of social networking in which geographic services and capabilities such as geocoding and geotagging are used to enable additional social dynamics"* [BAO 15]. For instance, some studies use LBSNs for the recommendation of social events [QUE 10] to discover user trajectories [ZHE 11] or discover community-based neighborhoods in a city [CRA 12]. However, these methods are only efficient and useful in the case of very active social networks and a large amount of data is required to draw precise and representative conclusions. Other methods have been used to track smartphones and estimate their trajectories in a city using WiFi. For example, Musa and Eriksson [MUS 12] show how Markov chains can be used to estimate trajectories using WiFi connection traces.

In our current case, LBSNs contain too little information concerning the city of Angers for them to be considered. Conversely, the existence of a city wide free public WiFi network with an infrastructure of 250 access points mainly in the city center makes the WiFi connection traces a very rich source of data from which location of users can be studied using methods such as Markov chains.

In section 2.3, we describe our framework, which proposes solutions to several of the issues presented above: data collection and sensing, data visualization and analysis, and implementation of a recommendation system for providing personalized services to mobile users in the smart city.

2.3. Our proposed framework

In the previous section, we introduced the main research studies in the field of MCSC, some illustrated by Citizen Centered Smart City applications. These studies tend to highlight the importance of concepts such as context and context awareness, and recommendation systems that use artificial intelligence methods.

In this section, we describe our proposed context-aware recommendation framework. First, we will define the notions of context and what we understand by context-aware services. We then present the method that we use for the context-aware recommendation of services to mobile users.

2.3.1. *Context and context-aware services*

The notion of context is the centerpiece of adaptability and personalization. Context-aware services constitute a mobile computing paradigm in which applications implemented as combinations of services capture and take advantage of contextual information to deliver the relevant service to the right person at the right time. This contextual information might be user location, date and time of day, neighboring users and devices, and user activity. The definition of context has been the subject of many works [CHE 04, BRO 07]. According to the literature, the most popular definition of the notion of context is given by Dey [DEY 01]: "*Context is any information that can be used to characterize the situation of an entity. An entity is a person, place, or object that is considered relevant to the interaction between a user and an application, including the user and applications themselves*".

Hammoudi *et al.* [HAM 15] synthesized different definitions and approaches for the notion of context and aimed to propose a generic context model that should satisfy the following three requirements:

– it must be sufficiently general to be used by different user-centered mobile applications;

– it must be sufficiently specific to cover the main contextual entities proposed in the state of the art of context-aware mobile applications;

– it must be sufficiently flexible to allow an extension and to take into account new entities specific to a given application domain.

Taking these three requirements into account, we are in line with Dey's definition. However, we can specify the context more precisely in particular for MCSC [GUO 15]. Therefore, the following two remarks are considered in our approach:

1) a user should not need to explicitly interact with the application to receive recommendations. Push recommendations could be very relevant for mobile users and the system could decide to recommend a given service to a user because of his or her context current;

2) the notion of context is defined in a very general manner and would benefit from being more precise. We argue that the *profile* and the *environment* are two main components of the context, and should be precisely defined, specifically for mobile context-aware services.

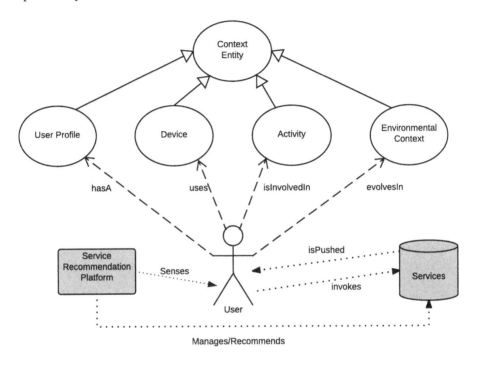

Figure 2.1. *Context model*

Figure 2.1 illustrates our generic context model involving its main components. The figure also shows how our proposed framework interacts with the context model.

With respect to context-aware computing, our model focuses on the *who*, the *where*, the *when* and the *what* (i.e. what activities are occurring) of entities and uses this information to determine *why* a situation is occurring [KRU 09]. Among these 5 Ws, the *why* should thus be deduced from the other four Ws (who, where, when, what) that can be captured: user, location, time and activity.

– *User*: a person who has a state and a profile. A user evolves in an environment and uses computational devices to invoke or receive services. The state of a user can be mobile or static.

– *Profile*: profile is strongly attached to the user and contains the information that describes them. A user can have a dynamic and/or a static profile. The static profile gathers information that describes the user and that does not change over time (or very rarely). It can be their date of birth, name or gender. On the contrary, the user's dynamic profile contains properties that can change over time and reflect her present situation, e.g. the user's goals, preferences, intentions, desires and constraints. For example, the goal of a tourist searching for a restaurant is to have dinner. A profile in this case can give information concerning the tourist's culinary preferences or whereabouts.

– *Activity*: the activity in which the user is involved may be a key to decide which service is relevant to her. However, recognizing users' activities is still a tough task.

– *Device*: the device is the mobile computing system used by the user to access the services and capture contextual information from the environment. The device can obtain information concerning its type (e.g., tablet, laptop, smartphone), the application and the network.

– *Environment*: the environment contains all of the information that describes the surroundings of the user and its device, and that can be relevant for the application. It includes different categories of information such as:

- *spatial context information*, e.g. location, city, destination and speed;

- *temporal context information*, e.g. time, date and season;

- *climatic context information*, e.g. temperature and type of weather.

Our framework senses users in the city in real time and manages a set of services from which it selects specific services, which it recommends to users according to their context. The recommended services can later be explicitly invoked by the user or pushed by the framework to identified users. Now that the notions of context and context awareness have been clarified, we can consider another major component of our framework: the recommendation system.

2.3.2. *Recommendation systems for personalized services*

Recommendation systems have been popular in the field of human–machine interaction for many years. They are decision support tools that offer users personalized suggestions of services or information according to who they are, what they like or what they are used to doing. Because of the growing quantity of available data, information recommendation systems have become very popular on the Internet to recommend products to customers of e-commerce websites, to recommend music or movies to users and to provide personalized travel information to tourists.

In the case of smart cities, the recommendation system should take in consideration the user's context and be a context-aware recommendation system. Just as Internet vendors combine user profile with browsing or buying habits to recommend websites to visit, goods to buy or destinations to visit, our aim here is to also consider data that reflect actual life in the city and thus make the city a part of our information system. The main challenge for the recommendation system is thus to fit the contextual information into traditional mathematical and systematic recommendation algorithms. To solve this issue, we propose to consider our problem as a contextual multi-armed bandit (CMAB) [LI 10] problem and use a reinforcement learning algorithm (*LinUCB*) to solve it.

2.3.3. *Main components of our framework*

According to the descriptions given in sections 2.3.1 and 2.3.2, we have designed a global framework, as shown in Figure 2.2:

– the mobile crowd sensing component senses data related to our mobile users in the smart city;

– the context-aware recommendation system is the "artificial intelligence" component and allows the recommendation of services to mobile users;

– the *Ur-MoVe* component that we have developed for studying the human mobility/activity and predicting the geolocation of users in the city;

– transverse issues, such as security, privacy, performance and energy consumption, will need to be considered in our future work and will be handled by a dedicated component.

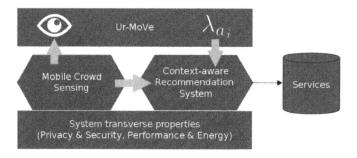

Figure 2.2. *Our proposed framework*

More precisely, data sensed by the mobile crowd sensing component is used as input by both *Ur-MoVe*, to carry out its predictions, and by the context-aware recommendation system, to be used as context data. Moreover, the prediction results obtained by *Ur-MoVe* (referred to as λ_{a_i} in the figure) are also integrated in user contexts and considered by the recommendation system.

2.4. Urban mobility and prediction with *Ur-MoVe*

The global description of our framework has introduced key concepts such as context, context awareness and recommendation systems. In this section, we will concentrate on a critical part of our framework: the *Ur-MoVe* prediction and visualization tool that we have developed. *Ur-MoVe* is able to visualize and predict the mobility of users through the analysis of the traces of their connection to a citywide WiFi network. The data that we have used in this work are provided by the Afone Group, a virtual operator based in Angers, France, which has launched a project called Wifilib – meaning free WiFi – as a continuous WiFi network in the busiest areas of the city of Angers. Using these data, we can monitor and predict various indicators of network activity and urban dynamics. The *Ur-MoVe* tool is the entry point to fully understand the users' mobility and behavior patterns. We believe that by analyzing mobility, we could exhibit contextual information that characterizes users and the city, and thus enhance the accuracy of the recommendation system.

2.4.1. *Urban statistics*

This part of our study is the data storytelling part that every data scientist has to go through in order to explain observed data according to a global purpose. For the time being, our data are profiles and geolocation data and our main purpose is to study urban mobility. We have considered both types of data and interpreted them to understand what they depict in the real world. In order to achieve our analysis, we have developed *Ur-MoVe*, an urban mobility visualizer. It is designed to display statistics and mobility patterns in a city and to give a representation of these statistics over time. For each access point identified by its ID linked to GPS coordinates, the data in the connection logs contain, for each connection, the anonymized users' profiles, the time of disconnection and the session's duration. Thus, our results, presented in Figure 2.3 and described below, are calculated with regard to a specific access point and displayed on the map at its position. When combined with Open Street Map (OSM) geographic information, our results can help us to discover interesting venues such as stores, tram lines and stations, popular places and streets.

1) *Density of connections*: the density of connections for each access point is drawn on a color scale from yellow to dark red according to the number of connected users at the selected time. These first results let us determine popular and busy places and infer specific periods of the day such as peak hours. Moreover, those data can allow us to further calculate flows in the city. They will be necessary when predicting a user's position.

2) *Duration of connections*: an indication of the duration of connections to an access point is very important when categorizing places and streets; for example, as walk-through places or as venues in which people stay for a while. Moreover, in our figure, which focuses on the downtown of Angers, we notice that people stay longer in the main city square *(Place du Ralliement)* or in the commercial streets where there are cafés and shops in which they can stop. On the opposite, streets such as *rue Saint-Laud* appear as connecting ways and connection times in these streets are short.

3) *Main languages*: in our example, we notice French-speaking users in blue and English-speaking users in red. This information could be very relevant to our recommendation system in the case of multilingual services, which should be provided in the users' language. This would be specifically interesting to applications in the field of tourism.

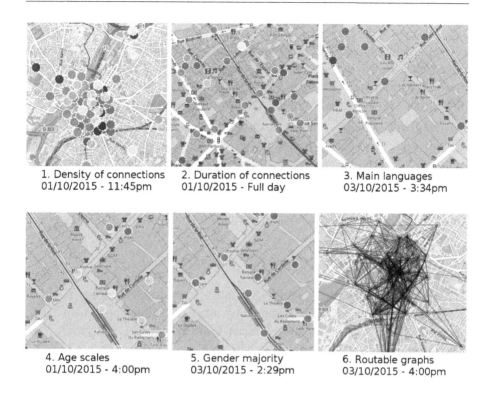

1. Density of connections
01/10/2015 - 11:45pm

2. Duration of connections
01/10/2015 - Full day

3. Main languages
03/10/2015 - 3:34pm

4. Age scales
01/10/2015 - 4:00pm

5. Gender majority
03/10/2015 - 2:29pm

6. Routable graphs
03/10/2015 - 4:00pm

Figure 2.3. *Results (in color) using* Ur-MoVe *from Wifilib
connections. For a color version of the figure, please
see www.iste.co.uk/sedes/information.zip*

4) *Age scales*: ages are grouped by decades from 0 to 100 and are displayed for each access point on a yellow-to-red color scale according to the average age of connected users. If used in combination with the time, this information seems very relevant in order to categorize the neighborhoods according to the ages of people in the area. For example, the figure shows that more people in the age range 40–50 are in the "culture superstore", whereas users in the age range 10–30 tend to *chill out* in the pubs and cafés around the main city square. Of course, this information will be a part of the context given to the recommendation system.

5) *Gender majority*: our application allows us to display connections to the access points by gender. The access point to which a majority of women are connected are represented in pink and turn blue when a majority of men are connected. In the figure, we notice that one category of people tends to be in

places like pubs, cafés or the "cultural superstore", whereas another category prefers shopping areas. The exact number of users belonging to each gender connected to an access point is displayed by clicking on it. This protects us from misinterpretation and should avoid stereotypes. This information will be fully part of the context given to the recommendation system.

6) *Routable graphs*: our data can also be used to infer more complex statistics such as routable graphs that give indications of popular routes in the city. We determine uncertain user routes by considering all connections between times t and $t + 15$ min. From these uncertain user routes, we then infer a graph of popular routes. This statistic is essential to compute results such as top-k routes and transition matrices used in the processing of Markov chains.

2.4.2. *Mobility and prediction*

Using the routable graphs introduced above, more results, such as popular routes, which gives an understanding of urban mobility can be inferred. Moreover, using Markov chains, we can estimate where a new user who connects to a given access point at t_0 will be from $t_0 + 1$ min to $t_0 + 15$ min. In this section, we will describe the methods we used and the results we obtained with regard to those mobility statistics.

2.4.2.1. *Top-k routes*

Our purpose is to highlight the best approximate and rebuilt top-k routes used at a selected date and during a given time span. We believe that this is the entry point to infer mobility patterns in our city. A variety of methods are described in the literature to obtain such results. For example, Han *et al.* and Bao *et al.* [HAN 14, BAO 15] describe how top-k trajectories can be calculated from user LBSN notifications or traveling time [HAN 14, BAO 15]. Most of the proposed methods use graph theory to efficiently solve such problems. Hence, before any further computation, we calculate the routable graph corresponding to a given interval of time.

1) For each user $u \in \mathcal{U}$, compute the list $\mathcal{L}_u$ of all of their route $l \in \mathcal{L}_u$ that occurred in the last 15 min. We consider a user's route l as being a set of at most five of her connections $c_{u,i}; \forall i \in [1; 5]$ to different and adjacent access points a_i ordered by timestamp over the interval $T = [t; t + 15 \min]$. Let $\mathcal{L} = \bigcup_{\forall u \in \mathcal{U}} \mathcal{L}_u$ be the set of all four-segment routes $f_{u,j}; j \in [1; 4]$ for all of the users.

2) Sum each segment flows f_j of all routes $l \in \mathcal{L}$. This corresponds to the user flows between each pair of adjacent access points between t and $t + 15\,\text{min}$. This enables us to highlight the best segments for an approximate and *rebuilt* route l.

3) Compute the top-1 rebuilt route by selecting $\arg\max_{f_j \in l} \sum_{j=1}^{5} f_j$.

For example, Figure 2.4 displays the top-1 route in Angers on October 3, 2015 between 4:00 pm and 4:15 pm. The next top-k routes are computed following the same method.

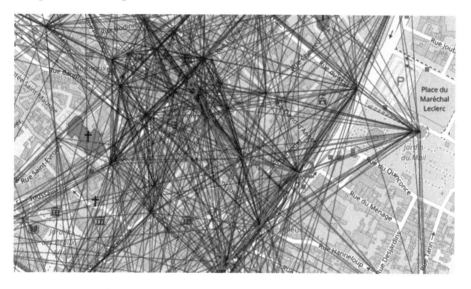

Figure 2.4. *Top-1 route calculated with Wi-Fi connections flows. For a color version of the figure, please see www.iste.co.uk/sedes/information.zip*

Combining our knowledge about the city of Angers and the computed top-k routes, we notice that the top-1 route corresponds to the city's tram line. Moreover, it fits with the main places of attendance and flows that we expected to obtain at the given time and day.

2.4.2.2. Predictions

The main issue of our architecture is predicting the future location of a user in order to recommend a service to them accordingly. Indeed, we believe that users interested in a located service have more chance of using it if going in the right direction (i.e., toward the geolocated service). Hence, it seems relevant to integrate both predicted and current user positions in their context. Moreover, the predicted positions of all users give an indication of the global oriented mobility flows in the city.

To solve our prediction problem, we propose using Markov chains. We consider the set $\mathcal{A} = A \cup \varepsilon$, where A is the set of all access points and ε represents an imaginary access point to which non-reconnecting users are "connected" (those that disconnected from an access point and never reconnected to another) to be the Markov chain states. $\mathcal{A}$ thus represents our countable set of state spaces. We have observed an average duration of connection of 9 min and 2 s and a standard deviation of 82.41 s in the studied population. Moreover, we have shown that there is no correlation between duration of connections and time of day. Hence, when computing the predicted location of a user, it does not seem relevant to consider instants longer than 15 min.

To calculate the Markov transition matrix, we mine the data to compute the flows between any two adjacent access points, the number of stationary users and the number of non-reconnecting users. This allows us to infer the probability of state changes over time. For each new connection of a user to any access point $a_i \in A$ at time t, $Ur\text{-}MoVe$ computes the probability that, at time $t + n; n \in \{0; ..; 15\}$, the user will be connected to another access point $a_j \in A$ such that a_i and a_j are adjacent access point, will still be connected to a_i, or has not reconnected and has thus reached state ε.

Figure 2.5 shows the prediction results obtained by $Ur\text{-}MoVe$ on October 1, 2015 at different times:

– The first experiment (see Figure 2.5(a)) aims to study one of the main connecting roads of Angers – *Avenue Foch* – where we expect people to be moving rather than staying still. In this case, $\{a_{421}; a_{388}; a_{406}; a_{366}\} \in A$ are the studied access points. In this figure we can observe that, after one minute, the predicted next connection of a user connected to a_{406} is estimated to be to a_{366} with a probability of 0.81. We believe that this is due to the characteristics of the road, which is a typical thoroughfare. For our demonstration, we have chosen to observe this place at 8:00 am on a usual working weekday.

– The second experiment (see Figure 2.5(b) aims to study Angers' main city square – *Place du Ralliement* – where people are expected to stay longer and where there is a tram station. In this case, $\{a_{275}; a_{331}; a_{271}; a_{409}\} \in A$ are the studied access points. In Figure 2.5(b) we can observe that, after 15 minutes, the predicted next connection of a user connected to a_{331} is estimated to be to a_{275} with a probability of 0.455 and they are estimated to be still connected to a_{331} with a probability of 0.372. Before predicting the mobility after 15 minutes, we have explored the first 14 minutes which showed that a user connected to a_{331} had more probability of staying connected to a_{331} than of moving to another access point. We believe this to be due to the characteristics of the main city square, which is a typical place where people stay for a while; in a café, shopping or waiting for the tram. For our demonstration, we have chosen to observe this place at 3:00 pm, which, according to our experience of the city, represents a good time for maximizing observations.

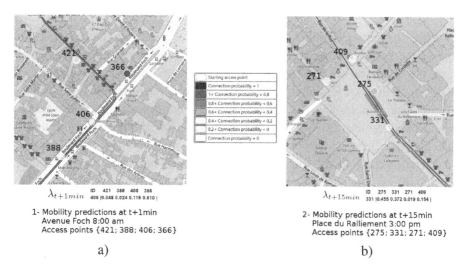

1- Mobility predictions at t+1min
Avenue Foch 8:00 am
Access points {421; 388; 406; 366}

a)

2- Mobility predictions at t+15min
Place du Ralliement 3:00 pm
Access points {275; 331; 271; 409}

b)

Figure 2.5. *Mobility predictions using* Ur-MoVe *from Wifilib connections. For a color version of the figure, please see www.iste.co.uk/sedes/information.zip*

In this study, we have worked with four days, worth of data collected from October 1 to 4, 2015. Thus, it allows us to validate the accuracy of our prediction by comparing it with the real data. Nevertheless, in our final platform, which will be deployed in the smart city, we will work with real-time data. Our predictions will thus need to be dynamically validated and corrected according to observed data.

2.5. Conclusion and future works

In this chapter, we have given a global description of our MCSC framework which aims to provide context-aware recommendations to mobile users in the smart city of Angers. Before fully deploying the framework, it seemed important to analyze urban mobility in the city. With this in mind, we developed *Ur-MoVe* as a first component, a tool that allows the precise analysis and prediction of human mobility using Wi-Fi connection traces.

Ur-MoVe allows the computation and visualization of several urban statistics such as the density of connections or information concerning the profiles of connected users over time and space. Moreover, it allows deeper and more complex analysis such as calculation of top routes and mobility prediction.

After our first experiments and analysis we can conclude that *Ur-MoVe* is one of the main entry points through which to understand the city and, as such, that it will be the centerpiece for further and more complex calculations such as predictions enriching our context-aware recommendation system. Considering what *Ur-MoVe* is able to provide to our system, we believe that it would be interesting to consider its results as part of the context. Indeed, information such as the density of connections or main languages of connected users give an indication of the crowd around an access point and thus could be considered as part of the environmental context used by the recommendation system. Also, a user's predicted future location could be considered to be related to that user's activity (the user's activity would thus either be *static* or *mobile* and in the latter case it would carry an indication as to an estimation of the direction of his or her mobility). Moreover, the transition matrices used for the location predictions, together with the routable graphs and top-k routes, are indicators of the global crowd mobility in the city and should thus enrich the users' environmental contexts.

To the best of our knowledge, only a few works using both location prediction and global urban mobility have been proposed in recommendation systems [ASS 16] and hence this represents an interesting direction of research to explore in our future endeavors.

For our domain of future application, emergency response systems and crisis management are among the most crucial dimensions of smart and future city design, due to the increase in various disruptions caused either by natural disasters, conflicts or terror attacks. Disasters cause great economic and human loss each year throughout the world. In this context, telecommunications play a crucial role in disaster response and management. In particular, the predicted movement of users could be very helpful in emergency situations.

2.6. References

[ALA 14] ALAZAWI Z., ALANI O., ABDLJABAR M.B. *et al.*, "A smart disaster management system for future cities", *Proceedings of the 2014 ACM International Workshop on Wireless and Mobile Technologies for Smart Cities*, pp. 1–10, 2014.

[ASS 16] ASSAM R., SATHYANARAYANA S., SEIDL T., "Infusing geo-recency mixture models for effective location prediction in LBSN", *Proceedings of the 2016 SIAM International Conference on Data Mining*, pp. 855–863, 2016.

[AUE 02] AUER P., "Using confidence bounds for exploitation-exploration trade-offs", *Journal of Machine Learning Research*, vol. 3, pp. 397–422, 2002.

[BAO 15] BAO J., ZHENG Y., WILKIE D. *et al.*, "Recommendations in location-based social networks: a survey", *Geoinformatica*, vol. 19, no. 3, pp. 525–565, 2015.

[BEN 11] BENGTSSON L., LU X., THORSON A. *et al.*, "Improved response to disasters and outbreaks by tracking population movements with mobile phone network data: a post-earthquake geospatial study in Haiti", *PLoS Medicine*, vol. 8, no. 8, p. e1001083, 2011.

[BOU 09] BOUIDGHAGHEN O., TAMINE-LECHANI L., BOUGHANEM M., "Vers la définition du contexte d'un utilisateur mobile de système de recherche d'information", MENGA D., SÈDES F. (eds), *Proceedings of the 5th Francophone Conference on Mobility and Ubiquity Computing, ACM International Conference Proceeding Series*, vol. 394, pp. 25–31, 2009.

[BOU 14] BOUNEFFOUF D., Recommandation mobile, sensible au contexte de contenus évolutifs : Contextuel-E-Greedy, Preprint, arXiv:1402.1986, 2014.

[BRO 07] BROLL G., HUSSMANN H., PREZERAKOS G.N. *et al.*, "Modeling context information for realizing simple mobile services", *Proceedings of the 16th IST Mobile & Wireless Communications Summit*, IEEE, 2007.

[CHE 04] CHEN H., PERICH F., FININ T. *et al.*, "SOUPA: Standard ontology for ubiquitous and pervasive applications", *International Conference on Mobile and Ubiquitous Systems: Networking and Services*, IEEE, pp. 258–267, 2004.

[CRA 12] CRANSHAW J., SCHWARTZ R., HONG J.I. *et al.*, "The livehoods project: utilizing social media to understand the dynamics of a city", *International AAAI Conference on Weblogs and Social Media*, p. 58, 2012.

[DEY 01] DEY A.K., "Understanding and using context", *Personal Ubiquitous Computing*, vol. 5, no. 1, pp. 4–7, 2001.

[GAL 15] GALICHET N., Contributions to multi-armed bandits: risk-awareness and sub-sampling for linear contextual bandits, PhD thesis, Paris-Sud University, 2015.

[GEO 16] GEORGAKOPOULOS D., JAYARAMAN P.P., "Internet of Things: from internet scale sensing to smart services", *Computing*, vol. 98, no. 10, pp. 1041–1058, 2016.

[GUO 15] GUO B., WANG Z., YU Z. *et al.*, "Mobile crowd sensing and computing: the review of an emerging human-powered sensing paradigm", *ACM Computing Surveys (CSUR)*, vol. 48, no. 1, pp. 7:1–7:31, 2015.

[HAD 14] HADERER N., APISENSE: une plate-forme répartie pour la conception, le déploiement et l'exécution de campagnes de collecte de données sur des terminaux intelligents, PhD thesis, Lille 1 University, 2014.

[HAM 15] HAMMOUDI S., MONFORT V., CAMP O., "Model driven development of user-centred context aware services", *IJSSC*, vol. 5, no. 2, pp. 100–114, 2015.

[HAN 14] HAN Y., CHANG L., ZHANG W. *et al.*, "Efficiently retrieving top-k trajectories by locations via traveling tim", in WANG H., SHARAF M.A. (eds), *Databases Theory and Applications*, Springer, 2014.

[HEY 09] HEY T., TANSLEY S., TOLLE K. (eds), "Jim Gray on eScience: a transformed scientific method", in *The Fourth Paradigm: Data-Intensive Scientific Discovery*, vol. 1, Microsoft Research, Redmond, 2009.

[KRU 09] KRUMM J., "A survey of computational location privacy", *Personal and Ubiquitous Computing*, vol. 13, no. 6, pp. 391–399, 2009.

[LEV 12] LEVANDOSKI J.J., SARWAT M., ELDAWY A. *et al.*, "Lars: a location aware recommender system", *2012 IEEE 28th International Conference on Data Engineering*, pp. 450–461, 2012.

[LI 10] LI L., CHU W., LANGFORD J. *et al.*, "A contextual-bandit approach to personalized news article recommendation", *Proceedings of the 19th International Conference on World Wide Web*, ACM, pp. 661–670, 2010.

[MUS 12] MUSA A., ERIKSSON J., "Tracking unmodified smartphones using WiFi monitors", *Proceedings of the 10th ACM conference on embedded network sensor systems*, pp. 281–294, 2012.

[NGU 14] NGUYEN H.T., MARY J., PREUX P., Cold-start problems in recommendation systems via contextual-bandit algorithms, Preprint arXiv:1405.7544, 2014.

[NOU 12] NOULAS A., SCELLATO S., LAMBIOTTE R. *et al.*, "A tale of many cities: universal patterns in human urban mobility", *PLoS One*, vol. 7, no. 5, p. e37027, 2012.

[QUE 10] QUERCIA D., LATHIA N., CALABRESE F. *et al.*, "Recommending social events from mobile phone location data", *2010 IEEE International Conference on Data Mining*, pp. 971–976, 2010.

[ROB 52] ROBBINS H., "Some aspects of the sequential design of experiments", *Bulletin of the American Mathematical Society*, vol. 58, no. 5, pp. 527–535, 1952.

[SAK 10] SAKAKI T., OKAZAKI M., MATSUO Y., "Earthquake shakes Twitter users: real-time event detection by social sensors", *Proceedings of the 19th International Conference on World Wide Web*, ACM, pp. 851–860, 2010.

[WAN 16] WANIGASEKARA N., SCHMALFUSS J., CARLSON D. *et al.*, "A bandit approach for intelligent IoT service composition across heterogeneous smart spaces", *Proceedings of the 6th International Conference on the Internet of Things*, ACM, pp. 121–129, 2016.

[WEI 17] WEI J., HE J., CHEN K. *et al.*, "Collaborative filtering and deep learning based recommendation system for cold start items", *Expert Systems with Applications*, vol. 69, pp. 29–39, 2017.

[ZHA 13] ZHANG W., WANG J., FENG W., "Combining latent factor model with location features for event-based group recommendation", *Proceedings of the 19th ACM SIGKDD International Conference on Knowledge Discovery and Data Mining*, pp. 910–918, 2013.

[ZHE 11] ZHENG Y., ZHOU X., *Computing with Spatial Trajectories*, Springer Science & Business Media, New York, 2011.

Smartphone Applications: a Means to Promote Emergency Management in France?

3.1. Introduction

When signaling an alarm regarding a current danger, real-time information and its diffusion to a large audience are crucial elements in avoiding risk behaviors (traffic jams, panic), indicating dangerous areas, and preparing the responsible actors to manage emergencies. Given the gravity of the situations it announces and the associated responsibility, the services offered by the State and its representatives at local level are the only services in France allowed to monitor, administer, perform and spread alerts throughout the population. However, institutional means RNA (*Réseau National d'Alerte*, National Alert Network) mobile alert systems, local alert systems) will not suffice so long as the timeframes necessary for their implementation are restricted by the administrative apparatus. Faced with this need, the fact that individuals are likely to have their smartphones with them and are capable of receiving or sending emergency messages through an application in an environment undergoing a disaster is an opportunity that the operational actors are aware of and that should be taken advantage of. However, the appropriation of technology (both by individuals and institutions) does not seem to be up to par in terms of the expectations and benefits attributed to it. The authorities seem little inclined to change their practices (the French government finally decided to drop SAIP on June

Chapter written by Johnny DOUVINET.

29th 2018) and citizens push the question of risk far from their daily concerns. With this in mind, what are the conditions for success and the factors blocking it? And how can the use of new technologies be promoted in such a context?

3.2. Investing in smartphones: a contextual opportunity

France is subject to a whole panoply of risks [VEY 04] which encompasses so-called "natural" risks (where chance lies partly at the origin of the material and human damage caused, without being deterministic), among which we can find hurricanes and cyclones (particularly in overseas departments), floods (which have affected 7 million inhabitants in France), earthquakes, landslides, mass movements, forest fires, etc., as well as so-called technological risks (the transport of dangerous materials and nuclear activity), sanitary risks (like dengue fever, which affects 5,000 people per year in French Guiana according to [MIN 04]), social risks (increased number of individuals under the poverty line), and emerging risks such as air pollution (which causes nearly 48,000 premature deaths each year) or bombings.

If a danger is likely to affect the physical integrality of individuals, institutions, or companies, several systems (the RNA, used since 1952, mobile automata, or local alert systems) can be activated by authorities. In a common manner, these tools call for timely responses on the part of the authorities (to ensure the security of goods and persons) but also on the part of the individuals who have to adapt the appropriate behaviors (specific to the nature of the risks at hand). However, institutional alert tools present technical and organizational limits [DOU 17a]. The siren, for example, remains the best-known sound signal [DIR 13] and yet it does not explicitly provide safety directives or even information on the type of danger [DOU 17b]. Various works [BOU 15, IRM 14, VIN 10] have also brought to light the problems encountered in the interpretation of messages mayors not wanting to alert their constituents needlessly or not understanding the different messages sent via various channels, and citizens not always taking the threat seriously (e.g. taking a selfie in front of a raging sea or kayaking during a flood).

In this context, smartphone use seems to provide an obvious opportunity for several reasons. On the one hand, 38% of French citizens in France (i.e. 33 million people) had a smartphone in 2017 (whereas it was barely

12 million in 2011) and the penetration rate will henceforth exceed that of desktop computers. As with the radio or even the television in the 20th Century, smartphones are turning society upside down [LAU 13, SLI 13] as they modify user habits [GOO 07, GRE 15]. This is also a scientific opportunity; a source of debates [BIR 12, CHA 04, GRA 16, LAN 16, PAL 07, WOY 14] that questions researchers, regardless of their field of work. Moreover, the abundance of applications is linked to the participation of several private structures (since 2007 on a global scale), which have developed and deployed their solutions at national and international levels. Without meaning to them more than 30 applications exist concerning risks (see the examples below) in France, and 12 are especially dedicated to facing natural risks. By studying their characteristics, we can quickly separate the applications with an advisory function (which allow the user to locate alerts and have access to instructions related to the danger) from those with a more participatory nature (those which offer the possibility to geolocate the danger in real time, allowing the user to sound the alarm and/or be alerted by other users) [KOU 16a]. Most applications have to be installed on cellphones and depend on an Internet connection to be functional (unless the notifications are sent using the phones' safe mode). They differ in their methods of diffusion (descending or ascending flow), the choices of policy centers, their actions (alert, warning), geographic coverage (local, national), risks, and selected operating systems (OSs) [KOU 16b].

EXAMPLES.– Numerous applications exist in France. To avoid listing them, we will use the first letter of their names. S., put online in 2013, is an application that functions on the basis of markers and intensity scales allowing recognized risks to be described in detail and in real time. The information is managed on a web platform and alerts are sent by an authority to app users in a given perimeter. V. (2013) offers the advantage of informing users based on where they are and not as a function of where they live based on phonebooks. The application is based on the idea that people have fewer and fewer landlines and that they are more and more mobile. M. centralizes the (geolocated) data and is free for users who subscribe to an alert list (based on keywords or event codes). M. notifies users about an event using a simplified formula (simplified terms and GPS coordinates). As for the French government, it launched its own application on June 8, 2016 following the attacks on November 13, 2015 and 2 days after the start of the 2016 European Championship organized in France. SAIP is presented as "quick and efficient" at alerting in case of emergencies (bombings, hydraulic structure breaks, technological or nuclear accidents). It was developed by a private enterprise (at the cost of 400,000 euros) but runs under the aegis of the Ministry of the Interior. Firefighters also have their own application (Géoloc18-112). Other examples can be cited on an international scale, such as the applications N., Fw, and Fi. in the United States, B. in Brazil, S.p. in Poland and Fw in Thailand. All of these applications are very recent, but they are followed attentively by the operational actors who benefit from high popularity rates, particularly for rescue services: firefighters benefit from an average confidence rate of 99% in France (compared with 90% on a global scale), according to a survey published on January 28, 2016 and conducted by the research institution *GfK Verein* in 25 countries on five continents.

3.3. Considerable benefits expected

3.3.1. *A tool to communicate more quickly*

One of the first contributions of smartphone applications is making communication between individuals and authorities easier. In emergencies, smartphone users can receive an alert no matter where they are located, which is a true capital gain compared to institutional tools (like sirens, which have a theoretical sound range of 3 km). They can also bring attention to a locally observed problem (except for the French Public Alert and Information System, SAIP, which currently only works from the top down) or upload different forms of information (e.g. photos, video, GPS coordinates) to decision-making centers. The faster the data are processed, the more quickly institutions can implement on-site action and send the alert to a greater number of individuals [CAV 16]. The Minister of the Interior hopes to reach 5 million inhabitants in France in 2018 with the SAIP application, for example. Since the technological advances of the late 1990s (robust telecommunications networks, increased memory spaces, digital photo devices), cellphones have also moved from the status of simple terminals to helpful tools for transmitting and receiving data [KOU 16b, DOU 17b]. Even if applications have the common goal of bringing individuals and institutions together, their goals are no less heterogeneous: the diffusion method, the fields concerned (expertise, alert, warning), spatial coverage, or the nature of the risk are diversified according to the solutions. Some applications allow us to foresee actions that could reduce the impacts of a crisis on goods and people. It is a matter of reinforcing the ability of communities to make the best choices when managing risks. Other solutions are based on the idea that citizens can become information vectors concerning risks that appear near their living spaces (see the example below)

[GOO 07] or use voice recognition technology to make individuals interact on their own within an environment [MAR 11, MUL 13]. However, all these studies show that smartphones can be used in a wide variety of situations, and with each new version, these terminals are equipped with a growing number of sensors that work in every direction [KOU 16b, DOU 17b].

EXAMPLE.– In the RAVEN project [PAL 12], an experiment was conducted with smartphone application users during an alert to evaluate the pertinence of collecting data in extreme situations, with an intuitive user interface that teaches in detail and is simple to use compared to classic standards (on an Android platform). Users can also create their application collaboratively within a matter of minutes and help to identify the affected areas, making it possible to anticipate the first emergency actions to implement.

3.3.2. *A tool to inform and provide reassurance concerning a situation in progress*

In the case of danger nearby (explosion, muffled sound), it is often difficult to know what really happened. Our first reflexes are thus to get informed (Table 3.1) or to seek information (no matter how incomplete or imprecise) through the classic communication channels or otherwise. Although the communication channels in the 1990s were the television or the radio, other means are preferred today, such as digital media and social networks [CRE 15, GIS 17, VIS 15, DOU 17]. By receiving an alert via an application, individuals feel more secure (particularly if the message comes from State services) and this limits their isolation or uncertainties associated with the situation, which they do not always understand. This is also a way for the authorities to reaffirm their role in risk management (see example below): in fact, they show that they have the event under control, while also controlling information flows.

EXAMPLE.– The SAIP application displays a red screen on the smartphone when its user is located in direct proximity to the crisis (on the condition that the application has been downloaded beforehand). No sound or vibration comes from the device. Only the authorities spread the message. The user can click on the "*Je m'informe*" (more information) button, which indicates the state of the situation and the appropriate actions to take (Figure 3.1). Unfortunately, the French government decided to give up on this application on May 29th 2018, because of the high number of errors, the limits in its application, and a polical choice giving priority to sirens in France.

Figure 3.1. *Communication display sent by the Ministry of the Interior to explain how the SAIP application works*

3.3.3. *A tool to help with individual decisions*

Being aware of the appropriate behaviors to adopt does not mean that it will be possible to apply them in a time of crisis (see *lessons learned*). Smartphone applications can remind users of the safety measures that each individual should adopt and help them make decisions. This is one of the expected advantages, in any case. The perception of risk is involved in this decision-making process and affects the level of acceptability and adherence to prevention tools [KOU 07]. It is this physiological awakening related to fear that prevents more detailed processing of information during emergencies [CRE 08] and the risk emanating from an unknown crisis is difficult to foresee [GIS 17, WIL 06]. By sending out an alert via applications, the goal is also to attempt to reduce cognitive and perceptual biases like the feeling of invulnerability (the danger concerns others and not me), comparative optimism or selective memory, for example, which depend on context, individual variables, social interactions and their role in a time period and culture [SJO 00]. The hope is also to act on the behaviors and motivations of the actors involved by going beyond a rational reading that often sets "good" behaviors against "bad" ones [SJO 00, GIS 17].

LESSONS LEARNED.– A survey conducted by the Vaucluse Prefecture on December 1, 2016 in Sorgues, France, during a civil security exercise (activation of the PPI, Individual Intervention Plan, following a fictitious scenario of a toxic gas leak) allowed the population's knowledge of appropriate behaviors during an alert to be tested and compared to the behaviors actually adopted during the alert. The PPI siren was set off at 8:45 am, then the community siren at 9:15 am. The surveys conducted "on the run" in the streets from 8:45 am to 11:30 am show the lack of seriousness on the respondents' parts (65% were not aware of the exercise) and the difficulty that they have foreseeing and applying what is expected of them (Table 3.1).

In case of alert...	What should you do?	What did you do?
Continue what I'm doing	67	133
Get informed	103	28
Panic	27	5
Call my loved ones	59	6
Look for my children	26	5
Get inside	95	13
Try to escape	54	5

Table 3.1. *Differences between people's knowledge of the appropriate behavior (left) and their actual behavior (right) as evaluated by a survey conducted during a civil security exercise in Sorgues (Vaucluse)*

3.4. Potential that should not be overestimated

3.4.1. *Hard-to-change institutional situations*

A very strict regulatory framework establishes the rules for sending an alert in France [DOU 17b], in particular decree no. 2005-1269 (October 12, 2005) and articles L. 1111-1 and L. 1111-2 of the French Defense Code. Applying policing powers defined in paragraph 5 of the General Code for Territorial Collectives (CGCT), the mayor remains the common law authority in charge of alerting and informing the population during ongoing dangers [DIR 13]. As Director of Rescue Operations, the mayor plans for situations likely to take place in the territory they are responsible for, and they must set the alert and population-informing institutions into motion when faced with such situation [INS 14]. The prefect can also send an alert and take over rescue operations by activating the ORSEC plan when the mayor is no longer capable of managing the situation, when a crisis spreads over multiple communities, or when the various capacities (logistic, technical, financial) at local level are exceeded. Legal texts also regulate the form of these messages, taking into consideration their psychological effect and their social dimension, and list the public or private structures involved in spreading the alert to the populations. The chosen vectors (radio, television, or other structures of interest) are selected according to various criteria: their ability to alert the population, their ability to inform the population, the quality and performance of the message broadcast, their ability to adjust the target of messages and to cover different areas. In view of the precision of this regulatory framework, State services hesitate to turn to applications, due to a lack of practice more so than desire (see *lessons learned*), and in France, this political position does not seem to be evolving. Whereas, the European commission announced on June 4th 2018 that a European SMS geolocation system would be launched in 2019 to alert the population in the case of natural or terrorism-related disasters.

LESSONS LEARNED.– An event (terror attack) that took place on April 21, 2017 in Paris is a good illustration of the degree to which institutions hesitate to turn to applications. SAIP did not send any form of alert, whereas the police prefecture indicated (at 9:06 pm then at 9:20 pm) on Twitter that the Champs Elysées district should be avoided. Numerous Internet users received a push alert at the same time, spread by the media and televisions, reporting the first death at 9:12 pm. People who downloaded the application (750,000 as of January 1, 2017) could not understand SAIP's intention, especially as the Minister of the Interior (the day after) justified not having used the application because the situation was under control (quick arrival of numerous police officers in less than 15 min). For them, the alert would have arrived once the danger had disappeared (according to the statements made by the Minister's speaker). However, this strategy sounds paradoxical: either the situation requires a message to be sent to the population, in which case the use of all existing means is necessary, or the goal is to avoid senseless panic, and in this case, why advise them to avoid one sector on social media? This hesitation is nothing new: even if the alert should have arrived sooner during the attack on July 14, 2016 in Nice (spread at 1:33 am, whereas the attack started at 10:30 pm) (this delay was linked to technical problems that were resolved), it went out much faster in September 2016 (attack mistakenly announced at a church on the Rue Saint-Denis in Paris), was never used during the Paris floods in early June 2016 and remained mute during the Louvre attack on February 3, 2017.

3.4.2. Solutions targeted at various technical problems

Applications have several pitfalls, notably technical ones. On the one hand, they present certain risks concerning people's rights to personal freedom; the recent GDPR law in March 2018 (which aims to reform the use of personal data) strongly reinforces this point. In France, the *Commission Nationale de l'Informatique et des Libertés* (CNIL) advises people to read the conditions of use closely, as these must specify the nature of data collected and their use before installing an application. Information (location, emails, contacts, attached documents, etc.) can be collected without user consent. In 2009, for example, a Swiss company had one of its applications withdrawn from the Appstore because it was transmitting the contact details of users who were then solicited. The traces left behind by sensors are still considered a means of surveillance over movement [FEN 12, OLT 15], and the implementation of GPS/GMS can be used for electronic tracking. Other studies also show permanent access to internal memory [MON 13, XIN 14].

Internet or cellphone communications may also be out of service during a crisis (see example below) due to a blackout or due to the violent nature of the disaster, which may interrupt connections between relays and then between authorities and citizens [DOU 17a]. Even if 3G is present in essentially the entire territory, the connection time and speed are no less disparate on a finer scale. Less than one-third of the French population has access to 4G (July 2016). An alert sent via cellphone also has an intrusive character, which requires a prior user agreement to access geolocation services (Figure 3.1). These are dependent on the OS: even if the mechanism is identical between one OS and another, its implementation may actually be different (the SAIP application is available on Windows 7) and obtaining acknowledgment of receipt from a person in danger is not guaranteed. For S. Gudnitz, head of UNOCHA in the Pacific (2013), the possibility of having rapid access to precise information must be considered a fundamental need and can be a question of life and death. This dependency on networks is worth reconsidering with regard to the potential offered by applications concerning individuals' ability to take control of their safety, but also with regard to the increase in vulnerability that threatens resilience in a broader sense [DOU 17, GIS 17, VIL 15].

EXAMPLE.– During the floods that took place on June 15, 2010 around the Var River (France), firefighters had to get involved (2,357 helicopter rescues between 4:38 pm and 11:15 pm) in multiple areas (over 35 km) while transmissions were nonexistent (no landlines, no GSM, no analogue radios and only a few text messages sent from time to time – according to Colonel E. Grohin SDIS06). More than 200,000 people lost electricity.

Another recent example: on October 3, 2015, more than 300 inhabitants were impossible to reach for 2 h (between 10 pm and midnight), in one neighborhood (le Hameau du Carimaï) in Biot, France, when the locals had more than 2.5 m of water in their houses.

3.4.3. Applications whose utility remains unclear

Data exist on the number of application downloads (which may be skewed because users may have deleted them in the meantime), or on the number of messages sent. However, no detailed, exhaustive study has been conducted on their efficiency [CLE 16, DOU 17a]. To evaluate such efficiency, a study could be conducted, for example, on their adequacy for the timeframe of the danger (a flood comes about within a few hours or a few days, whereas an earthquake or an eruptive toxic cloud can arise within a matter of minutes, as with the 1902 eruption of Mount Pelée), their ability to reach people in a dangerous situation, or to estimate individuals' reception and understanding of the signal. There are also no data on individual reactivity during the alert procedure, nor on the effects brought about by awareness-raising actions performed beforehand in connection with digital tools that have been created since the 1980s. A certain lack of knowledge concerning these applications has also been confirmed at local level (see *lessons learned*), whereas the population remains inclined to use emergency applications [CRE 15]. As such, the efficiency of applications is not well known and more detailed studies would need to be conducted to measure their real utility.

LESSONS LEARNED.– In the framework of a convention with a private partner, Signalalert, a survey was conducted with 622 participants living in four rural communes in the French Var and Vaucluse departments in 2015 to measure the level of knowledge of the application S. in regions that have a "more elderly" population but one exposed to multiple risks. As a whole, the responses confirm a lack of knowledge of alert tools (103 people identified the siren well, which is nevertheless not many out of 622 participants), and particularly of smartphone applications (only 22 knew of their existence). However, 178 respondents confirmed that they had a smartphone (particularly in the age range 20–39) and 102 did not turn this off at night (100% for people over 40). Surprisingly, quite a few inhabitants (135) even felt the need to have a more efficient alert tool via smartphone, and they would be willing to contribute to this by uploading information. This can be explained by the absence of communication concerning these applications; the lack of preparation and training exercises (there is, to our knowledge, no tutorial or training on their use) is an obstacle that is just as discriminatory for us.

3.5. How can we encourage recourse to smartphone applications?

Proven practices (both from an individual and institutional standpoint) are far from reaching the range of expected benefits. With this in mind, what ways can be investigated to increase smartphone application use as we move forward?

3.5.1. *Guiding practices and co-constructing applications*

It is not possible to impose "ready-for-use" tools (material or software) without ensuring dissemination and training. Top-down information has already shown its inefficiency, both in the fields of prevention and alerts [BOU 15, VIN 10]. As such, we must avoid making the same errors. For applications to be used, there must be a sort of "social breeding ground conducive to seizing these tools to fertilize it" [VIL 15]. In this regard, smartphone applications feed discussions around resilience, which defends the idea that a population must be autonomous (it may be isolated in times of danger), united, engaged and concerned by the stakes of its territory before it is capable of using the existing tools. Practices must therefore exist prior to this, which leads to the organization of exercises, role playing, dramatizations based on various scenarios, or the creation of tutorials. We must be prepared for the unimaginable [LAG 03] in order to be aware of our own reactions in case of emergencies or crises. Another aspect deserves our attention: the levels of language are different among the individuals themselves, and they also do not correspond to those of the authorities. By implicating each actor in the application design phase, it would thus be possible to clarify everyone's needs, evaluate the gaps in understanding according to the dangers, understand the obligations (results/means) of institutions and, in short, propose efficient tools that are understood by everyone. Applications constitute an additional means of alert with no real appropriation, and they could disappear as fast as they appeared if nothing changes in the short term.

3.5.2. *Deploying solutions independent of networks*

Network failures (electricity, telecommunications) can often disrupt the reactivity of operational actors, particularly the establishment of connections between victims and rescue workers [BOY 08, COR 12]. Therefore, more flexible solutions must be found, solutions that do not depend on telecommunications or Internet networks. In this regard, "opportunistic networks" (Figure 3.2) seem like an interesting possibility to explore, as smartphones become relays to establish "peer-to-peer" networks between smartphones, all while freeing ourselves from the telephonic network. Routing networks, called BATMAN (Better Approach To Mobile Ad-hoc Networking) or AODV (Ad-hoc On-demand Distance Vector), already exist and are quickly operational when networks are out of service [WIR 11]. Other systems remain functional through Wi-Fi terminals, using mobile devices connected to Wi-Fi as new relay points (Figure 3.2).

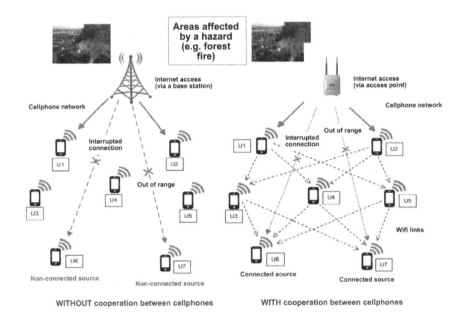

Figure 3.2. *Architecture allowing the absence of connectivity to be overcome with a relay antenna via mobile devices [DOU 15]*

Because of these advances, rescue service actors could be given smartphones and receive information from the operational command center, regardless of the state of networks. This architecture also allows terminals to be converted into interconnected multichannel devices. The conceptual network model is made up of two groups. The first group is composed of users directly connected to the base station with relay antennas. However, due to the effects of the environment on signal quality, some interruptions may give rise to irregular, intermittent connectivity. The second group would then be used as an indirect source based on Wi-Fi connections, thereby creating an ad hoc network. Such a network can be adapted by replacing the base station with a portable, wireless station or a 4G system, capable of being equipped with a satellite and short-range radio connection.

3.5.3. Creating an alert SYSTEM by integrating applications

All alert means are complementary, and there is thus a need to combine them if we want to reach populations that have different usages and references and who also live in different areas, whether in terms of population density, hazards (kinetics, duration, spatial range), population type (percentage of senior citizens or people with limited mobility) or tourism (some communities go from 2,000 to 20,000 inhabitants during the tourist high season). However, current policies more closely resemble actions on a case-by-case basis, with no comprehensive reflection and without displaying a will to harmonize all the existing means. The applications exist, but their use is not codified; telecommunications operators refuse to respect international norms (sending a text message to all cellphones in case of alert), which leaves the field open to private structures that develop other solutions. In the end, one alert SYSTEM (in the true systematic sense) would need to be created in France and this would have to be multirisk, multigenerational and multichannel, such as the *Common Alert Protocol* which has existed in the United States since 2014 or *BeAlert!* created in Belgium in 2016. Many countries (Israel since 2010, the United States, Japan or the Netherlands since 2012, Germany since 2015) also use national alert tools integrating Cell Broadcast technologies, using cellular stations and allowing for the diffusion of warnings via many means. These alert systems allow formats to be made uniform and real use of capitalized information to be guaranteed. However, for this, it would be necessary to change everyone's positions (both individuals and institutions) and to move forward in the same direction, with real political backing.

3.6. Conclusions

Numerous applications dedicated to natural risks have existed in France since 2013. They allow the population to be alerted, informed about the situation in progress or to communicate information about the appropriate behaviors. Despite obvious expectations, State services nevertheless remain reticent to the idea of using these new modern means, the defense of individual data property, the lack of credit attributed to citizen information and the technical barriers being the primary factors blocking progress. The population is also unaware of the existence of these new means of alert, and people will not see their utility so long as it they not faced with a serious crisis. The gap is nevertheless growing larger between the needs of the population (who want efficient and operational emergency applications, which is the case for a great number of them), on the one hand, and institutions that have trouble investing in digital tools and putting applications to use, on the other, because they feel that they are in control of the situation. We must therefore remedy this situation as fast as possible, especially as applications that are created but not used by the authorities will quickly be forgotten by the population, and this is the fear that may exist in relation to SAIP in particular.

3.7. References

[BIR 12] BIRD D., LING M., HAYNES K., "Flooding Facebook, the use of social media during the Queensland and Victorian floods", *Australian Journal of Emergency Management*, vol. 27, no. 1, pp. 27–33, 2012.

[BOY 08] BOYD D., ELLISON N., "Social network sites: definition, history, and scholarship", *Journal of Computer-Mediated Communication*, vol. 13, pp. 210–230, 2008.

[BOU 15] BOUDOU M., Approche multidisciplinaire pour la caractérisation d'inondations remarquables: enseignements tirés de neuf évènements en France (1910–2010), PhD thesis, Paul Valéry University, Montpellier 3 and IRSTEA Lyon, France, 2015.

[CAV 16] CAVALIÈRE C., DAVOINE P.A., LUTOFF C. *et al.*, "Analyser des tweets géolocalisés pour explorer les réponses sociales face aux phénomènes météorologiques extrêmes. Réflexions épistémologiques et verrous méthodologiques", *SAGEO Nice*, France, p. 12, 2016.

[CLE 16] CLEVER TECHNOLOGIES, Livre blanc – L'alerte et l'information des populations en cas de risque majeur, Internal Report, Clever Technologies, 2016.

[COR 12] CORVEY J.W., VERMA S. VIEWEG S. *et al.*, "Foundations of a multilayer annotation framework for Twitter communications during crisis events", *8th International Conference on Language Resources and Evaluation*, Istanbul, Turkey, 2012.

[CRE 05] CREDOC, Le baromètre du numérique, Report for ARCEP and GCE, 2015.

[CRE 10] CRETON-CAZANAVE L., Penser l'alerte par les distances : entre planification et émancipation, l'exemple du processus d'alerte aux crues rapides sur le bassin versant du Vidourle, PhD thesis, University of Grenoble, France, 2010.

[DIR 13] DIRECTION GENERALE DE LA SECURITE CIVILE ET DE LA GESTION DES CRISES, "Guide ORSEC, GT4, Alerte et information des populations", available at: http://www.interieur.gouv.fr/content/download/67723/491852/file/ GUIDE% 20ORSEC-juin%202013-T.G4.pdf, 2013.

[DOU 17a] DOUVINET J., GISCLARD B., KOUADIO J. *et al.*, "Une place pour les technologies smartphones et les Réseaux Sociaux Numériques (RSN) dans les dispositifs institutionnels de l'alerte aux inondations en France?", *Cybergeo: European Journal of Geography*, available at: http://cybergeo.revues.org/27875, 2017.

[DOU 17b] DOUVINET J., JANET B., "Effectiveness of Institutionnal Alert Tools in Flood Forecasting in France", in VINET F. (ed.), *Floods 2*, ISTE Press Ltd, London and Elsevier Ltd, Oxford, 2017.

[FEN 12] FEN-CHONG J., Organisation spatio-temporelle des mobilités révélées par la Téléphonie mobile en Ile-de-France, PhD thesis, Pantheon-Sorbonne University (Paris 1), France, 2012.

[GIS 17] GISCLARD B., DOUVINET J., MARTIN G. *et al.,* "From public Involvement to Citizen-Based Initiatives: How Can Inhabitants Get Organized to Face Floods?", in VINET F. (ed.), *Floods 2*, ISTE Press Ltd, London and Elsevier Ltd, Oxford, 2017.

[GOO 07] GOODCHILD M.F., "Citizens as sensors: the world of volunteered geography", National Center for Geographic Information and Analysis, available at: http:// www.ncgia.ucsb.edu/projects/vgi/docs/position/Goodchild_VGI2007.pdf, 2007.

[GRA 16] GRANELL C., OSTERMANN F.O., "Beyond data collection: objectives and methods of research using VGI and geo-social media for disaster management", *Computers, Environment and Urban Systems,* vol. 59, pp. 231–243, 2016.

[INS 14] INSTITUT DES RISQUES MAJEURS, "Dossier thématique sur l'alerte et l'information à la population, avec 12 onglets présentant les différents systèmes", available at: http://www.irma-grenoble.com/05documentation/, 2014.

[KOU 17] KOUABENAN D.R., CADET B., HERMAND D. *et al.*, *Psychologie du risque: Identifier, évaluer, prévenir*, Editions De Boeck, Brussels, 2007.

[KOU 16a] KOUADIO J., DOUVINET J., "Diffuser une alerte aux crues rapides via une application smartphone en France: de la théorie à la mise en pratique", *Ingénieries des systèmes d'information*, vol. 21, no. 4, pp. 49–66, 2016.

[KOU 16b] KOUADIO J., Les applications smartphone comme outils d'aide à l'alerte face aux crues rapides en France, PhD thesis, University of Avignon, France, 2016.

[LAG 03] LAGADEC P., "Faire face à l'imprévisible", *La Recherche*, vol. 13, pp. 66–69, 2003.

[LAU 13] LAURILA J.K., GATICA-PEREZ D., AAD I. *et al.*, "From big smartphone data to worldwide research: the mobile data challenge", *Persuasive and Mobile Computing*, vol. 9, no. 6, pp. 752–771, 2013.

[MAR 11] MARQUARDT P., VERMA A., CARTER H. *et al.*, "(sp)iPhone: decoding vibrations from nearby keyboards using mobile phone accelerometers", *Proceedings of the 18th ACM Conference on Computer and Communications Security*, pp. 551–562, Chicago, October 17–21, 2011.

[MIN 04] MINISTERE DE L'ENVIRONNEMENT ET DU DEVELOPPEMENT DURABLE (MEDD), Les évènements naturels dommageables en France et dans le monde en 2003, Publications de la DGPR, Ministère de l'Environnement, Paris, p. 39, 2004.

[MON 13] MONTJOYE Y.-A., HIDALGO C.A., VERLEYSEN M. *et al.*, "Unique in the crowd: the privacy bounds of human mobility", *Science Report*, vol. 3, p. 1376, 2013.

[MUL 13] MULHERN N., MCCAFFREY N., BERETTA N. *et al.* "Designing android applications using voice controlled commands for hands free interaction with common household devices", *39th Annual Northeast Bioengineering Conference*, Syracuse, USA, 2013.

[OLT 15] OLTEANU A., VIEWEG S., CASTILLO C., "What to expect when the unexpected happens: social media communications across crises", *18th ACM Conference on Computer-Supported Cooperative Work and Social Computing*, Vancouver, Canada, 2015.

[PAL 07] PALEN L., LIU S.B., "Citizen communications in crisis: anticipating a future of ICT-supported participation", Proceedings of the 2007 Conference on Human Factors in Computing Systems, CH1 2007, San Jose, USA, pp. 727–736, 2007.

[PAL 12] PALMER N., KEMP R., KIELMANN T. *et al.* "Raven: using smartphones for collaborative disaster data collection", *Proceedings of the 9th International ISCRAM Conference*, Vancouver, Canada, 2012.

[SLI 13] SLINGSBY A., BEECHAM R., WOOD J., "Visual analysis of social networks in space and time using smartphone logs", *Persuasive and Mobile Computing*, vol. 9, no. 6, pp. 848–864, 2013.

[SLO 04] SLOVIC P., FINUCANTE M., PETERS E. *et al.* "Risk as analysis and risk as feelings: some thoughts about affect, reason, risk, and rationality", *Risk Analysis*, vol. 24, no. 2, pp. 1–12, 2004.

[SMI 15] SMITH A., RAINIE L., MCGEENEY K. *et al.*, U.S. smartphones use in 2015, report, Pew Research Center, available at: http://www.pewinternet.org/files/2015/03/PI_smartphones_0401151.pdf, 2015.

[VEY 04] VEYRET Y., *Géographie des risques naturels en France*, Editions Hatier, Paris, 2004.

[VIN 10] VINET F., *Le risque inondation. Diagnostic et gestion*, Tec & Doc, Lavoisier, Paris, 2010.

[VOL 15] VOLONTAIRES INTERNATIONAUX EN SOUTIEN OPERATIONNEL VIRTUEL, Guide d'utilisation des médias sociaux en gestion d'urgence (MSGU) pour améliorer la connaissance de la situation et l'aide à la décision, VISOV francophone association, available at: http://www.visov.org/guide-msgu/, 2015.

[WIL 06] WILSON T., "Les risques de blessures et de décès par imprudence lors des inondations", *Responsabilité & Environnement*, vol. 43, pp. 57–63. 2006.

[WOY 14] WOYKE E., *The Smartphone, Anatomy of an Industry*, The New Press, New York, 2014.

4

Mobiquitous Systems Applied to Earthquake Monitoring: the SISMAPP Project

Modern smartphones are embedded with sophisticated technologies and could become *de facto* mobile seismic stations capable of being easily deployed on a large scale at a low cost. With M.A. students specializing in CS "Mobiquitous, Big Data/databases, integrated systems" (MBDS, www.mbds-fr.org) at the University of Nice–Sophia-Antipolis (www.unice.fr) in France and the European-Mediterranean Seismological Centre (EMSC, www.emsc-csem.org) partnership, we have studied the use of mobiquitous technologies applied to earthquake management in the framework of the SISMAPP project. In this chapter, we present our work around the prototyping of a mobiquitous platform to monitor before, during and after earthquakes based on the use of smartphones and the exploitation of their features: among other things, we used their inertial sensors to detect potentially seismic events and collect motion measurements that could be useful for seismology research and the discovery of new models, their connectivity to establish a peer-to-peer mesh to broadcast alerts and make local instant messaging available even when cellular networks are down, and last known GPS data for victim geolocation.

4.1. Introduction

With the advent of the Internet and broadband, digital services have spread from a professional platform to an individual platform with

---

Chapter written by Anne-Marie Lesas.

deployment on the web, opening access to personal computers. Desktop computers, laptops, telephones and mobile devices have become smart: "today somebody who holds a smartphone in her hands has more computing power than the computer that was used for the Apollo mission; the smartphone gives access to much more information than President Kennedy had" [LES 17]. We have entered the era of mobiquity, "a portmanteau word created with the arrival of the mobile Internet at the end of the 1990s" [MIR 11], which designates the ubiquity of the Internet combined with the mobility of the smartphone and the concept of ATAWAD (AnyTime, AnyWhere, AnyDevice) that allows the individual to access digital services anytime, from anywhere and with any device.

Mobile devices equipped with smart systems involve all kinds of electronic components and sensors (accelerometers, gyroscopes, magnetometers, global positioning system (GPS), gravity, lighting, atmospheric pressure, etc.), sparking a new digital revolution: with the possibility of knowing who, where, when, whereabouts and what, the user's identity (with their habits and preferences), space and time ("here and now"), the event raised (motion, stillness, connection, disconnection, etc.), and the result obtained, the user equipped with a smartphone has become the provider and source of valuable information that can be collected in real time or retrospectively. Nearly 1.5 billion smartphones were marketed in 2016[1], making smartphones the most deployed computers in the world: their strong involvement in the user's daily life, their connectivity (cellular network, WiFi, Bluetooth, near field communication (NFC)), and the sophisticated technologies that they implicate make them a powerful tool that can be applied to the field of seismology. Since the release of the first models in 2007, smartphone functionalities have been the subject of scientific interest, and there are numerous references that demonstrate the pertinence of their use in the scope of crowdsourced seismic surveillance with the use of their connectivity and their on-board sensors [FAU 11, OLS 11, DOL 13, NAI 13a, NAI 13b, REI 13, MIN 15].

Since 2013, teams of M.A. students from the MBDS have chosen SISMAPP projects [LES 16a] from among the proposed subjects in order to put into practice the knowledge they have acquired at the University of Nice–Sophia-Antipolis (UNS) for the prototyping of a platform of services

---

1 Source IDC via ZDNet: http://www.zdnet.fr/actualites/chiffres-cles-les-ventes-de-mobiles-et-de-smartphones-39789928.htm.

dedicated to the management before, during and after earthquakes. With the advice of seismology experts from the European-Mediterranean Seismological Centre (EMSC), our work involved creating functional "proof-of-concept" bricks to be applied to the pervasive technologies studied.

In this chapter, we will present the result of research and development (R&D) work performed as part of the SISMAPP project. The sections of this chapter are organized in the following way:

– we will dedicate the first section to briefly discussing our reasons for contributing to prototype computer tools on the subject of earthquake management;

– the second section proposes a synthetic state of the art relative to our work and more particularly to the use of cellphones and shipped sensors applied to the domain of seismology;

– the synthesis of the work performed and applications prototyped is dealt with in the third section;

– in the fourth section, we will present our mobile application and its original algorithm for motion detection of potentially seismic origin and collecting acceleration measurements captured on the cellphone's triaxial accelerometer meant to monitor and scientifically analyze real-time or postevent data;

– in conclusion, we will summarize the advances of our contribution and the extent of our work on two comprehensive projects concerning connected objects into the smart home and smart lampposts;

– finally, we will dedicate a section to thanking the contributors to the SISMAPP project.

4.2. Motivations

Geoscience research networks and institutions for observing and preventing seismic risks have allowed an assessment and a fine-grained location of seismic hazards to be established. However, seismologists are still not capable of anticipating the onset of seismic activity and, each year, earthquakes affect tens of thousands of victims and destroy infrastructures with the catastrophic repercussions that are brought about in the environment, as we saw, for example, during the earthquake on the Pacific

Coast of Tōhoku, Japan in 2011 [BAU 11] and its consequences including the tsunami that caused the nuclear disaster at the Fukushima power plant [INT 15].

Any contribution to the seismology research effort is a humanitarian cause with a general interest concerning every population across the entire planet; at the UNS, on the French Riviera, we are all the more sensitive to the problem given our geographic situation at the center of a network of seismic faults in one of the regions in France most exposed to seismic risks: "The Provence-Alpes-Côte d'Azur region is the French metropolitan region most subject to the seismic risk" [VIR 14]. Already made aware by the devastating earthquake that shook Haiti in 2010 and led to the destruction of Haitian antenna sites set up by the MBDS M.A. program, our contribution to the development of digital tools in the framework of the SISMAPP project and earthquake management came from the source. Our objective with the SISMAPP project and the implementation of technological teaching was to study the state of the art and to propose and implement original software solutions that would be applied and find interest in managing seismic events. Several themes were studied between 2013 and 2016 (see Table 4.1):

– the analysis, collection and interpretation of data from fixed and mobile sensors;

– the automatic correlation of data and real-time instant messaging within a peer-to-peer (P2P) mobile network independent of cellular networks;

– the location of victims and tracking crowd movements during earthquakes;

– the implementation of interactive dashboards and monitoring screens on a dedicated platform.

By presenting the prototyping work that we performed in the framework of the SISMAPP project, we hope to share a perspective on the implementation of mobiquitous technologies for earthquake management and, why not, raise awareness and mobilize the scientific pluridisciplinary and regional university or national community to create an open prototyping platform dedicated to managing earthquakes so as to sustain the successful initiatives and help them evolve. Thus, we hope to make our contribution to designing a system to collect (i.e. from mobile devices, the Internet, sensor networks and connected objects) and process massive heterogeneous referential (e.g. seismic data, sensor measurements, connection and disconnection counts, Internet and social network searches) and participatory data (e.g. textual, vocal, visual, etc.) that would allow indicators to be identified (i.e. observation and learning phase), models to be discovered (i.e. for reproduction and prediction), contextualized automata to be implemented (e.g. broadcasting geographic alerts) and target audiences to be informed (i.e. researchers, authorities, emergency services, populations).

Feature	Interest	Technology
Use of embedded and fixed sensors	Determine if the mobile can become a seismic sensor, detecting anomalies	Mobile development, Android and Windows Phone, manipulation API sensors, signal processing
P2P mesh network communication	Determine if the mobile can: (1) become a distress beacon; (2) corroborate the detection of an earthquake; (3) substitute for telecoms.	Mobile development, Android and iOS, manipulation API WiFi, Bluetooth API, design and implementation of a protocol (connection management) and disconnects from the network, system "heartbeat"
System of notification (mobile to mobile)	Send emergency messages, communicate with the victims	Web and mobile development, handling API GPS, systems grouped or targeted broadcasts, systems of notifications, web sockets (NodeJs, JavaScript), alerts on social networks
Monitoring platform	To provide dashboards for the consultation and viewing data, map the victims, analyze behavior, inform: send messages to mobile phones, etc.	Web development, HTTP, web services (J2EE or Grails), data base relational, structured or semi-structured (NoSQL), graphics and statistics APIs, etc.

Table 4.1. Objectives covered by the SISMAPP project

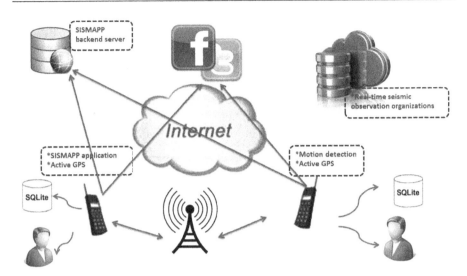

Figure 4.1. *SISMAPP architecture imagined in 2013–2014*

4.3. State of the art

Earthquakes are caused by a brutal rupture in an area accumulating natural terrestrial seismotectonic force or sometimes due to a trigger event (e.g. dam collapse) that brings about motion of the earth. These wave-like or seismic vibrations of the earth spread at a velocity that can reach 10 km/s.

4.3.1. *Seismic waves*

Body waves propagate through the earth's body from the source in every direction. There the *surface waves*, which are high amplitude and low frequency, generate complex interactions with the *body waves* at the surface of the globe.

Body waves: "P" (primary) waves are the fastest, a few seconds before the destructive phase of an earthquake; "S" (secondary) waves result from lateral (perpendicular) displacement in the sense of wave displacement.

Surface waves: shearing waves known as "Love" (LQ) waves and elliptical Rayleigh (LR) waves are the most destructive and are responsible for the collapse of buildings.

4.3.1.1. *Wave measurement: the seismometer*

The seismometer (electronic version of the seismograph, the principle of which is illustrated in Figure 4.2) is a device for measuring the motion of the ground, capable of perceiving and registering terrestrial oscillations on a seismogram that displays the intensity and the frequency of vibrations over time (see Figure 4.2). Paired with the graphic visualization of data, these are also called seismographs. Triaxial seismometers measure vertical and horizontal (lateral and longitudinal) oscillations.

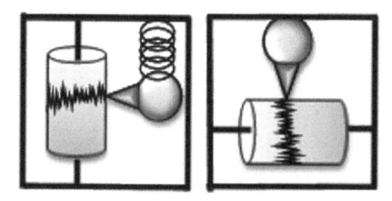

Figure 4.2. *Principle of the mechanical seismograph (vertical and horizontal)*

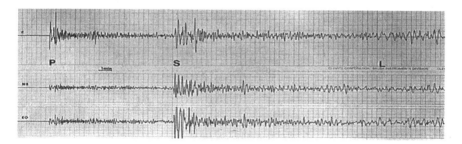

Figure 4.3. *Earthquake record in Mexico,*
August 28, 1973[2]

The magnitude of an earthquake is calculated either using the amplitude logarithm or the period of the signals registered. The "Richter" measurement

_____

2 Source: Larousse, http://www.larousse.fr/encyclopedie/images/Sismogramme/1012217.

is no longer commonly used; it has been expanded by two more sophisticated scales:

– the magnitude of the surface waves M_S is defined for the maximum amplitude of a 20 s period (generally the Rayleigh wave on the vertical axis), using the following formula:

$$M_S = \log_{10} \frac{A}{t} + b + c \ \log_{10} d, \qquad\qquad [4.1]$$

where A is the amplitude of the ground's motion (in microns[3]), d (in degrees) is the distance between the epicenter and the measurement location, and b and c are calibration constants;

– the magnitude m_b (for "body waves") of the body waves can be measured starting with the very first waves (P waves). m_b is defined by the following formula:

$$m_b = \log_{10} \frac{A}{t} + Q(d, h), \qquad\qquad [4.2]$$

where t is the period (in seconds) of the waves with the maximum amplitude A and Q is a calibration function as a function of the epicentral distance d and the focal depth h (in kilometers) of the earthquake.

NOTE.– The intensity that describes the force of an earthquake is based on the perception of witnesses and the extent of damage. It can be measured by the criteria of the European macroseismic scale EMS-98 (Roman numerals ranging from I for imperceptible shaking to XII for a catastrophe that overturns the landscape, an improved derivation of the "Mercalli" scale).

4.3.2. Sensors

Sensors are measurement instruments that transform physical, chemical or organic information into digital data that can be manipulated and interpreted. Nowadays, there are seismic sensors in pocket format, even much smaller. Seismic sensors are sensors (meant to function in a stable environment in normal time) that measure inertia by the acceleration perceived on a spatial axis at a given sample frequency. There are many diverse shapes and technologies used as seismic sensors: sensors to connect

---

3 1 micron = 0.001 mm, distance.

to a USB[4] port, piezoelectric sensors that generate a current when they are in motion or household sensors proposed for commercialization to individuals (e.g. Quake Alarm, Quake Guard, etc.); attached to the wall, they aim to detect P waves to warn inhabitants through the emission of an audio signal in the few seconds that precede destructive waves so that they can seek shelter.

4.3.2.1. MEMS[5] sensors

MEMS sensors are very small economical micro-electromechanical systems (tending toward nanotechnology) that use electromagnetic, thermal, optical, chemical or biological properties to make and collect measurements. MEMS seismic sensors (e.g., Figure 4.4) are generally made up of accelerometers that measure the variations in the force field exercised on a small reference mass (Newton's second law of motion: $F = m.a$), also known as a "seismic mass", moving between slides fixed to the surface of a silicon-integrated circuit. It is thus possible to measure horizontal and vertical accelerations as a function of position. Triaxial sensors return a scalar value (x, y, z) that corresponds to the magnitude of the acceleration vector in a three-dimensional space.

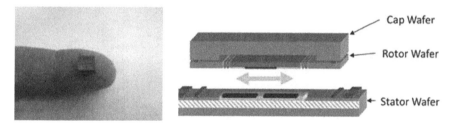

Figure 4.4. *Hewlett Packard[6] MEMS seismic sensor*

NOTE.– The accelerometers used in mobile devices are MEMS sensors.

4.3.2.2. Sudden motion sensors and active protection systems

Recent computers are equipped with active protection systems on the hard drive. These are based on accelerometers and they allow sudden motions to be detected (sudden motion sensors) in order to protect the hard drive by automatically parking the reader heads.

---

4 Universal Serial Bus to connect devices to computers.

5 Micro electro mechanical systems.

6 Source: HP, http://www8.hp.com/us/en/hp-news/press-kit.html?id=1096990

NOTE.– The collaborative program *Quake Catcher Network* (QCN, www. qcn.stanford.edu) and several projects like ShakeMapple [BOS 10], or even MacSeisApp [MEH 16], for example, aim to detect earthquakes by using information assembled by these hard drive protection sensors.

4.3.2.3. *Inertial sensors used in smartphones*

As a standard, most smartphones use inertial sensors measuring motion on three geospatial coordinates relative to the position of the mobile device (vertical, frontal and lateral axes). Motion in the geodesic system is reproduced by translating coordinates (with the help of a quaternion or a rotation matrix). Inertia is measured by physical sensors like the accelerometer, which sends an acceleration vector in $m.s^{-2}$ (gravity included), the magnetometer that sends a direction vector in micro-tesla[7], the gyroscope measuring the Coriolis effect in rad/s reproduced in the form of an angular velocity vector in relation to the axes and the sensor of the atmospheric pressure, measured in hectopascals (millibars).

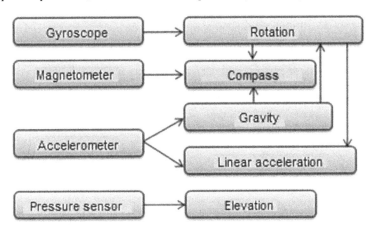

Figure 4.5. *"Fusion" sensors on Android platforms*

Figure 4.6 shows the smartphone rotation axes:

– the azimuth (yaw or pan) corresponds to the rotation of the cellphone around the vertical z axis between $0°$ and $360°$, with the direction North at $0°$, East at $90°$, South at $180°$ and West at $270°$;

---

7 In order to have a correct measurement in time, it is necessary to standardize the signal by taking a sample of the angular velocity, i.e. the square root of the sums of the squares.

– the pitch (tilt) corresponds to the rotation of the cellphone around the lateral x axis downwards or upwards between $-180°$ and $+180°$ ($0°$ in a horizontal position);

– the roll (horizon) corresponds to the rotation of the cellphone around the longitudinal y axis to the right or left between $-90°$ and $+90°$ ($0°$ in a horizontal position).

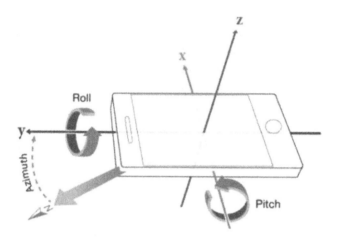

Figure 4.6. *Axes of smartphone geospatial coordinates*[8]

The fusion of information arising from the physical sensors provides a layer of software abstraction of the material whose relations, illustrated in Figure 4.5, show the dependencies of the source toward its use between the physical sensors (left) and the "fusion" sensors (right) based on calculations combining measurements noted by the source sensors. For example, the rotation vector indicates the direction with the azimuth (x coordinates), the pitch and the roll in degrees. The distribution of gravity ($g = 9.81$ m·s^{-2}) over the axes is measured in m·s^{-2} by combining acceleration and direction vector data; linear acceleration is calculated by subtracting gravity from acceleration; and elevation, given in meters, is deduced from the pressure sensor. Motion sensors are present in all modern smartphones, though with application programming interfaces (APIs) that differ in terms of

---

8 Image source: http://www.mathworks.com/matlabcentral/fileexchange/screenshots/9373/original. jpg.

software/middleware and data preprocessing (i.e. data filtering and fusion), e.g. the Windows Phone API cannot be used for background agents[9].

NOTE.– To find the amplitude A (in microns) used to calculate [4.1] and [4.2], it is possible to use the acceleration a measured by the accelerometer (in m/s^2) in the relation [4.4] deduced from [4.3], where x is the position at the moment t:

$$a = \frac{\Delta x^2}{\Delta t^2}$$
[4.3]

$$A = 10^{-4}\sqrt{a\Delta t^2}$$
[4.4]

Mobile platform	Raw data	Prefiltered data	Background application use	Data frequency	Fusion sensors (orientation)
Android	Yes	No (to be coded)	Yes	4 predefined periods: - normal (3 ns) - UI (2 ns) - Game - Fastest	Linear acceleration, gravity, rotation vector, elevation
iOS	Yes	Yes	Yes	To be specified in the code	Altitude, rotation vector, calibrated magnetic fields, compass, gravity, linear acceleration
Windows Phone	Yes	Yes	No	2 ms by default (to be specified)	Compass, inclinometer, orientation

Table 4.2. *Sensor API characteristics as a function of the mobile platform*

Motion sensors are present in all modern smartphones, though with some differences in the cellphone in terms of user friendliness, since sensor APIs differ in terms of the software/middleware layer that avoids the coding of some data preprocessing (i.e. value filtering and combination).

9 Source: http://msdn.microsoft.com/en-us/library/windowsphone/develop/hh202962%28v=vs. 105%29.aspx#BKMK_UnsupportedAPIs.

4.3.2.4. Sources of errors and correction of measurements stemming from inertial sensors

One of the primary concerns in sensor manipulation is the elimination of noise:

– the accelerometer presents a constant gap between the value produced and the real value, which accumulates over time and grows quadratically during double integrations;

– the offset in the gyroscope data causes an angular error that grows linearly over time, but an error in the calibration scale factors can add to the inaccuracy of calculations based on the skewed measurements, which has repercussions on the fusion sensors;

– the magnetometer is subject to interference from environmental magnetic contamination (proximity to ferrous materials).

However, the inaccuracy created by these errors can be significantly reduced after determining the offset coefficient [SHA 11] as a function of the sensor model. The fusion of multisensor data also implements filters from signal processing (e.g. low pass, Kalman, Butterworth) that allow the noise to be eliminated and inaccuracy to be compensated for.

4.3.3. Projects and cellphone applications dedicated to seismic surveillance

Among the cellphone applications designed for Android or iOS that we studied, Berkeley's iShake project [ERV 11, REI 13] and the Japanese i-Jishin prototype [NAI 12 NAI 13a] use sensors on the cellphone when this is placed or charging in a stationary position, whereas other applications are based on data from seismic surveillance systems like those proposed by the USGS[10], the EMSC, Earthquake Early Warning (EEW[11]), etc.; this information comes from stationary seismic stations located all over the plate and it is accessed upon demand with a time delay or in semi-real time (continuous requests with or without alert notifications) and, although the Japanese application Yurekuru Call from the EEW center uses an alert system disseminated via the cellular network, no application exploits

---

10 USA Geological Survey.

11 Japan Meteorological Agency.

peer-to-peer connectivity, which allows for continuous transmission even when cellular networks are unavailable (e.g. after infrastructures are destroyed by an earthquake). The common characteristic of these applications is that they are based on a network of sensors (external or internal to the device); the functionalities differ from one application to another, but they all present one interest: alerting users, confirmation by users, independence from the Internet (cellular network), sharing over social networks or on surveillance platforms (testimonies, videos/photos), recovery information (before, during, after), data exportation to Google Earth or in other formats (e.g. the KML format[12]), visualization on a map (with or without filtering); for example, Facebook has begun to offer an "I'm safe" button that informs families that their loved ones are safe in case of disasters. The EMSC has also unfurled its participatory contribution (crowdsourcing) mobile application meant for a large public, "Last Quake", which is available on iOS and Android platforms, as well as web browsers[13].

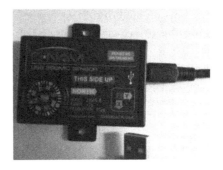

Figure 4.7. *USB O-NAVI seismic sensor*

Since 2008, the QCN project, initiated by Stanford University and the University of California, Riverside, uses the open calculation software "Berkeley Open Infrastructure for Network Computing" (BOINC[14]) developed by the University of Berkeley in California (USA). BOINC is an

---

12 Keyhole Markup Language is an XML language based on beacons, meant to manage the display of geospatial data in Geographic Information Systems (GIS).

13 Available for download on Google Play for Android: https://play.google.com/store/apps/details?id=org.emsc_csem.lastquake, on iTunes for iOS: https://itunes.apple.com/fr/app/lastquake/id890799748?mt=8, and as a plug-in version for web browsers: http://www.emsc-csem.org/service/Browser-extension/Lastquake.

14 See https://boinc.berkeley.edu.

open-source platform hosting scientific projects whose principle is to use part of the computer system resources from volunteer users connected to the network (use of computer sensors or those connected to the computer, e.g. the USB sensor in Figure 4.7). The trustworthiness of interpretations of data gathered by the QCN network has been demonstrated with data collected by inertial sensors placed within buildings in Christchurch, New Zealand [COC 11]: these data, compared to data from the GeoNet seismic stations (www.geonet.org.nz) in the region during the October 18 2011 earthquake, showed that the ground motion observed by GeoNet and QCN had comparable amplitudes at a given distance from the earthquake's epicenter.

The EMSC also proposes two programs as part of the QCN: the "QCN Sensor Monitoring Program", which functions in "trigger" mode, i.e. the information is only disseminated when the acceleration is significantly higher than that of the preceding seconds, based on the "Short-Term Average/Long-term Average" (STA/LTA) algorithm [CUE 03], and the "QCN Continual Monitoring Program", which functions in "continuous" mode to collect data samples. In January 2014, QNC also rolled out its mobile application using the smartphone accelerometer and working with the Android version of BOINC[15], still with a resting (charging) trigger. This application only uses 1–5% of the device's resources (CPU) and only a few kilobytes of data are sent over the network daily.

4.4. Overview of our work

In the scope of the student study and research work (TER) projects and transverse practical work (TPT) done during the three academic years from 2013–2014 to 2015–2016, we dealt with three primary issues:

– the analysis of signals from fixed or mobile inertial sensor (embedded in the smatphone), the detection of earthquakes and measurement collection;

– the connectivity of cellular devices (i.e. WiFi, Bluetooth) and fixed sensors made to communicate, applied to the spread of early alerts (in real time, at the start of an earthquake) and to replace the loss of the cellular network in case of telecom infrastructure destruction in order to allow backup communication during an earthquake (i.e. via a mesh network and in peer-to-peer mode);

---

15 See http://qcn.stanford.edu/qcn-app-available-for-android-using-boinc.

– the use of geolocation to locate victims and the gathering of data used to filter alert notifications according to the location, as well as to analyze behavior.

NOTE.– Since 2016, we have been working on the "MASLOW" (Mobiquitous Autonomous and Antiseismic Sustainable LOW-cost home) project for homes and the "2LIFI-R" (*Lampadaire LIFI Intelligent Facilitant l'Intégration des Risques*) project for smart, energy-autonomous (solar and wind) streetlights that can communicate and that are equipped with a Linux microserver (Raspbery PI or Wismote) with all kinds of embedded sensors (camera, energy consumption, lighting, temperature, presence, pollution, motion, noise, pollinization, etc.) and a range of location-based and contextualized services.

4.4.1. *Analysis of the signal from intertial sensors*

During an initial approach, we prototyped and studied the reliability of an early warning system with an eye to detect an earthquake when the smartphone is moving: thus, the system was meant to differentiate between "normal" user activity and a motion potentially linked to an earthquake. Despite the original solution that we will present in this section, our tests have shown that the system could be improperly triggered in the metro or in a crowd and that, given the current state of technology, we could not keep improving the system enough for it to be efficient. We thus adopted a more traditional approach [REI 13] and implemented an application to detect potentially seismic motion and to collect measurements [LES 16b] based on the sensors installed on Android smartphones; we will present this in detail in section 4.5. We implemented the same algorithm in this cellular application as we use on the fixed sensors to detect and spread potential alerts over surrounding networks and to collect data that will be analyzed in real time and retrospectively with the long-term goal of discovering predictability models.

4.4.1.1. *The cellphone's motion recognition demonstrator*

The first demonstrator that we prototyped on Android (see Figure 4.8) and Windows Phone platforms (see Figure 4.9) allowed information to be collected in order to analyze and extract indicators as a function of the signal's characteristics during an initial stage because of the functionalities proposed:

– selection of an activity to be analyzed;

– graphic visualization and initiation of measurement collection based on the three axes of the accelerometer;

– calculation of functions applied to the measurements (maximums, minimums, average);

– selection of a filtering algorithm to be applied to the measurements (high-pass, low-pass, band-pass, Kalman);

– location of the user and estimation of the displacement velocity;

– recognition of user activity.

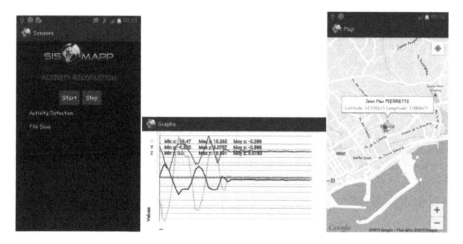

Figure 4.8. *Screens from the Android demonstrator*

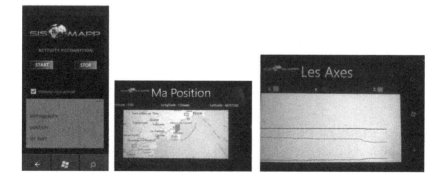

Figure 4.9. *Screens from the Windows Phone demonstrator*

The data collected have allowed indicators to be identified as a function of the signal characteristics, the device from which the measurements were collected, and the activity they were associated with in order to establish a behavioral reference used to identify user activity; by comparing the model to the data analyzed during mobile device use, the prototype was able to determine user activity during normal use: immobile, walking activity, running, elevation and jumping.

4.4.1.2. *Use of filters*

Filtering techniques find applications in several domains, e.g. in electronics, for signal processing; they are used to correct, attenuate or accentuate a signal (be it continuous or discrete) at the onset in order to amplify, smooth, or isolate a part of the output signal. In the framework of the demonstrator, the application of filters aims to test their utility for improving the detection and utility of motions "felt" by the cellphone.

NOTE.– There are numerous filtering techniques that can be applied to earthquake detection [ELM 08] and that we have no dealt with. We finally decided to keep the values measured by the accelerometer sensor as they were and to only take into account signals that were greater than the sensor interference measured while stationary (see section 4.5), because we have proven that the sensors were precise enough and that every value could be used as an indicator.

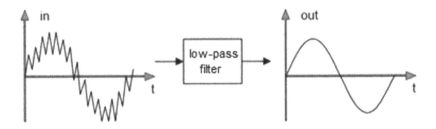

Figure 4.10. *Example of a low-pass filter[16]*

Low-pass filter (see Figure 4.10): As its name indicates, the low-pass filter (or high-cut filter) only allows signals past that are below a given level,

16 Source Polytechnique Montréal: http://www.groupes.polymtl.ca/mec6405/Labo%20A06/ Filtres%20passe-bas.pdf.

known as a "cutoff frequency", by eliminating signals above the cutoff frequency.

Example of the low-pass filter [4.5]: the filtered acceleration A' at the moment t is obtained by multiplying the acceleration A measured at the moment t multiplied by the cutoff coefficient α and then adding the acceleration measured at the previous moment $t - 1$ multiplied by the complement of the cutoff coefficient $(1 - \alpha)$:

$$A'_t = A_t * \alpha + A_{t-1} * (1 - \alpha) \qquad [4.5]$$

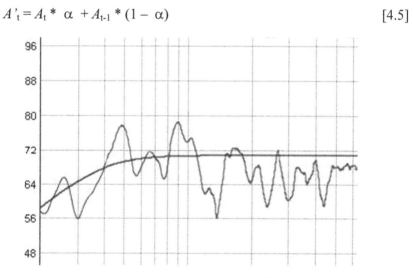

Figure 4.11. *Example of the high-pass filter[17]. For a color version of the figure, please see www.iste.co.uk/sedes/information.zip*

High-pass filter (see Figure 4.11): the opposite of the low-pass filter, the high-pass (low-cut) filter only allows signals above the cutoff coefficient through.

Example of the high-pass filter [4.6]: the value filtered at the moment t is calculated by multiplying the double of the measurement at moment t by the cutoff coefficient and then subtracting the value measured at the previous moment:

$$A'_t = \alpha \times 2A_t - A_{t-1} \qquad [4.6]$$

---

17 Measured signal in green, filtered signal in blue.

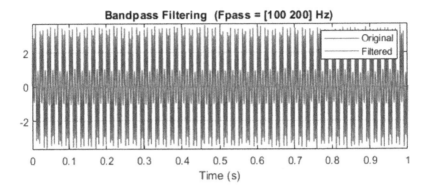

Figure 4.12. *Illustration of the bandpass filter[18]. For a color version of the figure, please see www.iste.co.uk/sedes/information.zip*

NOTE.– The bandpass filter (see Figure 4.12) is a combination of the low-pass and the high-pass filters that only allows an interval of the signal between the low cutoff frequency and the high cutoff frequency through.

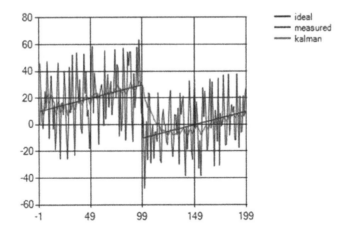

Figure 4.13. *Example of the Kalman filter[19]. For a color version of the figure, please see www.iste.co.uk/sedes/information.zip*

---

18 Source: MathWorks® documentation, https://www. mathworks.com/help/signal/ref/bandpass.html.

19 Source open source project HoshiKata on Code Project: https://www.codeproject.com/Articles/326657/KalmanDemo.

Kalman filter (see Figure 4.13): the Kalman filter (named after mathematician Rudolf Kalman[20] who invented it) is used in many fields to eliminate interference, smoothing or even prediction. The Kalman filter integrates two phases: an estimation (recursive) phase based on the preceding signal and a correction phase based on the actual signal.

Example of the Kalman filter [4.7]: the value filtered at the moment t is calculated by adding the value measured at the previous moment $t - 1$ to the difference weighted by the cutoff coefficient between the measured value at moment t and $t - 1$.

$$A'_t = A_{t-1} + \alpha \times (A_t - A_{t-1}) \qquad [4.7]$$

4.4.1.3. Battery consumption linked to the use of GPS and sensors

Mobile devices, i.e. smartphones, have evolved in less than a decade to the point of rivaling desktop computers – 2.5 GHz processors versus 470 MHz for the first iPhone in 2007, in 64-bit dual-cores or quadri-cores, with an initial RAM of 128 Mb today at 4 Gb in the most powerful models with a storage capacity that can reach up to 64 Gb versus 16 Gb in 2007 – we think the current constraints will no longer exist in a few years. However, the use of sensors and GPS in particular lead to excessive battery consumption; as an example, we examine the consumption for a Google Nexus S smartphone in Table 4.2, which shows that the combination of using the accelerometer, the GPS and the direct peer-to-peer WiFi network can lead to an additional 61% consumption (much lower consumption has been proven in recent smartphone models).

This is why it is important to program in the activation and deactivation of services using functionalities with an impact on battery consumption and to monitor the state of the battery, e.g. by activating notifications on the charge status and possibly stopping the service (and notifying the user) when the battery is low.

---

20 See Wikipedia: https://en.wikipedia.org/wiki/Kalman_filter.

Continuous use (Google Nexus S)	Time to use 1% of the battery	Recalculated time to use 100% of the battery	Additional consumption
Normal (78% charge)	00:03:28	05:46:40	–
Accelerometer	00:03:01	05:01:40	13%
Accelerometer + GPS	00:01:38	02:43:20	53%
Accelerometer + GPS + WiFi access	00:01:21	02:15:00	61%

Table 4.3. *Additional battery consumption*

4.4.2. *P2P correlation to spread a seismic alert*

Despite our ability to identify a particular user activity (i.e. change in direction, walking, running, stationary state, shaking, the device falling) by comparing the signals to a preestablished reference point, it has not been possible for us to efficiently differentiate seismic motion from a single device (e.g. passage of a truck, train, etc.).

We therefore worked on a semiautomatic algorithm, "Did You Feel It?" (DYFI) to corroborate alerts between nearby peripheries including a request for user confirmation:

– in the initial state, the system is in phase zero: no anomaly has been detected yet;

– the first stage consists in collecting the measurements from the accelerometer over a sliding period that is short enough for early detection (e.g. 1 s);

– the second stage (see Figure 4.14) involves comparing the measurements collected to a reference in order to detect a potentially seismic anomaly: if an anomaly is detected and the system is in phase zero (no alert), the system moves to phase 1, unconfirmed anomaly detection, then sends out a "DYFI" message to nearby devices connected to the peer-to-peer network over direct WiFi (Android feature) or Bluetooth with an automatic search for/creation of the dedicated mesh network and connection;

– the third stage (see Figure 4.15) deals with the receipt of a "DYFI" message on a device connected to the peer-to-peer network: if the device detected an anomaly itself and is already in phase 1, it moves onto stage 2, anomaly sensed by at least one other device;

– when the system moves to phase 2, the program displays a request to confirm that the user felt the movement (see Figure 4.16) in the fourth stage: if the user confirms having felt it, the system moves to phase 3, confirmed detection;

– in phase 3, a messaged about user-confirmed detection of seismic activity is broadcasted over the peer-to-peer network, predefined actions like the automatic activation of the GPS system to locate the user (the user's location already being spread in the messages sent over the peer-to-peer network), and a screen with useful information is displayed, including a "cancel alert" button (see Figure 4.17).

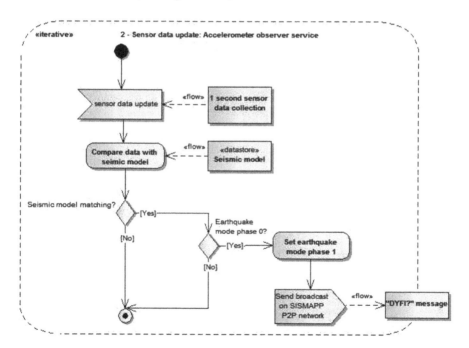

Figure 4.14. *Analysis of collected measurements*

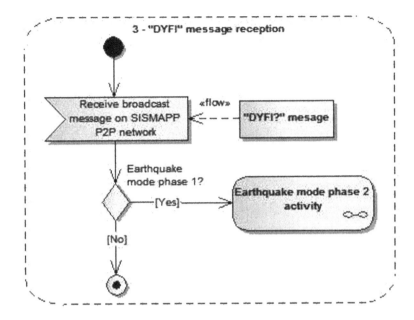

Figure 4.15. *Receipt of a "DYFI" message in phase 1*

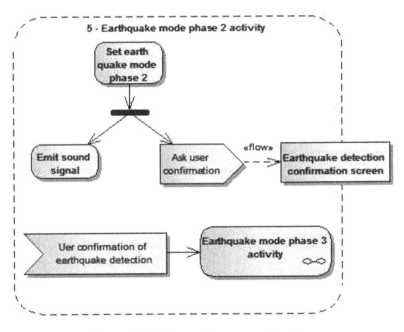

Figure 4.16. *Request for user confirmation*

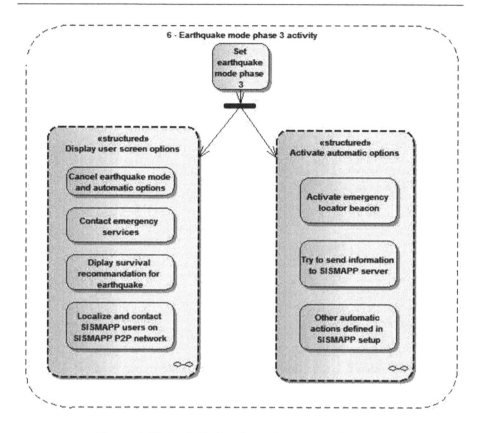

Figure 4.17. *Available functions after user confirmation*

4.4.3. Notification server

The system was then spread so that mobile applications subscribe to a notification server (NodeJs technology) to which they regularly send their position and the potential alerts that have been detected through the analysis of accelerometer sensors (see Figure 4.18): as a function of the user's location, the server only sends alert notifications to devices whose positions are in the concerned radius using the Haversine formula[21], which allows the distance between two geodesic coordinates to be calculated by taking into consideration the earth's curvature (see Algorithm 4.1):

---

21 See Wikipedia: https://en.wikipedia.org/wiki/Haversine_formula.

```
1:  /* Calculation of the distance in km between two geographic coordinates */
2:  ComputeDistanceInKilometers (lat1, long1, lat2, long2): decimal value
3:  {
4:      /* Earth's circumference: 2 * 6371 km */
5:      C ← 12742
6:      /* PI = 3.14159265359 */
7:      PI ← 3.14159265359
8:      /* degrees between latitude 1 and latitude 2 */
9:      d1  ← (lat1-lat2) * PI/180
10:     /* degrees between longitude 1 and longitude 2 */
11:     d2  ← (long1-long2) * PI/180
12:     /* latitude 1 in degrees */
13:     dlat1 ← lat1 * PI/180
14 :    /* latitude 2 in degrees */
15:     dlat2 ← lat2 * PI/180
16:     /* temporary variable */
17:     a  ← sin² ( ½ d1 ) + cos( dlat1 ) * cos( dlat2 ) * sin² ( ½ d2 )
18:     /* distance between the two coordinates in km */
19:     km ← C * arctan2(a², ( 1 – a )²)
20:     return km
21: }
```

Algorithm 4.1. *Calculation of the distance between two locations*

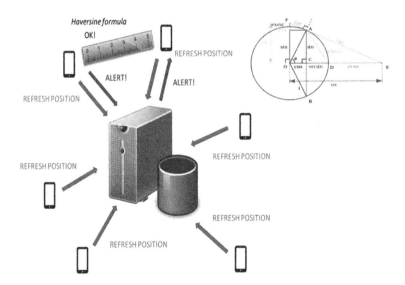

Figure 4.18. *Notification server. For a color version*
of the figure, please see www.iste.co.uk/sedes/information.zip

This same technique is used to send seismic events received from the EMSC[22] portal, which can be consulted on the mobile device and located on a map (see Figure 4.19).

Figure 4.19. *Consultation and display of seismic events*

NOTE.– The notification server has a web monitoring interface that allows notifications to be sent manually or automatically, be they collective, geographically targeted, or individual, e.g. postseismic, to indicate the location of rescue services, to disseminate rallying instructions, to contact a user, etc. The monitoring console also allows the subscribed users to be mapped (automatic subscription performed by the mobile application); in fact, we find it relevant to be able to follow the movements of the crowd by sending position updates via the mobile application.

4.4.4. Network loss in case of infrastructure destruction

The use of a peer-to-peer network via direct WiFi on Android was already tested in corroborating potentially seismic anomalies detected through the analysis of measurements collected on the accelerometer of

22 The EMSC portal can be found at: http://www.emsc-csem.org/Earthquake

mobile devices. The use of a peer-to-peer network can also prove useful when telecommunication networks are no longer available in case of infrastructure destruction by an earthquake.

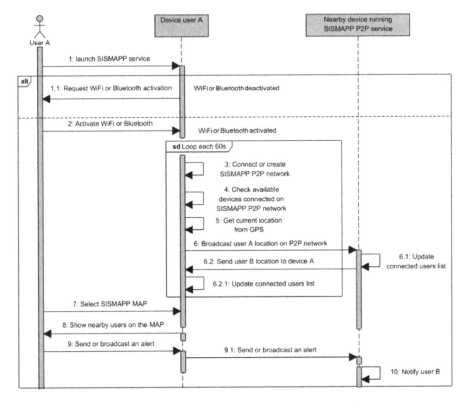

Figure 4.20. *Connecting SISMAPP P2P network*

For example, the use of the application WhatsApp[23], which uses smartphone connectivity with Bluetooth or WiFi, allows communities to communicate peer-to-peer (see Figure 4.20) over a linked network independent of the cellular network, which made it possible to denounce the Chinese government's repression during the 2014 manifestations and this despite the government's attempt to block telecommunication networks. Based on the establishment of a peer-to-peer network using the available WiFi access points and Bluetooth, we thus prototyped a system for the iOS

23 See www.whatsapp.com.

platform regardless of the cellular network with the primary functionalities (see Figure 4.21) of disseminating alerts and emitting an audio and visual signal on the device that receives the notification (see Figure 4.22), the users' GPS locations and instant messaging.

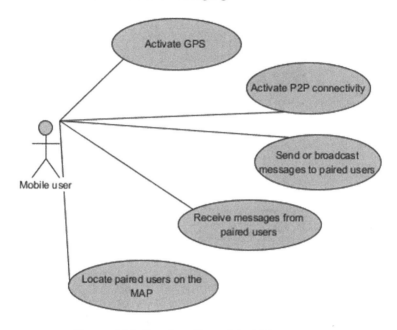

Figure 4.21. *Functionalities of the iOS prototype*

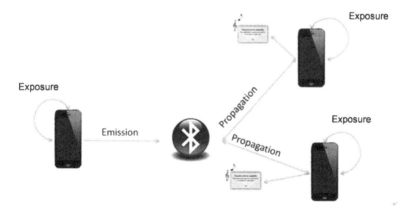

Figure 4.22. *P2P alert dissemination (iOS)*

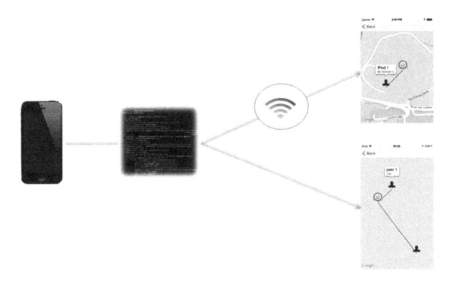

Figure 4.23. *P2P user location (iOS)*

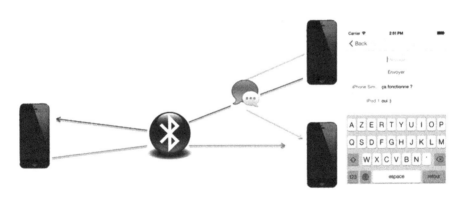

Figure 4.24. *P2P instant messenger (iOS)*

NOTE.– Prototyping the dissemination of a (simulated) confirmed seismic alert over the SISMAPP peer-to-peer client–server network (introduced and managed by the first device that launches the alert, thus assuming the role of a server) was performed on the iOS[24] platform starting with version 7

24 Demo available at: https://youtu.be/GCiibgdfppQ.

(iPhones, iPods and iPads); instant messaging allows the list of devices (users) detected nearby to be displayed by calculating their distance expressed in 10 m units (see Table 4.4, which shows the imprecisions measured during a period of 5 min with a location request performed every 3 s with the university buildings in Sophia-Antipolis in 2014) or their position (last known GPS location) to be displayed on a map. The connection is established via the first communication interface activated on the devices found nearby with WiFi or Bluetooth® connection. The network may be heterogeneous; devices can join it and exchange information in a transparent way for users.

Mode	HP[25] min	VP[26] min	HP max	VP max
WiFi	10 m	15 m	65 m	40 m
Cellular network	30 m	57 m	200 m	180 m
3G	30 m	57 m	280 m	114 m

Table 4.4. *GPS precision measured on an iPhone in the UNS buildings*

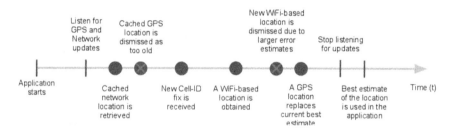

Figure 4.25. *Google API: position estimate window over time*[27]

Geolocation represents an indispensable interest for earthquake management: in fact, the measurement of a seismic event represents no interest if it does not show the date and time and the geolocation. Locating also has applications in mapping users to locate victims or analyze behaviors. Even if the site of fixed sources (e.g. seismic stations, fixed sensors) is determined in advance and therefore does not require dynamic location, this is not the case for mobile devices. Whatever the chosen mobile

25 HP: horizontal precision.

26 VP: vertical precision.

27 Source of the illustration: https://developer.android.com/guide/topics/location/strategies.html.

platform (Android, iOS, etc.), the location APIs are based on data from the GPS, WiFi, and the cellular network. Two modes are possible: continuous subscription to periodic location updates at a given frequency when motion is detected (see Figure 4.25) or one-time recovery of the last-known position (more economic for the battery). However, location is not available in areas that do not have network coverage and precision can vary from 2 to 200 m as a function of coverage (e.g. no GPS within buildings).

NOTE.– On the iOS platform, it is still not possible to create a direct WiFi network; an "ad hoc" network is available via cellular networks, but this functionality is not accessible through programming. It is therefore necessary to have a local network to connect the devices on a peer-to-peer Wi-Fi network. This is why we also used Bluetooth connectivity, which has a range limited to 50 m (equivalent to the Wi-Fi indoor range). However, on the iOS platform, it is still not possible to activate Bluetooth through programming, which is only possible through the use of a private API.

4.4.5. *Trustworthiness of alerts and fixed sensors*

Our experiments have led to the conclusion that it is difficult to eliminate the false positives in real time because the correlation of the accelerometer signals from mobile devices based on a peer-to-peer network does not eliminate the inappropriate triggering of an issue from an event that could not be seismic in nature; for example, in a stadium or the metro, the vibrations could trigger the system at an untimely moment and cause users to get rid of the application. However, the management of alerts based on a server can cause highly significant delays for an early alert system. Moreover, the unavailability of networks could quite simply make the system useless. We have concluded from this that the triggering of trustworthy early alerts should come from fixed sensors located in locations slightly exposed to vibrations other than those of the ground and that should use a connection independent of the cellular networks in order to transmit the notifications of alerts to mobile devices located in the proximity: a planned solution is based on high-performance sensors positioned at strategic locations with limited exposure to false positives, e.g. the sensor can integrate Bluetooth or WiFi connectivity (i.e. Arduino or Raspberry Pi microcontrollers).

As a proof of concept, we also implemented the potentially seismic anomaly detection algorithm based on the measurements from the USB O-NAVI seismic sensor (see Figure 4.7) initially meant for the QCN network provided by the EMSC (http://qcn.emsc-csem.org/sensor). We plugged the sensor whose use we reoriented towards a fixed location to test the dissemination of alerts over mobile devices connected to the available WiFi networks and to show that the smartphone can receive early warnings from locally fixed sensors.

4.5. Measurement collector from the mobile accelerometer sensor

In this section, we will show how our mobile application is capable of detecting and triggering potentially seismic alerts and collecting measurements by using the accelerometer sensor installed on smartphones. The data collected are meant to feed a massive data storehouse meant for studying predictability models. The intended goal is to demonstrate the pertinence and trustworthiness of using smartphone sensors in detecting earthquakes through the presentation of our ready-for-use prototype implementation. The added value of our solution focused on analyzing data from the mobile accelerometer sensor can be found in the flexibility that it offers and the possibility of collecting not only locally but also transmitting the data to a distant server, which is actually a portable measurement device specially adapted for research. In fact, unlike other applications, the proposed solution allows multiple configurations to be tested and potentially seismic alert notifications as well as measurements collected over a predefined period of time before and after alerts to be recorded. The data are recorded on a database (DB) on the cellphone and they can be sent automatically to a (configurable) server in the NoSQL[28] format (JSON[29] key-value format). The server makes a Representational State Transfer (REST) web service accepting text with no formatting constraints available in order to allow later evolution without any impact on the interface: this architecture was designed in order to gather heterogeneous data in different formats and with different origins that could later be the subject of map reduce (Hadoop) processing.

28 "Not Only SQL".
29 Java Script Object Notation.

4.5.1. *Motivations*

In August 2014, the recording of a magnitude 6 earthquake in South Napa (CA, USA) was captured by chance 38 miles from the epicenter with the "MyShake" application (see Figure 4.26) developed in the seismology laboratory of Berkeley University (www.seismo.berkeley.edu). The recordings of the Napa earthquake with a mobile application showed that data from smartphone sensors are of high quality when the device is positioned on a stable support and that they could be used by seismologists.

Detection based on the sensors installed on smartphones is a new field of study, e.g. a scientific study conducted by several researchers [MIN 15] mentions that an earthquake could be detected in 5 s with community participation by only 0.2% of cellphone users (~5,000 devices) in a 5-km radius around the epicenter of a densely populated area like San Francisco or San Jose (in the United States). The article explains that detection is only possible during high-magnitude earthquakes: the precision of the mobile sensors used limit the detection to earthquakes above a magnitude of two. However, technologies evolve much faster than usage and today's limitations should not limit research.

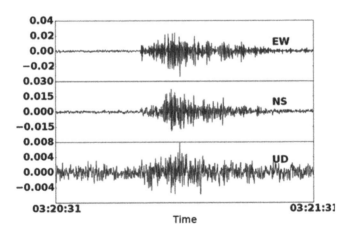

Figure 4.26. *Recording of the Napa earthquake captured by the MyShake application with a Samsung Galaxy 4[30]*

---

30 Source: [BOS 15].

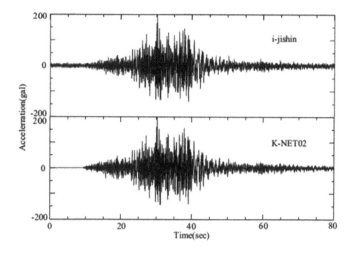

Figure 4.27. *Comparison of the recordings from K-NET02 network and the i-Jishin mobile application*

4.5.2. *Use of the mobile service*

The SISMAPP mobile service (Android) analyzes the data from the triaxial accelerometer sensor in smartphones in real time in order to detect motions likely resulting from an earthquake. In order to avoid impacting battery consumption (see Table 4.2) and limit data consumption, the service is only activated when the device is charging and connected to a WiFi network. The analysis is only activated when the stationary state of the mobile is detected. The service implementation we propose is inspired by the principle of detecting events beyond a threshold, a principle commonly used in alert systems. This technique allows an anomaly in a sufficiently dense network to be determined efficiently [CUE 03]. The background execution is based on different settings that the user can modify to adapt the sensitivity as a function of the expected result: sensor frequency, minimum and maximum acceleration for a stationary state, minimum variance to leave a stationary state, timed switching of the data analyzed and collected. Moreover, the settings allow the collection and notification options to be modified: the address of the server and web services, activation and deactivation of the service or data transmission, collection time, delays between two notifications and the interval between locations.

The method for crossing the threshold over a period is illustrated by the algorithm [4.8] where the a_t are the accelerations measured at the moment t and $\delta(M)$ is the acceleration differential that activates processing:

$$\forall\, t > t_0,\, a \in [a_{t0}\,..\,,a_{tn}],\, si\, |a_t - a_{t-1}| > \delta(M) \rightarrow \text{Processing} \quad [4.8]$$

4.5.2.1. Accelerometer data analysis and processing

Our adaptation of the threshold-crossing method takes place over a very short configurable sliding period (~1 s) whose activation is proposed in Algorithm 4.2: during application launch, the service subscribes to events connecting to and disconnecting from the electric source, to the change in network connectivity (WiFi), to the location service[31] and to the event of service activation and deactivation accessible from the application's "Setup" menu. When receiving events, the update of Boolean indicators conditions the initiation or stoppage of accelerometer data analysis or collection processing.

```
1:    /* Subscription to the events that condition processing */
2:    SubscribeEvents (power, connectivity, location, activationService)
3:
4:    /* Management of processing as a function of events */
5:    ReceptionEvent(Event)
6:    {
7:        Record the state related to the event
8:        if located then
9:            /* Update localization with the event "localization" */
10:           Updtate latitude and longitude
11:       else
12:           if (inCharge ∧ connectedToWiFi ∧ serviceActivated) then
13:               /* If all conditions are met, data analysis is stopped */
14 :              start of sliding ← timestamp
15:               collection duration ← ∅
16:               maxX ← 0
17:               maxY ← 0
18:               maxX ← 0
19:               stationary ← false
20:               collecting ← false
21:               StartAccelerometerReading(frequency)
```

31 GPS and GPS fusion available as a function of network and coverage.

```
22:          else
23:              /* If not, analysis is stopped */
24:              StopAccelerometerAnalisis()
25:          endif
26:      endif
27: }
```

Algorithm 4.2. *Subscription to events*

Accelerometer data reading is also presented in the form of a subscription to the API sensor events at the chosen frequency (see Table 4.5).

Reading frequency option	Intervals between readings
SENSOR_DELAY_NORMAL	0.2 s
SENSOR_DELAY_UI	0.06 s (suitable for display refresh)
SENSOR_DELAY_GAME	0.02 s (suitable for games)
SENSOR_DELAY_FASTEST	No delay: maximum frequency

Table 4.5. *Sensor reading frequency*

The timed and dated measurements of three axes x, y and z of the accelerometer sensor (linear[32]) are received in the *AnalysisValues Accelerometer* method in which they are analyzed and processed according to Algorithm 4.3.

```
1:   /* Accelerometer data analysis processing */
2:   AnalysisValuesAccelerometer(accelerometer current values, timestamp)
3:   {
4:       x, y, z ← accelerometer current values
5:       collection ← {x, y, z, timestamp} ∪ collection
6:
7:       /* Sliding of the analysis on the read values during the configured period */
8:       if (collection duration > sliding parameter) then
9 :
10:          /* Verification of the stationary state: */
11:          if ¬stationary ∧ ¬collecting then
12:              stationary ← VerifyStationary(collection)
13:          endif
```

---

32 Minus gravity.

```
14:
15:              /* When the stationary state has been detected: */
16:         if stationary then
17:              /* Verification of collected data crossing threshold */
18:                   collection ← VerifyAlert(collection)
19:         endif
20:
21:              /* When threshold crossing has been detected: */
22:         if collecting then
23:                   id_ collection ← id_ collection + 1
24:                   /* Sending alert notification to the user */
25:              ProcessAlertUser(timestamp)
26:
27:                   /* If the server is configured, send notification to server */
28:              ProcessAlertServer(timestamp, id_ collection, last location)
29:
30:                   /* Verify whether the set collection duration is reached */
31:              if (collection duration – sliding parameter) > collection parameter then
32:                        /* Processing collection and pausing */
33:                        collecting ← false
34:                        ProcessCollection(id_collection, collection)
35:                        ProcessPause(timestamp)
36:              endif
37:         else
38:                   /* Deleting the first values collected to only keep */
39:                   /* the configured slide time and update */
40:                   /* the time and date from the start of collection...        */
41:              ProcessSlide(collection)
42:         endif
43:    endif
44:
45:    sliding duration ← (timestamp – start of sliding)
46: }
```

Algorithm 4.3. *Accelerometer measurement analysis and processing*

Algorithm 4.3 shows that the timed and dated data on the measured values (x, y and z) are collected over a sliding period in a list. The activation of a notification and the saved collection are only processed after the detection of the stationary state (see Algorithm 4.4): if the threshold is exceeded (see Algorithm 4.5), an alert notification is propagated (in the notification bar) and, according to the settings, sent to the server. The collection is continued over the set period before being processed according to Algorithm 4.6. After collection, the variables are reinitialized and the service is paused for the set time (which avoids untimely notifications and limits sensor deviation over that time). If there is no detection of threshold crossing, the first measurements are deleted so as to only keep the sliding period in the memory.

```
1:    /* Verification of the stationary state */
2:    VerifyStationary(collection)
3:    {
4:        ∀ x, y, z ∈ collection:
5:        stationary ← false
6:        avgX ← ∑ x > 0 / nb(x > 0)
7:        avgY ← ∑ y > 0 / nb(y > 0)
8:        avgZ ← ∑ z > 0 / nb(z > 0)
9:
10:       /* comparison of the values at the minimum threshold established during setup */
11:       if (avgX < minAccel) ∨ (avgY < minAccel) ∨ (avgZ < minAccel) then
12:
13:               /* if at least one of the average values measured on an axis is below */
14:               /* the minimum value, then the stationary state is considered and */
15:               /* the average maximum values of the stationary state are memorized */
16:               stationary ← true
17:               maxX ← avgX>maxX ?avgX :maxX
18:               maxY ← avgY>maxY ?avgY :maxY
19:               maxX ← avgX>maxX ?avgX :maxX
20:       endif
21:    }
```

Algorithm 4.4. *Verification of the stationary state*

In order to exclude potential parasite values, the stationary state is verified against the average of all collected data (sliding period): if the average measured on one of the axes is below the minimum threshold for a stationary state, this is enough to consider the stationary state because this allows a potential shift from the zero of one of the axes to be dismissed. The maximum averages are memorized to calculate the delta of the acceleration alert threshold in relation to the delta established during setup (see Algorithm 4.5).

NOTE.– Because detection takes place based on a stationary state and positive acceleration is normally followed by negative acceleration, only positive acceleration is taken into consideration.

```
1:    /* Verification of an alert via deviation from the method of crossing the threshold */
2:    VerifyAlert(collection)
3:    {
4:        ∀ x, y, z ∈ collection :
5:        deltaX ← (∑ x > 0 / nb(x > 0)) – maxX
6:        deltaY ← (∑ y > 0 / nb(y > 0)) – maxY
7:        deltaZ ← (∑ z > 0 / nb(z > 0)) – maxZ
8:
9:        /* If the average delta is greater than an established maximum value */
10:       /* then the motion that caused it is too brusque to be                */
11:       /* seismic in nature...                                               */
12:       if (deltaX > maxAccel) ∨ (deltaY > maxAccel) ∨ (deltaZ > maxAccel) then
13:
14:           stationary ← false
15:
16:           /* Potential collection must then be stopped */
17:           if collecting then
18:               /* Potential collection must then be stopped */
19:               collecting ← false
20:
21:               /* However, collection is still processed before the pause */
22:               ProcessCollection(id_collection, collection)
23:           endif
24:           ProcessPause(timestamp)
25:       else
26:           /* If not, if the average delta is greater than the delta of acceleration */
26:           /* established for an alert, the collection to be saved initiates */
27:           if (deltaX > deltaAccel) ∨ (deltaY > deltaAccel) ∨ (deltaZ > deltaAccel) then
28:               collecting ← true
29:               start of collection ← timestamp
30:           endif
31:       endif
32:   }
```

Algorithm 4.5. *Verification of crossing the threshold for an "alert"*

The initiation of an alert verifies two conditions (see Algorithm 4.5): (1) the average deltas of acceleration in relation to the average maximums calculated in a stationary state in Algorithm 4.3 do not exceed an extreme threshold (e.g. due to the user picking up the device); and (2) at least one of the deltas measured on the x, y or z axes exceeds a minimum activation delta of acceleration. When the calculated delta of acceleration exceeds an extreme threshold and a collection was in progress, the collection is stopped but the data are nevertheless processed for a local save and sent to the server (see Algorithm 4.5) because this crossing of the threshold could have been caused by the device falling during an earthquake.

```
1:    /* Verification of an alert via deviation from the method of crossing the threshold */
2:    ProcessCollection(id_collection, collection)
3:    {
4:        if sendServer ∧ serverIsKnown() then
5:            sendCollection(id_collection, collection, start slide,
6:                           start collection, timestamp, last location,
7:                           sensor type, frequency, device model)
8:        endif
9:        saveLocally(id_collection, collection)
10:   }
```

Algorithm 4.6. *Processing data collection following an alert*

4.5.2.2. *Processing alerts and collected measurements*

We mentioned before that it is possible for networks to be saturated or damaged during an earthquake. As an alternative to the inability to contact the server and in a research context, local records allow the collected data to be analyzed at a later time.

The alert notifications that activate collection and measurement are stored locally in an embedded DB (SQLite[33]) accessible in a folder created by the application in the cellphone's storage memory (see Figure 4.28).

Figure 4.28. *Model of the service's local DB*

---

33 See https://www.sqlite.org.

The collected data can be deleted from the mobile application or even retrieved for analysis (e.g. in a spreadsheet). The time t elapsed at the moment n for the collected values is given in milliseconds; then, one needs only to calculate the t_n of a temporal (horizontal) axis in seconds, starting at t_0 such that: $t_0 = 0$ and $t_n = (t(n) - t(0)) \times 10^{-9}$ and to select the series of values x, y and z represented in m/s^{-2} on the vertical axis: Figure 4.29 shows the graphic visualization of data where the acceleration peak corresponds to a cellphone vibration (obtained through testing) that activated an alert and a collection save.

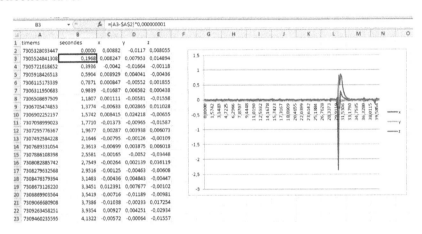

Figure 4.29. *Graphic visualization of the data collected. For a color version of the figure, please see www.iste.co.uk/sedes/information.zip*

If delivery to the server has been configured and a connection can be made, the notifications (in real time) and the measured accelerations (at the end of collection) can be sent in the key-value format (JSON). Below is an example:

– Alerts: "{"notifications":{"id_device":1,"id_notification":4,
"timestamp":"2015-03-15_10:01:59","latitude":43.7055339,"longitude":
7.2820472, "id_collection":4}"

– Measurements: "{"collections":{"id_device":1, "id_collection":4,
"sensor_type":"Linear acceleration", "sensor_delay":3,
"start_timestamp":"2015-03-15_10:01:49", "end_timestamp":"2015-03-
15_10:02:19", "latitude":43.7055339, "longitude":7.2820472,
"device_model":"Android 21 - LGE NEXUS 5", "values":"
[{"timestamp_ms":63382020019531, "x":0.0019194632768630981,
"y":1.209452748298645E-4, "z":0.0025548934936523438},
{"timestamp_ms":63382218017578, "x":0.0013000965118408203,
"y":0.006275080144405365, "z":0.02202129364013672},
{"timestamp_ms":63382416015625, "x":8.293241262435913E-4, "y":-

0.012210480868816376, "z":0.010548591613769531},
{"timestamp_ms":63382614013671, "x":-0.014498397707939148,
"y":0.0084128007292747, "z":0.02068042755126953},...]}

4.5.2.3. Prototype experimentation and limitations

Threshold determination: in an initial stage, threshold determination for alert triggering takes place empirically through observation of several smartphone models (Google/Samsung Nexus S, Samsung Galaxy S3, Microsoft/Nokia Lumia 720 and Google/LG Nexus 5): without a vibrating table, the experiment involved detecting a very light vibration (minimum threshold) from the support (caused manually) over a sufficient arbitrary time period (i.e. 1 s) after the stationary state is detected. The maximum threshold was determined by measuring several natural recoveries of the smartphone. At this stage, a more rational approach for determining thresholds is foreseen in collaboration with industrial partners (e.g. in the scope of an experimental pilot).

Loss of network in case of infrastructure destruction: as mentioned above, smartphone connectivity with Bluetooth or direct WiFi allows urban peer-to-peer communication via a linked network when telecommunication networks are no longer available. We have integrated the two connectivities into our protocol; however, the system is only functional when devices are covered by this connectivity (a maximum distance of approximately 30 m from one another).

Identification of false positives and data correlation: we started with the idea that it is not possible to eliminate individual false positives; this is why we focus all of our attention on the correlation of events and massive data processing. Several paths can be foreseen: the study of collected data (in real time or not), from the moment they are timestamped and geolocated, allows retrospective analysis from which predictability models could be extracted. However, we also think that the correlation of sources of information and the implementation of a network of fixed sensors communicating with the smartphone at sites chosen for their limited exposure to motion likely to cause false positives could be a customized solution for early alerts.

4.5.2.4. Other possible uses of the service

The SISMAPP mobile service is ideally designed to initially allow the determination of efficient sensitivity threshold establishment in a laboratory. However, a pilot phase is necessary to evaluate the frequency of notifications and the volume of relevant information. The use of prototyping in the context of seismological research is still at an early stage, but its flexibility makes it a portable measurement tool that could prove useful in other domains, for example, measuring the resonance of waves from an explosion (e.g. in mineral extraction careers).

4.5.3. *Description of the mobile service*

The Android mobile application (see Figure 4.30) includes a background service, a settings screen and a notification history screen.

Figure 4.30. *Android application icon*

Upon launching the application, a folder named SISMAPP (see Figure 4.31) is created within the phone's storage space (recreated upon each subsequent launch if the folder has been deleted); this contains the SQLite database file called *SismappDb*, which could eventually be transferred to a personal computer to process its content on another system (with an SQLite tool presented later in this section), as well as the transaction journal and the database created while installing the application.

The SISMAPP folder also contains the (optional) configuration file called *sismapp.xml* containing the application settings in XML format (see Figure 4.32) installed with default settings that can be personalized by the user (from the settings screen) and adapted to use (e.g. as a function of the smartphone model).

Figure 4.31. *SISMAPP file and its content*

```
1   <setup>
2       <!-- Server URL -->
3       <server_url>http://www.emsc-csem.org</server_url>
4       <!-- Server port -->
5       <server_port>80</server_port>
6       <!-- Web Service path -->
7       <ws_path>sismapp</ws_path>
8       <!-- Delay between 2 notifications sending in milliseconds -->
9       <delay_notification>600000</delay_notification>
10      <!-- Collection duration in milliseconds when possible earthquake detection -->
11      <collection_duration>120000</collection_duration>
12      <!-- Delay between 2 collections in milliseconds -->
13      <delay_collection>600000</delay_collection>
14      <!-- Sliding collection duration before detection in milliseconds -->
15      <sliding_duration>30000</sliding_duration>
16      <!-- Delay for location update in milliseconds -->
17      <location_update>60000</location_update>
18      <!-- Delay for location update in milliseconds -->
19      <location_fast_update>10000</location_fast_update>
20      <!-- Sensor delay one of: Normal | UI | Game | Fastest -->
21      <sensor_delay>Normal</sensor_delay>
22      <!-- Max acceleration m/s^2 for detection -->
23      <max_acceleration>1.0</max_acceleration>
24      <!-- Min acceleration m/s^2 for stationary -->
25      <min_acceleration>0.05</min_acceleration>
26      <!-- Delta acceleration m/s^2 for collection -->
27      <delta_acceleration>0.03</delta_acceleration>
28  </setup>
```

Figure 4.32. *config.xml file with default settings. For a color version of the figure, please see www.iste.co.uk/sedes/information.zip*

4.5.3.1. *Mobile application screens*

The application offers two screens that are accessible from the application menu (see Figure 4.33):

– the settings screen (*Setup*);

– the notification history screen (*Data*).

Figure 4.33. *Application menu*

NOTE.– The settings screen is displayed when the application is launched.

4.5.3.2. *Settings screens (Setup)*

The data are initialized either with fixed values within the application or with the XML file's configuration content if it is found to be present (in the SISMAPP folder). Consideration of modifications may be confirmed by the user, who has the choice to save, delete or cancel modifications when the user leaves the screen.

NOTE.– The settings screen scrolls; the user must scroll/slide toward the bottom to display the next settings.

Figure 4.34. *Settings screen (Setup)*

List of settings offered:

– *server URL*: address of the server notifications must be sent to;

– *server port*: port of the server notifications must be sent to (default value: 80);

– *web service path*: web service path/domain notifications must be sent to;

– *send collection to server*: activation or deactivation of sending collections to the server; when this option is deactivated, the data are collected locally, but they are not sent to the server;

– *delay for notification*: delays between sending two successive notifications in milliseconds; this option aims to avoid saturating the network in case of notifications in rapid succession;

NOTE.– The value entered for the delay between two notifications must be greater than the value of the slide time. Service use and data transmission via Internet can impact costs depending on the mobile subscription (but only WiFi mode is used by the application).

– *service activation*: service activation/deactivation; when this option is deactivated, the data are neither analyzed nor collected (service is stopped);

– *sliding duration*: sliding time in milliseconds of data collection from sensors that precede potential seismic detection;

– *location update interval*: time interval given in milliseconds for location updates;

– *sensor delay*: delays/frequency of data uploaded from accelerometer senses to be chosen from among the following:

- normal (default);

- UI (screen display frequency);

- game (designed for video games);

- fastest (quickest setting).

– *minimum acceleration (m/s²) for stationary*: minimum acceleration (m/s²) to determine the device's stationary (immobile) position; this makes use of a minimum low value for a stationary state (greater than sensor signal interference);

NOTE.– Only positive values are observed. The given value for the minimum acceleration in a stationary state must be less than the maximum value.

– *maximum acceleration (m/s²) for stationary*: maximum acceleration (m/s²) to determine the device's stationary (immobile) position; this makes use of the minimum high value for a stationary state (less than a brusque signal like when the phone is picked up by the user);

NOTE.– Only positive values are observed. The given value for the maximum acceleration in a stationary state must be greater than the minimum value.

– *delta acceleration (m/s²) for stationary*: minimum average variation of acceleration (m/s²) over slide time in relation to the values collected in a stationary state, which will determine the potential detection of an earthquake. This value corresponds to a differential greater than the one resulting from interference and fluctuations of the stationary state and less than that of interactions by the user when the phone is not immobile;

NOTE.– Only positive values are observed. The given value for the minimum average variation added to the minimum value for acceleration must be less than the maximum value for acceleration in a stationary state, all previously defined. This value was chosen, by default, to be deliberately high at 0.03 m/s^2 to be able to activate a simulation during a test. The value requires refinement to find a value (less than the default value) that is just above sensor fluctuations.

4.5.3.3. Notification history screen (data)

The history screen is displayed as a scrolling list that contains the description of the notifications present in the *SismappDb* database (in the SISMAPP folder) with notification time and date, as well as the latitude and longitude at which the data were collected. A check box allows users to select notifications they wish to delete; they then just need to click on the delete icon (trashcan) and a pop-up will ask if they are sure they want to delete notifications, with options to delete all notifications (including those not selected), delete the selected notifications or cancel the request (see Figure 4.35).

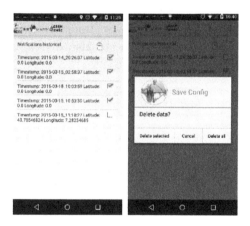

Figure 4.35. *Notification history screen (data)*

NOTE.– Deleting a notification deletes all recordings, including the data and values collected.

4.5.4. Service behavior

During installation, the SISMAPP folder is created with the settings file and database. The settings file can then be substituted for another file containing different values. The database can be copied and consulted outside the mobile device. Once the settings have been modified, those changed are saved in the application's preferences and are used rather than the defaults, which come from the application or the XML file. To delete the settings saved by the user, one must simply manage the application via the Android application management menu and delete the application data: the deletion will stop the service if it is in progress (deactivate the service before any use); the user will then need to return to the setting screen to find the default values and record them.

NOTE.– If the file is deleted, it will be recreated during the next application launch, but if the service is stopped, this will cause a glitch and the service will stop brusquely just like if the DB file is deleted or renamed.

When the *Setup* screen is active (displayed on the screen), the service is stopped. If the service is activated, the process restarts upon leaving the screen.

During detection of an anomaly or transmission of a notification (collection) to the server, notifications are also disseminated in the user's Android notification bar (see Figure 4.36).

Figure 4.36. *Notifications sent to the user*

4.5.5. *Previous conditions to activate collection*

The service is active from the moment the "Service activation" option is activated upon leaving the *Setup* screen, but accelerometer and location data collection are initiated when the two following conditions are verified:

– device plugged in and charging both currently and for the needs of the production tests via USB port;

– connected to a WiFi network.

If these conditions are not verified, or one of these conditions is not verified, data analysis, collection and location are stopped. When the two conditions are verified again, data analysis, collection and location are restarted.

NOTE.– Localization is only possible if the user has activated GPS in the mobile device's settings. If not, latitudes and longitudes are saved with a value of zero.

4.5.6. *SQLite DB management of the SISMAPP folder*

A simple way to recover the DB is to send an email attachment from the smartphone. Several software tools allow SQLite DBs to be manipulated on computers; for example, the following screenshots show the user interface of the "SQLite Expert" [34] software (personal version), which allows relational data to be managed (see relational schema Figure 4.28) from the graphic interface and which also offers an interface for manipulation with SQL request language (see Figure 4.37–Figure 4.39).

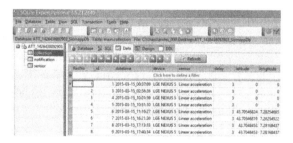

Figure 4.37. *"Collection" table*

---

34 See http://www.sqliteexpert.com.

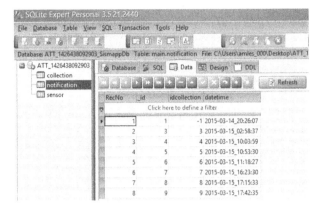

Figure 4.38. *"Notification" table*

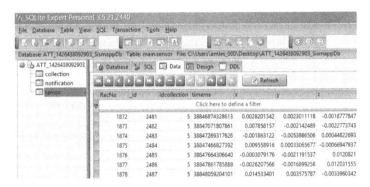

Figure 4.39. *"Sensor" table*

4.5.7. *Data recovery on the server*

If the "Send notification to server" option is activated on the *Setup* screen and the conditions are met (prerequisites, delays respected), the notification is sent to the web service URL indicated in the *Setup* (i.e. in the form http://URL:port/chemin/) in *JSONObject* format with the "PUT" method and the header "content-type" containing "application/json". The HTTP request entity thus contains a chain of characters as follows:

{"_id":8,"sentdatetime":"2015-03-
19_00:20:04","collection":{"idcollection":9,"begindatetime":"2015-03-
19_00:19:23","detectiondatetime":"2015-03-
19_00:19:23","delay":3,"latitude":0,"longitude":0,"device":"LGE NEXUS

5","sensortype":"Linear
acceleration","values":{{"timems":11137067016601,"x":0.010202288627624512,"y":0.0
03160327672958374,"z":-0.030803680419921875},{"timems":11137264038085,"x":-
0.011219501495361328,"y":-
0.0062153637409210205,"z":0.00882720947265625},{"timems":11137461029052,"x":-
0.012072324752807617,"y":-
0.003899902105331421,"z":0.015831947326660156},{"timems":11137658050537,"x":0.
006931900978088379,"y":-
0.009602516889572144,"z":0.016912460327148438},{"timems":11137855072021,"x":0.
006333649158477783,"y":0.008010119199752808,"z":-
0.0129241943359375},{"timems":11138052093505,"x":-0.013565599918365479,"y":-
0.007970929145812988,"z":0.0012922286987304688},{"timems":11138249084472,"x":-
1.4066696166992188E-5,"y":-0.010918229818344116,"z":-0.015429496765136719}, ...
}}}

NOTE.– Our tests were performed on the EMSC test server (which kindly made a web service available for us); the last data sent could be consulted in the navigator by typing the web service URL.

4.6. Conclusion and continuation of the project

In this chapter, we have presented our university and prototyping work with a mobiquitous platform designed for earthquake management before, during and after the event in the framework of the SISMAPP project and its applications with:

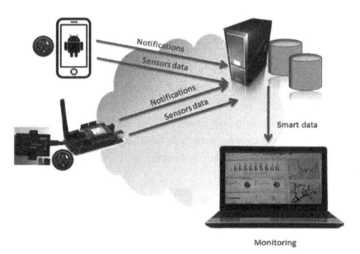

Figure 4.40. *Monitoring SISMAPP data*

– an algorithm for analyzing signals from fixed or installed inertial sensors;

– a linked mobile network in peer-to-peer mode (WiFi and Bluetooth) independent of the cellular network;

– a mobile alert dissemination and instant messaging system;

– the on-phone cartography of users connected to the peer-to-peer network;

– a location system for victims subscribed to the service;

– monitoring from a centralized server;

– real-time cartography of mobile application users from a web server interface;

– the delivery of group and/or geographically targeted or individual messages to mobile application users from a web interface;

– a mobile application to collect data from an installed accelerometer intended to feed a data warehouse (see Figure 4.40) with an aim to later deduce models that could contribute to earthquake prediction.

Our work has captured the interest of the EMSC seismologists, who have followed the project from the start by making us part of their expert vision the entire time. The EMSC also allowed us to test our application by making a web service available for us on their test server for uploading collected data.

In its current form, the SISMAPP project has been integrated into two innovation projects in which the smartphone becomes a remote control, a universal connector that allows communication between connected objects in a smart environment: in the MASLOW[35] house (see Figure 4.41 and Figure 4.42) and installed in the 2LIFI-R[36] streetlamp (see Figure 4.43 and Figure 4.44). The seismic sensor is one of many sensors meant to manage security and environmental risks (camera, sensors for pollution, pollen, noise, weather, etc.).

---

35 Mobiquitous Antiseismic Autonomous Sustainable LOW-cost home.
36 *Lampadaire LIFI Intelligent Facilitant l'Intégration des Risques.*

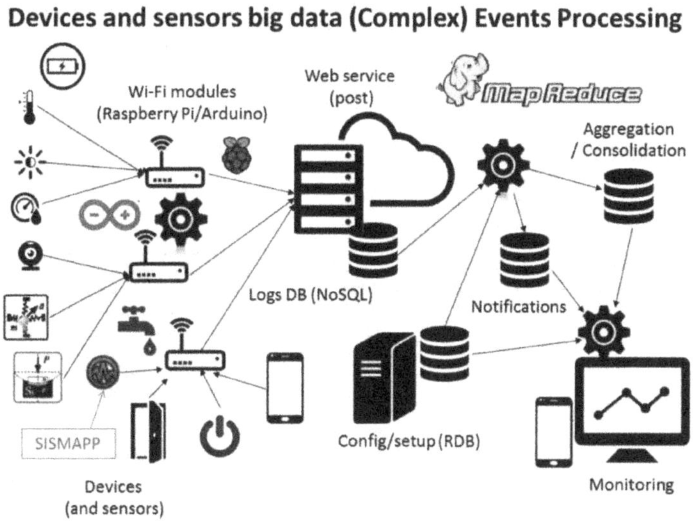

Devices and sensors big data (Complex) Events Processing

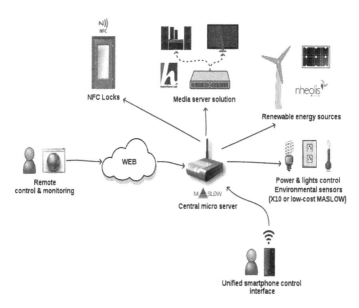

Figure 4.41. *Architecture of the Big Data system from the MASLOW project*

Figure 4.42. *Architecture of the connected house from the MASLOW[37] project*

37 Illustration source: MASLOW and 2LIFI-R projects.

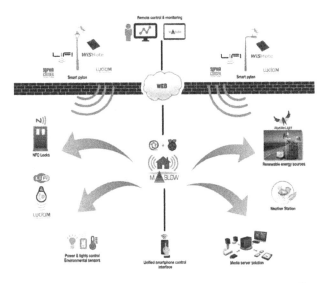

Figure 4.43. *Connection between the MASLOW and 2 LIFI-R[36] projects*

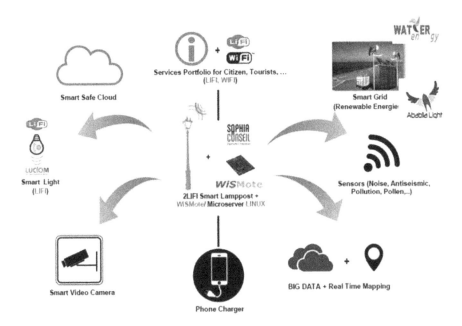

Figure 4.44. *2LIFI-R[36] smart lamppost*

4.7. Acknowledgments

Most of the experiments performed as part of the SISMAPP project result from a collaborative team effort motivated by the interest that our scientific partners gave us; I would personally like to thank all the contributors who participated in the project in any way, especially the students whose work we presented in this chapter:

– Béatrice Pierrette Noël, Jean-Max Pierrette and Francis Dolière Some (first-year M.A. students, 2012–2013 academic year);

– Axel Ardoin, Gilles Miraillet, Robin Dreux, Sébastien Cano and Jean-Max Pierrette (second-year M.A. students, 2013–2014 academic year);

– Anna Repousi, Guillaume Adam and Feny Fercouch (second-year M.A. students, 2014–2015 academic year).

In addition, I would like to thank Professor Serge Miranda on behalf of the SISMAPP project for his active supervision, as well as the partners who followed the projects:

– Rémy Bossu and Frédéric Roussel (EMSC);

– Anne Deschamps, Emmanuel Tric and Damienne Provitalo (GéoAzur[38]);

– Pierre-Jean Barre (IMREDD[39]).

Most of all, I want to thank Professor Florence Sedes (IRIT[40]), thanks to whom we can present our work in this publication.

4.8. References

[BAU 11] BAUMONT D., Séisme de Tohoku au large de l'île d'Honshu, Report, IRSN, 2011.

[BOS 10] BOSSU R., MCGILVARY G., KAMB L., "ShakeMapple: tapping laptop motion sensors to map the felt extents of an earthquake", *European Geosciences Union (EGU) General Assembly*, Vienna, Austria, 2010.

---

38 See www.geoazur.oca.eu.

39 *Institut Méditerranéen du Risque, de l'Environnement et du Développement Durable*, www.unice.fr/imredd.

40 *Institut de Recherche en Informatique de Toulouse*, www.irit.fr

[BOS 15] Bossu R., "Earthquake risk mitigation using social media and sensor-based citizens' participation", *AAAS*, San Jose, United States, February, 2015.

[COC 11] Cochran E.S., Lawrence J.F., Kaiser A. *et al.*, "Comparison between low-cost and traditional MEMS accelerometers: a case study from the M7.1 Darfield, New Zealand, aftershock deployment", *Annals of Geophysics, Citizen Empowered Seismology*, Special Section, pp. 728–737, 2011.

[CUE 03] Cuenot O., "Les algorithmes de détection automatique d'ondes sismiques", *CNAM*, 2003.

[DOL 13] Dolui K., Mukherjee S., Kanti Datta S., "Smart device sensing architectures and applications", *International IEEE Computer Science and Engineering Conference (ICSEC)*, Bangkok, Thailand, 2013.

[ELM 08] El Mhamdi J., Regragi F., Harfani F. *et al.*, "Traitement adaptatif appliqué au signal sismique," *Bulletin de l'Institut Scientifique*, vol. 30, pp. 13–22, 2008.

[ERV 11] Ervasti M., Dashti S., Reilly J. *et al.*, "iShake: mobile phones as seismic sensors – user study findings", *International Conference on Mobile and Ubiquitous Multimedia (MUM)*, Beijing, China, 2011.

[FAU 11] Faulkner M., Olson M., Chandy R. *et al.*, "The next big one: detecting earthquakes and other rare events from community-based sensors", *International Conference on Information Processing in Sensor Networks (IPSN)*, Chicago, United States, 2011.

[INT 15] International Atomic Energy Agency, The Fukushima Daiichi Accident, Vienna International Centre, 2015.

[LES 16a] Lesas A.-M., "Une perspective de la mobiquité au service de la gestion avant/pendant/après des séismes (Prototypage autour du projet SISMAPP)", *Informatique des Organisations et Systèmes d'Information et de Décision (INFORSID) Conference*, Grenoble, France, 2016.

[LES 16b] Lesas A.-M., "Détecter et monitorer les séismes grâce aux capteurs embarqués dans les smartphones", *Congrès Informatique des Organisations et Systèmes d'Information et de Décision (INFORSID) Conference*, Grenoble, France, 2016.

[LES 17] Lesas A.-M., Miranda S., *The Art and Science of NFC Programming*, ISTE Ltd, London and John Wiley & Sons, New York, 2017.

[MEH 16] Mehrazarin S., Tang B., Leyba K., "A MacBook based earthquake early warning system", *IEEE Conference on Computer Communications Workshops (INFOCOM WKSHPS)*, San Francisco, United States, 2016.

[MIN 15] MINSON S.E., BROOKS B.A., GLENNIE C.L. *et al.*, "Crowdsourced earthquake early warning," *Science Advances*, vol. 1, no. 13, 2015.

[MIR 11] MIRANDA S., "Introduction aux systèmes d'Information mobiquitaires: de l'utilisateur au nuage," *Ingéniérie des Systèmes d'Information (ISI)*, vol. 16, pp. 3–8, 2011.

[NAI 13a] NAITO S., AZUMA H., SENNA S., *et al.*, "On-site experiment of seismic monitoring network by utilization inside sensors of mobile terminal", *Japan Geoscience Union Meeting*, Makuhari, Japan, 2013.

[NAI 13b] NAITO S., AZUMA H., SENNA S. *et al.*, "Development and testing of a mobile application for recording and analyzing seismic data", *Journal of Disaster Research*, vol. 8, no. 15, pp. 990–1000, 2013.

[OLS 11] OLSON M., LIU A., FAULKNER M., "Rapid detection of rare geospatial events: earthquake warning applications", *Distributed Events-Based Systems' Conference*, New York, United States, 2011.

[REI 13] REILLY J., DASHTI S., ERVASTI M. *et al.*, "Mobile Phones as Seismologic Sensors: Automating Data Extraction for the iShake System", *IEEE Transactions on Automation Science and Engineering*, vol. 10, no. 12, pp. 242–251, 2013.

[SHA 11] SHALA U., RODRIGUEZ A., Indoor positioning using sensor-fusion in android devices, Master's thesis, School of Health and Society, Sweden, 2011.

[VIR 14] VIRIEUX J., Le Sud-Est est la région française la plus exposée au risque sismique, Le Figaro, April 7, 2014.

5

Information Systems for Supporting Strategic Decisions and Alerts in Pharmacovigilance

5.1. Introduction

The works presented in this chapter focus on one of current societal issues: how can the quality and the safety of health products available on the market be guaranteed to every citizen? This topic is directly related to the notion of pharmacovigilance and in the broader sense that of surveillance and strategic foresight (SF).

Pharmaceutical accidents of the industrial era bring about issues related to the implementation of a security system in this area, similar to what already exists in the civil nuclear, space and aerospace areas.

The main topic of pharmacovigilance concerns the surveillance of drugs and the prevention against the risk of adverse effects resulting from their use, whether this risk is potential or supported by proof. It constitutes a guarantee that remains valid throughout the lifetime of a drug[1]. It thus comes under the umbrella of the science concerned with the detection, assessment,

---

Chapter written by Yannick BARDIE and Thérèse LIBOUREL.

1 http://social-sante.gouv.fr/soins-et-maladies/medicaments/la-surveillance-des-medicaments/article/la-pharmacovigilance.

understanding and prevention of adverse effects or any other problem related to drugs[2].

More specifically, we focus on pharmacovigilance implemented by national and international health institutions and pharmaceutical industries[3] during trials and clinical studies.

We will first define the intrinsic difference that exists between the clinical study and clinical trial. The clinical study is a scientific approach whose purpose is to evaluate a technique devised for the prevention, diagnosis or treatment of a pathology (the assessment can be done using existing data, without exposing subjects). For its part, the clinical trial studies new and experimental therapies, according to the stage of development of the health product, which precedes marketing authorization (MA). The primary objective of the clinical trial is to confirm the safety of the molecule to measure its efficacy and evaluate its safety.

Pharmacovigilance organizations can be seen as complex systems and, analogously to any complex system, they are based on a structure, a functioning and a dynamic. Their operation can be nominal but can migrate toward an accidental functioning (provided by various random or intentional causes).

In this context, the main interest lies, on the one hand, in the analysis of the system *in toto* and its two areas (business and information systems), and second in the choice of a holistic strategy making it possible to avoid the migration toward accidental functioning, while at the same time satisfying the various multidimensional and multiorganizational requirements of pharmacovigilance.

At the moment, ongoing works in this area, to our knowledge, are in their early stages and our contribution focuses on a methodology for anticipatory and SF as well as on proposals for the strategic alignment of information systems (ISs) within the framework of new institutionalism. The institutional theory [DIM 83, MEY 77, SCO 13, MIG 09] indicates that parties involved passively adopt institutionalized practices; some authors suggest that there is a wide range of responses to institutional pressures, ranging from

---

2 This can easily be widely extended to the medical device, for which the term medical devices vigilance is appropriate.
3 As well as manufacturers of medical devices for medical devices vigilance.

acquiescence to manipulation including compromise, avoidance or provocation.

The structure of the chapter will be as follows. Section 5.2 details the origin, the current context and good practices of pharmacovigilance. Section 5.3 is dedicated to the analysis of the project system and the organization of a clinical trial based on a methodology recommended for the analysis of IS infrastructures and processes during the implementation of a biomedical experiment. Section 5.4, dedicated to the state of art, will recall the notions of SF and risk-based monitoring. This will allow us to then detail the issue in question in section 5.5. Finally, section 5.6 will present the recommended solution before addressing section 5.7, a conclusion which will position current perspectives.

5.2. Pharmacovigilance

5.2.1. *The origin of pharmacovigilance*

The first major accident of the industrial era of contemporary pharmacy was that involving thalidomide in 1957. The cause and effect relationship between the administration of the drug and its deleterious effects has been objectified by a university department of Uppsala University: the Uppsala Monitoring Center (www.umc.org).

Thalidomide has been marketed since 1957 by the Grünenthal laboratory under the commercial name CONTERGAN©, and along with the indication of being a sedative and a treatment for nausea, it was marketed in over 40 countries. Two years after its release, cases of phocomelia (phocomelia is a malformation by anomaly in development during pregnancy leading to atrophy and direct implantation of hands and feet on the torso) were reported. The active ingredient caused serious adverse effects in the form of a teratogenic action[4] on the embryo. By blocking the vascularization of developing members, it causes their atrophy. The drug inhibits angiogenesis[5]

---

4 Teratogens are pharmacological agents that, when used, cause the development of abnormal cell masses during fetal growth, leading to physical defects in the fetus.

5 Angiogenesis is a process describing the growth of new blood vessels (neovascularization) from pre-existing vessels. It is a normal physiological process, particularly encountered during embryonic development, but it is also a pathological process, primordial in the growth of malignant tumors and the development of metastases.

by interfering with the development of blood vessels of the fetus. Phocomelia children can be identified by their vestigial upper and sometimes lower members. After investigation, it was demonstrated that certain side effects that occurred during the preclinical phase had been ignored such as studies on animals showing weak drowsiness. Nonetheless, it should be pointed out that this major accident and the feedback therefrom have led to the strengthening of coordinated international pharmacovigilance. This scandal was decisive in the creation of the world center for pharmacovigilance, at present based in Uppsala in Sweden.

This center operates under the umbrella of the WHO (http://www.who-umc.org/) for the detection of pharmacovigilance events since 1978.

Over the last 40 years, regulatory constraints and ethical requirements related to clinical trials [LEF 95] have increased in developed countries. This has led to the relocation of trials to countries at a lower cost and having lower regulatory constraints (this is the case for many Eastern countries).

During this same period, the number of sites outside the United States has multiplied by 10, whereas the clinical trials in traditional countries has significantly declined. According to a study of the U.S. public database of clinical trials (www.clinicaltrial.gov) carried out by the 20 largest U.S. laboratories, one-third of trials were conducted entirely outside the United States (157 of 509) and the majority of investigating sites, regardless of the type of studies, were located outside the United States (13,521 sites outside the United States of the 24,206 sites identified). However, 80 diseases are affecting developing countries, whereas there are only 10 research projects devoted to them [THA 10].

5.2.2. *Present context*

Recent accidents have raised public awareness regarding the need for transparency and safety in the evaluation of health products. The case of VIOXX® can be identified as the most representative industrial, global, contemporary pharmaceutical accident similar to that of thalidomide in 1953 and Distilbene in 1977.

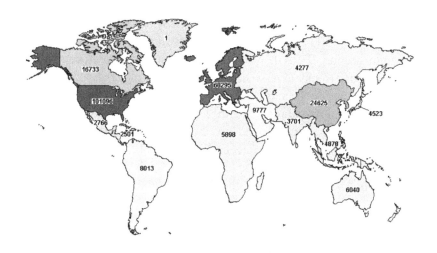

Figure 5.1. *Global distribution of clinical trials in the world (source: www.clinicaltrial.gov). For a color version of the figure, please see www.iste.co.uk/sedes/information.zip*

Rofecoxib (Common International Denomination) is a non-steroidal anti-inflammatory drug marketed that was under the proprietary name VIOXX® by the Merck and Co. laboratory until September 30, 2004, at which time Merck decided a worldwide withdrawal of the drug was necessary. The latter was a follow-up to a study against a placebo (named APPROVe) conducted on 2,600 patients, which was suddenly interrupted due to the near doubling number of myocardial infarctions in the group receiving treatment.

This NSAID (Non-Steroid Anti-Inflammatory Drug) of the coxib class was mainly used in the treatment of osteoarthritis, acute painful states and dysmenorrhea. The advantages of this new class of drugs were to provide an anti-inflammatory action similar to conventional NSAIDs with substantially fewer unwanted side effects such as burns or gastric ulcers.

Since the early stages of its commercialization in 1999, VIOXX® became the center of controversy concerning the real truth of its "therapeutic innovation". Despite this, the drug quickly became a blockbuster. Sold in more than 80 countries and representing 80 million prescriptions, this drug yielded to the Merck and Co. laboratory an average of $2.5 billion per year between 1999 and 2004, which is a total profit of about $11 billion. This success in a result of very aggressive marketing strategies ($100 million per year for direct advertising to consumers). When VIOXX® was withdrawn from the market in 2004 (while the drug was still approved by the Food and Drug Administration (FDA)), Merck acted as a transparent company and claimed that it has found adverse heart effects in its medication. This proved to be a false assertion because as early as 2000, in a double-blind study named VIGOR against naproxen, with 2,000 patients, twice the number of myocardial infarctions was found in the VIOXX® group. Merck then explained these results by a "protecting" the role of naproxen (which has never demonstrated) in strokes. The cardiovascular risk could thus have been detected nearly 4 years before its withdrawal from the market.

As a result, serious concerns were expressed within the scientific community; neither Merck nor the powerful FDA (U.S. competent authority) could recommend further studies to verify these allegations. Meanwhile, Merck initiated a $100 million advertising campaign to praise the benefits of VIOXX® for treating arthritis and other inflammatory diseases. The FDA could have (and it had all the powers necessary to do so) required that such a study be carried out. It could even have required that Merck included with its product a warning of the possibility of heart or vascular problems as long as the study did not demonstrate otherwise.

The cardiac risks of VIOXX® were predictable from the outset; they were part of its action mechanism and it was not possible for them to *not* occur. Its anti-COX-2 inhibits the prostacyclin synthesis and leaves the door wide open to thromboxane, a proaggregant, and therefore in principle, a risk of arterial, coronary or cerebral thrombosis. This is written, engraved in advance, into an inescapable biological logic.

From February 2001, an advisory committee recommended the FDA issue a warning about the possible link between VIOXX® and cardiovascular problems. In September 2001, the FDA asked Merck and Co. to stop misleading medical doctors on cardiovascular problems occurring due to VIOXX®. Then, in April 2002, the FDA required Merck to add information about cardiovascular problems in the product insert.

VIOXX® caused around 88,000–140,000 heart problems in the United States, of which 30% (about 27,000) were fatal from 1999 to 2003. Concerning Merck and Co., the complaints against this laboratory will amount to about $5 billion.

5.2.3. *Good pharmacovigilance practices*

Pharmacovigilance is the surveillance of drugs and the prevention against the risk of adverse side effects resulting from their use, whether this risk is potential or supported by proof. It is based on:

– the collection of adverse reactions based on spontaneous feedback provided by health professionals, patients and approved patient associations and manufacturers with the support of the network of 31 regional pharmacovigilance centers in France;

– the recording and the evaluation of this information, the implementation of surveys or studies to analyze risks, participation in the implementation and the follow-up of risk management plans;

– the assessment of the safety profile for use of the drug based on the collected data;

– the implementation of corrective actions (precautions or restrictions for use, contraindications or even product withdrawals) and communication with health professionals and the public;

– the communication and dissemination of any information related to the drug's safety of use;

– the participation in the public health policy to combat drug iatrogenesis[6].

Pharmacovigilance relies on a national and European regulatory basis: laws, decrees, directives and good pharmacovigilance practices published by order Good Clinical Practice (GCP)).

In France, on January 26, 2013, the minister entrusted the chief executive officer of health services with a mission concerning the redesigning of health vigilance. The goal of the mission was to identify means for:

– turning patients into the key players of the health and safety policy, by facilitating the reports that they provide;

– promoting the involvement of professionals, regardless of the manner they exercise, in the reporting of adverse events (AEs);

---

6 Drug iatrogenesis refers to adverse effects caused by drugs.

– clarifying the role of regional health agencies (Agences Régionales de Santé (ARS)) both for sharing reports and the management of signals and alerts, including in the debate of the future of regional structures supporting the ARS;

– optimizing the information system in the sense of better completeness, of greater relevance of collected signals and their treatment, by formalizing the conditions of use at the national and regional levels;

– reorganizing the chain for processing alerts by the different national agencies, to the first rank of which the ANSM (Agence Nationale de Suritdu Médicament et des produits de santé or French National Agency for Medicines and Health Products Safety) and the InVS (Institut de Veille Sanitaire or French Institute for Public Health Surveillance), specifying the articulation of the respective skills.

5.3. System and clinical trial project organization analysis

According to Rasmussen [RAS 97], the study of risk management involves an analysis of sociotechnical systems. The understanding of the roles, actions and strategies of the system actors requires the knowledge of the requirements and constraints of the system to which they belong.

Within the context of a clinical trial project organization[7], one can make a distinction between external business and IS strategies to this organization and internal business and IS strategies.

Figure 5.2 highlights the interactions within each area as well as between external, internal levels and cross-domain interactions.

The external business area defines a strategy: utilization safety and effectiveness of health products and to this end internally implements an infrastructure and institutional processes. In the era of digital technology, strategy as well as the set up of processes and the underlying information system infrastructure are based on advances in computer technology.

---

7 The project is a single process that consists of a set of coordinated and controlled activities, comprising start and end dates, undertaken with the purpose of achieving a goal in accordance with specific requirements, including time, cost and resources constraints (according to the ISO 10006:2003 standard and reformulated by the AFNOR as the X 50-105 standard).

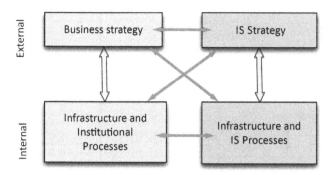

Figure 5.2. *Information system business areas interactions*

Rasmussen's vision relies on the structural hierarchy of key players and the implementation hierarchy (system dynamics).

An adaptation of this vision (see Figure 5.3) emphasizes the structural hierarchy of the actors of the global organization facing the technical system for implementing vigilance.

We will therefore dwell on this vision in order to better understand its different aspects.

5.3.1. *Pharmacovigilance and IS business view*

For any project, the pharmacovigilance system includes, from the business perspective, the following institutional stratifications:

– global level: the World Health Organization (WHO), the Uppsala Monitoring Center (UMC, umc.org);

– European level: the European Medicines Agency (EMA), which is the European agency for pharmacovigilance and drug evaluation;

– French national level: the ANSM, which is the French agency for the safety of health products;

– French regional level: the regional pharmacovigilance centers (CRPV).

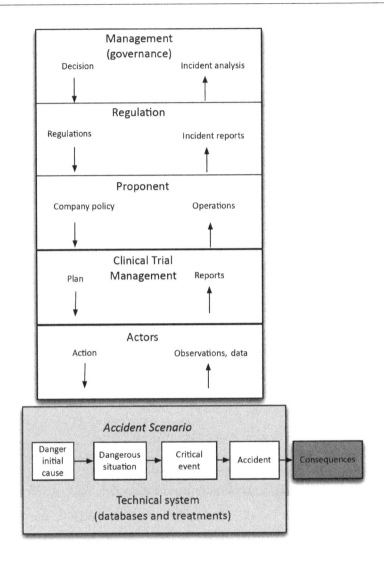

Figure 5.3. *Adaptation of Rasmussen's vision*

The national system is thus integrated to the EMA in compliance with the European regulatory context.

Beyond this, institutional personnel of other actors are directly involved at the clinical trial level:

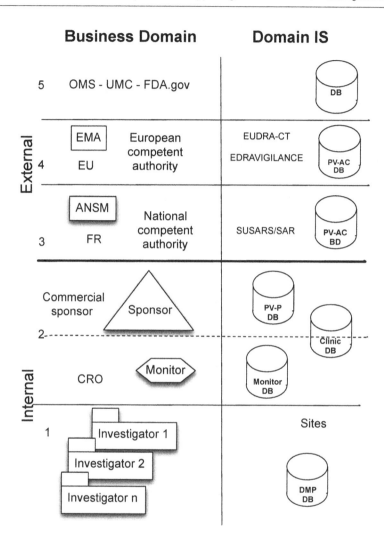

Figure 5.4. *Pharmacovigilance and IS business overview*

– health professionals (medical doctors, pharmacists) and investigators responsible for the practical implementation of the trial proposed by the sponsor, and for the synthesis of data collected in the form of a report;

– patients and/or patient associations;

– the sponsor and the pharmaceutical company (pharmaceutical laboratory or medical device manufacturer) who assumes the initiative of conducting the clinical trial;

– the monitor, as the person chosen and mandated by the sponsor, is responsible for monitoring the trial and ensuring that it is conducted, recorded and reported in accordance with the protocol (Standard Operating Procedures (SOP)), with GCP and with the regulatory requirements applicable. It serves as a link between the proponent and the investigator and reports her/his activity to the sponsor[8].

On the information system side, various data sources are involved in the overall process:

– at the investigator site level, the databases related to the patient medical records (PMR), filled in by doctors and nurses, etc., who communicate with various IS (see Figure 5.5);

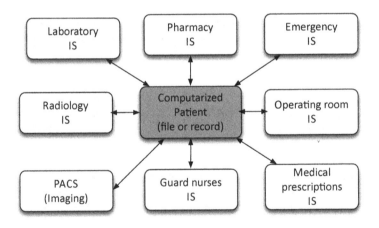

Figure 5.5. *Patient medical file*

---

8 The monitor should be trained appropriately and should have the scientific and/or clinical knowledge necessary to adequately control the trial process.

– at the sponsor-cro (Contract Research Organization: private subcontracting body in the given field) couple level, the clinical databases including, in particular, the Case Report Forms (CRF), which are records destined for the collection of all the data required by the study protocol, as well as the databases related to the vigilance plan comprising the documents identifying AEs (which are pages of the CRF, and which consequently will enhance the clinical database) and serious AEs (SAEs) (being the subject of a reporting based on AEs – the SAE is first an AE – as part of a process of acquisition separate from that of clinical data, into the pharmacovigilance database of the proponent);

– at the national level, the databases of the reported adverse reactions of serious adverse reaction (SAR) and suspected unexpected serious adverse reaction (SUSAR);

– at the European level, the Edravigilance database collecting SAR/SUSARs and the Eudra-CT database (for the Eudra-Clinical Trial) that lists the protocol numbers of clinical trials at the European level;

– on a global level, the UMC.org database (referring body for the WHO).

All are interesting from the vigilance point of view, especially SAR and SUSAR data. The Edravigilance database contains three types of SUSAR records: those originating directly from clinical trials, those originating from spontaneous reports in view of commercial use and finally those originating from meta-analyses. We consider that the acquisition of SUSARs based on meta-analyses is of great interest. As a matter of a fact, a meta-analysis is a crossover study between the results of various clinical experiments (high-quality randomized controlled trials) and points out aspects that are not directly taken into account by investigators and monitors on the ground. Thereby, they make it possible to officially collect detected adverse reactions, especially cases that could have gone unnoticed in one of the *princeps* clinical trials.

5.3.2. *Protocol overview*

The information transmission process involves numerous interactions between the various actors.

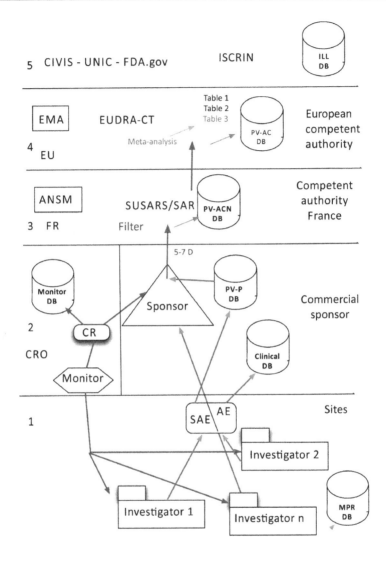

Figure 5.6. *Transmissions. For a color version of the figure, see www.iste.co.uk/sedes/information.zip*

In the context of clinical trials, perceived as a project-based enterprise, the trio sponsor, investigator and monitor is the basic organizational architecture underlying the course of the protocol and the flow of information and critical communications. The sponsor takes the initiative, implements and finances the trial until its conclusion; they are responsible for it. The investigator executes the protocol by recruiting patients within its investigative center (hospital), in order to provide the sponsor with evaluable clinical data. The monitor can assist the proponent in the design and the implementation of the protocol, but they are mainly responsible for controlling the execution (monitoring or quality assurance) of the protocol (referenced and referred to by its EUDRA CT number) in the investigational center.

Accordingly, the monitor (who may be a CRO – Contract Research Organization) is the "guardian angel of the clinical trial" because they protect the rights of participants and ensures the quality of data (true and verifiable in the source documentation). They ensure that the research is conducted according to the protocol and supported by appropriate documentation.

The monitor should specifically verify (and formulate in a monitoring report carried out after every site visit) that:

– data required by the protocol are reported accurately in the CRF and are faithful to the data source[9] (contained in PMR);

– any changes in the dose and/or therapy is well-documented for every participant (subject) of the trial;

– adverse events, concomitant treatments and intercurrent diseases are reported according to the protocol in the CRF;

– visits that subjects do not make, the tests which are not conducted and examinations that are not performed are clearly indicated as such in the CRF;

– all the samples and biopsies from subjects enrolled in the trial are reported and explained in the CRF;

– appropriate corrections, additions or deletions are established, dated, explained (when necessary) and reported by the investigator or by a staff member of the investigator who is allowed to initially modify the CRF on their behalf.

In addition, they must:

– inform the investigator of any input, omission or irregularity error at the CRF level;

_____

9 Original documents, data and records presenting a research interest: medical records, radios, evaluation booklets.

– determine whether all adverse events (AEs) are correctly reported within the timeframe required by the GCP, the protocol, the ethics committee, the proponent and the applicable regulatory requirements;

– determine whether the investigator retains essential documents (source documentation and investigator folder);

– communicate deviations from the protocol, SOP, GCP and the regulatory requirements applicable to the investigator and take appropriate measures devised to prevent the recurrence of detected deviations.

The investigator, the monitor and the sponsor have the imperative duty to transmit specific information on the occurrence of AEs and SAEs.

Lastly, it is the sponosr who will decide to send to national (ANSM) and European (EMA) health authorities the cases of the most serious and severe reactions, attributable to the product under study (SUSAR unexpected/SAR expected).

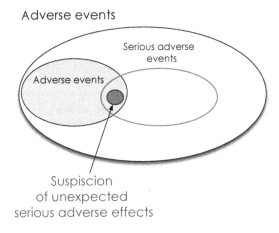

Figure 5.7. *Adverse events and reactions*

Expected SARs and serious reactions that are neither fatal nor life threatening must be reported as soon as possible, but not later than 15 calendar days after first knowledge by the sponsor. On the other hand, unexpected fatal or deadly SUSARs occurring during clinical trials must be notified (by email, phone, fax or in writing) as soon as possible, but not later than 7 calendar days after first knowledge by the sponsor.

A supplementary report as comprehensive as possible may follow within 8 additional calendar days. The sponsor declares the fact to the authority by using form CIOMS-I (Suspect Adverse Reaction Reaction)[10]. The monitor will ensure on-site that these documents have been received and read by the investigator. These notifications are to be classified in the Investigator Site File (ISF).

Apart from the project concerned by the current clinical trial, there is a community comprising all actors of all protocols that are conducted with this product. A copy of the CIOMS-I form associated with any SUSAR occurring during the current clinical trial form will be sent electronically by the promoter to this community:

– to the member state in which the reaction occurred;

– to the other member states concerned;

– to the agency (Eudravigilance CT module);

– to investigators and monitors using the product (in other protocols).

5.3.3. *Overview of essential records*

The permanent record of the research must be established from the beginning of the research: with the sponsor (Trial Master File or SMF) and in the centers (Site files/Investigator files: ISF). This folder contains all the documents referred to as *essential*. These mentioned in article R.11-23.61 of the Public Health Code individually or all together allow the evaluation of the conduct of the research (BPC, 1.16). They serve to demonstrate the compliance of the investigator, proponent and monitor with the GCP standards and with all regulatory requirements applicable.

They also serve a number of other important objectives:

– their proper management in a timely manner with the investigator and the promoting institution can greatly contribute to the successful management of the trial based on the triplet of sponsor, investigator and monitor, in that they are part of the information system of the clinical trial;

---

10 http://www.cioms.ch/images/stories/CIOMS/cioms.pdf expedited reports – CIOMS Council for International Organizations of Medical Sciences.

– these are the documents that are generally verified by the independent audit function of the sponsor and inspected by the regulatory authority or authorities within the framework of the trial to confirm the validity of its conduct and the integrity of the data acquired.

They are verified before the end of the trial, and must be kept (for 15 years or the lifetime of the product on the market, the longer of the two periods) in order to be able to be quickly made available; any changes to records must be able to be tracked and inspected by the regulatory authorities. The investigator, the sponsor and site managers shall take all measures necessary to prevent the accidental or premature destruction of the documents or data.

The minimum list of essential documents comprises various documents grouped in three sections according to the phase of the trial during which they are generated: (1) before the beginning of the trial clinical phase, (2) during the conduct of the clinical trial process, and (3) after completion or at the end of the process.

Each section gives a table describing the list of documents, a description of the purpose of the document and also specifies whether it will be delivered to the investigator or to the sponsor or to both.

| Document title | Object | Level storage | |
		File Investigator IS	File Sponsor IS
8.2.1 XXXXX	XXXXX	X	
8.2.1 YYYYY	YYYYY	X	X

Figure 5.8. *Table of essential documents*

5.4. The state of the art

SF is defined as the proactive process by which the company (or part of it) tracks and assimilates information of an anticipatory nature about changes in its socioeconomic environment, with the objective of finding business opportunities as well as acting quickly and at the right time.

We use the following definition: "Strategic Foresight (SF) is the proactive information process by which an organization initiates an anticipatory process of looking for early signals in its socio-economic environment for the creative purpose of opening opportunities and reducing risks associated with its uncertainty" [ANS 75].

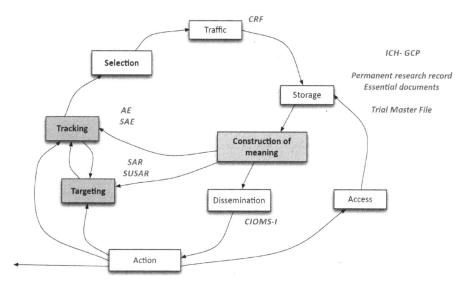

Figure 5.9. *The strategic foresight cycle*

According to Lesca [LES 00], "strategic foresight is a process comprising four critical phases: the targeting of the players to be monitored; the tracking of targeted information; the transmission and dissemination of the information gathered and the processing of collected information into meaningful form so that it will support management processes".

We can transpose the cycle in Figure 5.9 in the context of the study in question, information flow via the CRF and the on-site storage (research document) accessible to investigating participants that track AE and SAE events in order to feedback the targeted information; in this case, SAR and SUSARS through the CIOMS-I.

Publications dedicated to strategic foresight in the pharmacovigilance area are virtually nonexistent.

The process of monitoring however focuses on the issue of risk management (risk-based monitoring (RBM) – transposition at the level of the ISO 31000:2009 standard onto risk management). This has been the subject of studies, two of which serve as references to institutions: OPTIMON and ADAMON that are cited by the FDA and the EMA and destined to proponents of clinical trials.

OPTIMON (monitoring optimization) [JOU 11] observes that monitoring, in the current state, is not optimal and relies on an analytical grid including three steps: (1) definition of the topic(s) for study; (2) identification of one or several conditions of increased risk and (3) determination of the risk level.

ADAMON [BRO 09] is a proposal for a tool able to systematize risk assessment and for the implementation of measures targeted for quality management.

On the other hand, we have focused on the concept of weak signals: the designation weak signals introduces a parallel between the fields of electromagnetism, electronics and that of information and decision systems that multiply as part of the company's management framework[11] [COH 64], [JAR 08]. Similarly to generalized or specialized types of computing platforms affected by the civil and military surveillance of space areas, strategic foresight can rely on a device equivalent to a radar (radio detection and ranging) in order to capture primary, emerging information of unclear origins.

It is likely that weak signals are particularly significant in specific procedures that organizations can implement so as to increase the probability of being capable of releasing warnings in the presence of an emerging event?

5.5. Issues

Was it possible to anticipate risks? Could industrial pharmaceutical accidents be avoided? What are the risks nowadays? Where and when will they occur? Assessments concerning therapeutic accidents are partial. They would be responsible for 130,000 hospital admissions (1% of admissions) and

---

11 Organization, business.

18,000 annual deaths (3% of deaths), of which experts claim half could have been avoided. It is thus useful and necessary that a maximum amount of foresight information be available, in order to temporize and map the global pharmaceutical risk and global pharmacovigilance.

The core of the problem can therefore be formulated: can we design specific procedures to increase the probability of being able to signal warnings in the presence of an emerging event?

As part of the framework of new approaches to pharmaceutical safety (under legislation[12] and new regulations[13]), are we able to identify at an early stage threats and opportunities by organizing SF and targeting early warning signs [LES 97, LES 11].

The purpose of the work that we wish to undertake is to provide a scientific basis for the emergence of new instruments (instruments, in the sense given by Engerstöm [QUE 12] for security monitoring in the field of the clinical development of health-related products.

According to Gilbert *et al.* [GIL 13], "to use a tool, it should be appropriated, and this appropriation involves changes at the user's level. What is trivially called a 'tool' does not forcibly constitute an instrument. To qualify as an instrument, constructions, methodologies for use, are necessary that organize the action".

These instruments would be capable of preventing serious AEs affecting patients and subjects but also of detecting, preventing or providing evidence of fraud or bad practices in unethical trials, and thus of maintaining the clinical research approach within an "acceptable safety envelope" [ARE 13].

How can one design structured, reticulate and pro-active instruments at the internal organizational level that allow this organization to explore its external environment to acquire, distribute and use forward-looking information for the purpose of anticipating plausible future changes? How *in fine* can disaster be made unlikely to happen [FRI 61]?

---

12 Law concerning the strengthening of drug health-related and health products safety and application of the European regulation in 2018.

13 In Europe, the reference text for pharmacovigilance is: "detailed guidance on the collection, verification and presentation of adverse reaction reports arising from clinical trials on medicinal products for human use" (April 2004).

5.6. Proposal: considered solution

The solution considered is built from various findings given in section 5.3 and takes into account the emergence of advanced management and technology.

Based on the interactions between fields described in section 5.3, Henderson [HEN 92] describes and categorizes strategies making use of information technology as levers for decision-making and in which the IS plays a critical role in the transformation of the institutional process (see Figure 5.10).

Alignment, according to this model, can be achieved by the following four strategies:

– implementation strategy (the external institutional business strategy induces the implementation of infrastructures and internal processes and the IS infrastructure follows);

– technological influence (the external business strategy generates external changes in IS strategies (standards) that in turn induces changes in infrastructures and internal IS processes);

– technological operation (it is the external IS strategy and its technological breakthroughs that drive internal processes and infrastructures);

– technological implementation (the infrastructure of the global external IS influences and improves the quality of the institutional process).

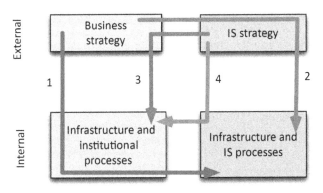

Figure 5.10. *Alignment strategies*

Within the pharmacovigilance context, the process of aligning information systems according to objectives and business strategy is, in our view, a major challenge. The specificity and sensitivity of pharmacovigilance[14] will depend on the quality of the strategic alignment [HEN 92].

European and American authorities preferentially advocate strategy 3 because of the evolution of information technology in connection with the notion of *integrity*.

As a matter of fact, the issue related to integrity covers various dimensions, which are as follows:

– the integrity of voluntary participants (patients and subjects) to medical research and end users of health solutions; in the field of studies, which is biomedical research and in particular in the area of clinical trials, the integrity of participants is crucial. The possibility of conducting a clinical trial is under the control of ethics committees or people protection committees as well as pharmacovigilance authorities;

– the integrity of the research and development processes of data used for security analyses. The integrity of the data generation process is supported by the study protocol framework. This is the process of data generation where the early stages of the production of weak signals can be found [ANS 75];

– the integrity of actors (in a moral sense) within the organizations conducting health solutions development projects;

– data integrity (source documentation, namely the PMR, clinical, monitoring, surveillance and pharmacovigilance).

First of all, we thus propose following the choice of strategy 3 and under legal injunction of European[15], French and also American authorities (EMA, FDA, ANSM) responsible for implementing the surveillance of risk (RBM) in the field of clinical trials.

---

14 The terms specificity and sensitivity as in the statistical sense.

15 These injunctions emanate from neo-institutional consortiums that have established studies and standards on the subject (CTTI: Clinical Trials Transformation Initiative, and Transcelerate).

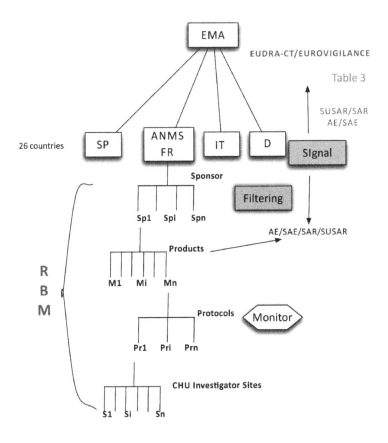

Figure 5.11. *Overall view within the RBM context. For a color version of the figure, see www.iste.co.uk/sedes/information.zip*

Figure 5.11 shows the overall view of the organizational structure of work (work breakdown structure (WBS)) of projects related to clinical trials within the RBM context. The WBS is a hierarchical decomposition of works necessary to achieve the objectives of the project, that is to say the organizational structure of the key players (especially of the monitor) and the actions in the trial.

As a reminder, during a test and according to the feedback of information administered by the monitor, the sponsor redirects toward Eudravigilance the SAR/SUSARS signals and eventually the AE/SAE signals after filtering, and therefore it is actually at the filtering level of the interpretation that the problem arises.

Unlike "standard" monitoring that consists of checking 100% of source data (at the investigation center) and in identifying source data transcription errors (in the patient's medical record) in the CRF in paper or electronic form, RBM is intended to optimize and reduce on-site monitoring. The intensity of on-site data verification will therefore be adapted to the risk level, preset at the beginning of the study in the risk management plan (by type of test, medication, development stage, by country, etc.) but also through adaptation during testing, according to the risk signals perceived in the databases created. Among other things, this will make it possible to optimize on-site monitoring, and therefore to decrease the time spent on-site, and as a result, the cost allocated to global monitoring (almost 30% of the budget of a study are dedicated to monitoring).

This requires in particular remote monitoring, a monitoring system that relies on information technologies to transmit field data almost in real time and without physically traveling. It should be noted that the verifications of consents, of eligibility criteria, and security data (SAE) remain necessarily unchanged during on-site monitoring. In its guide, the FDA encourages proponents to "perform global statistical analyses of study data to identify sites that are aberrant compared to others". In other words, the proponent is able to identify centers whose data differ considerably from others based on statistical algorithms. The sponsor will seek to detect incompatible information generated by a center by comparing with the data produced by all of the other sites participating in the clinical trial. Preventing and identifying risks (error detection, carelessness, fraud, falsification) at the earliest by means of statistics allows for the problem to be anticipated and corrected before it aggravates[16].

On the infrastructure side, the disparity of systems and databases involved in the transmission of the various types of information (see Figure 5.12) can obviously cause defects in terms of missing data or data redundancy in the variety of information stored and consequently possible distortions at the interpretation level in tracking AEs and SAEs.

---

16 CTTI, Transcelerate, EMA, FDA, available at: https://www.ctti-clinicaltrials.org/ and at: http://www. transceleratebiopharmainc.com/Initiatives/risk-based-monitoring/.

The correlations between data (represented by red links in Figure 5.12) pertaining to pharmacovigilance databases, clinical databases and *in situ* control databases (monitoring) are not operational (when they exist they are achieved on a case-by-case basis and manually).

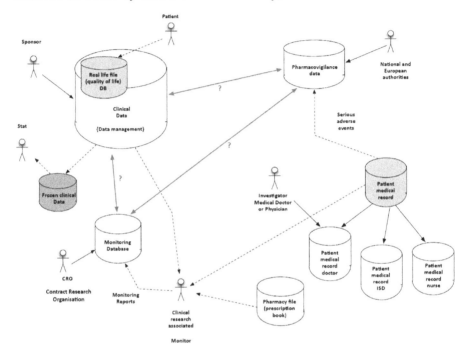

Figure 5.12. *A heterogeneous set of ISs. For a color version of the figure, see www.iste.co.uk/sedes/information.zip*

The implementation of information systems "integrated" in this area of activity would thus be a major innovation because it would allow remote monitoring, mentioned earlier, which relies on information technologies to transmit field data in near real time[17].

The cluster structure, a geographical spin-off of project resources and their necessary optimization in addition to the necessary planning-based time management to develop the drug ("time to market" or better "time to cure"),

---

17 It should be noted that verifications of consents, eligibility criteria and security data (SAE) remain unchanged during on-site monitoring.

makes the use of a global information system of the enterprise resource planning (ERP) indispensable.

Therefore, ERP is used in the presence of an information system that allows the management and the monitoring on a daily basis by means of an automated system (workflow engine) of complete information and operational services of an organization. All the information is thus linked together like a chain-link data flow.

Besides the fact that this is a new generation system, the advantage of such solutions lies in its capability to provide tools for business intelligence (data mining) enabling the real-time analysis of data on a very large scale on all of the user's data.

This would have two main effects: to increase the quality and productivity of agents around what we call an *information organization matrix* or *organizational matrix* including the possibility to build a first-choice statistical and forward-looking instrument centered on this matrix.

With this in mind, the solution under consideration is based on the intuition that one should be able to proceed to a "spectral analysis" of the information (data and knowledge) present in this matrix with the purpose of improving the monitoring around the process of the trial.

The organizational matrix is the result of a vision created by the various interactions taking place based on the essential documents that should enable the perpetuation of the data pertaining to these interactions. The underlying idea is to study in an innovative manner the protocol and the workflow that govern the clinical trial.

To build this, we rely on Section 8 of the GCP-ICH (CPMP/ICH/135/95ICH 2002) of the Good Clinical Practices according to the ICH consensus (International Conference in Harmonization), which details the documentation of the trial. It is used as a chronological checklist of the actions to be carried out before, during and after the active phase of the trial. The traceability principle prevails in the ICH consensus, thereby to every action there are corresponding documents. It is also necessary to obtain a system for securing data by way of encryption, while allowing the authorized person, in accordance with the rules established in the world of clinical research, to have access to the useful and necessary information, whether it concerns information having a direct connotation with the progress of the trial, or critical information that requires a different treatment. For this purpose, we will thus sequence chronologically (following the order of generation of documents and records) the set of tasks of the trial and subsequent documents. The milestones 8.2.x, 8.3.x and 8.4.x correspond to the three most important moments of the trial: (1) 8.2.x: before the start of the on-site trial, that is, before the inclusion of the first patient, (2) 8.3.x: active phase of the trial between the first patient first visit and the freeze of the database (namely after the LPLV (Last Patient Last Visit) but especially once all corrections requests have been resolved) (3) 8.4.x: closure phase of the trial that comprises the closing visit and the drafting of the final study report.

Therefrom, we are able to design and fill in a matrix table (see Figure 5.13) for each case study.

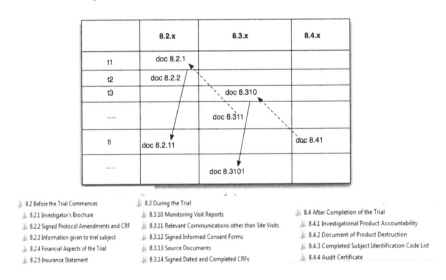

	8.2.x	8.3.x	8.4.x
t1	doc 8.2.1		
t2	doc 8.2.2		
t3		doc 8.310	
....		doc 8.311	
ti	doc 8.2.11		doc 8.41
....		doc 8.3101	

8.2 Before the Trial Commences	8.3 During the Trial	8.4 After Completion of the Trial
8.2.1 Investigator's Brochure	8.3.10 Monitoring Visit Reports	8.4.1 Investigational Product Accountability
8.2.2 Signed Protocol Amendments and CRF	8.3.11 Relevant Communications other than Site Visits	8.4.2 Document of Product Destruction
8.2.3 Information given to trial subject	8.3.12 Signed Informed Consent Forms	8.4.3 Completed Subject Identification Code List
8.2.4 Financial Aspects of the Trial	8.3.13 Source Documents	8.4.4 Audit Certificate
8.2.5 Insurance Statement	8.3.14 Signed Dated and Completed CRFs	

Figure 5.13. *Matrix table originating from the organizational matrix*

This table should next be submitted to various treatments [ARQ 94] in order to detect weak signals in the correlations. These could be, for example, sparse and discrete algorithms. These sparse (algorithmic) methods for estimation and detection have, since the development of the theory of wavelets 25 years ago, enabled a large body of work in the field of the sparse and flexible representation of functions (signal, images).

We believe that the processing of weak signals in the matrix table of each trial could lead to an *instrument* which, based on collective intelligence, would ensure a process of SF [AMA 99] at the level of the various key players involved (laboratories, Contract Research Organization, health authorities and interested parties (shareholders and insurers)).

5.7. Conclusion

The various events described in 5.4 have contributed to strengthening pharmaceutical foresight, in particular due to the emergence of phase-IV studies[18].

These accidents have driven the development of laws and "guidelines". The assessment of the benefit/risk ratio before releasing the drugs to the market has become the rule for recording government agencies.

Are we not within a context of primariness[19] and in the presence of a situation of limited rationality [SIM 57][20] due to incomplete information on the question raised by the study? In this context, can clinical research managers make objectively rational decisions, and rational from the organization's point of view [SIM 57], as they would in a situation of substantive rationality (Vienna School)? In other words, in this context of limited rationality, related to the ontological dilemma of the clinical trial, is it possible to consider computational procedures in order to develop tools for supporting decision-making? Therefore, would it be possible to program in this context of uncertainty? Would it be possible to develop a heuristic model of factual analysis of perceived signals in the trial organizational matrix (as per GCP-ICH)? Moreover, will we observe resistance to change [JIA 00]

---

18 So-called phase-IV trials are performed under conditions close to the usual decision-making process. These tests are designed to identify potential rare adverse effects not detected during previous stages (pharmacovigilance) and to specify the conditions of use for certain groups of patients at risk. See http://www.sanofi.com/innovation/essais-cliniques-et-resultats/phases/phases.aspx.

19 Primariness: according to PEIRCE, the semiotic process is a triadic relationship between a sign or represent a men (primary), an object (second) and an interpretant (third).

20 In the field of the theory of organizations, the hypothesis of limited rationality has focused researches on the analysis of collective decision-making and on the interactions of actors whose strategies are subjected to constraints

when implementing such systems? How can acceptance be guaranteed by the actors? Could the matrix thus defined provide support for an IS for health monitoring in clinical trials as part of a process of risk analysis and management in the field of pharmacovigilance? To develop computer-based, cybernetic tools for modeling trials is tantamount to developing a new sector in Europe and France, by optimizing health monitoring and SF to increase the safety of health products and improve the efficiency of research and clinical development.

On a neo-institutional level, how will monitoring be structured in governmentality? How and by whom will the control, static and dynamic organizational management in clinical research be carried out within the framework of the new European regulation on clinical trials? Will we witness resistance to change? Will we witness resistance and conflicts when implementing information systems able to manage risk-based monitoring? As such, will we observe resistance to change during the implementation of such systems? How can acceptance be guaranteed by the actors? Would such IS be chosen by managers? Is it technologically and sociotechnologically possible to develop safe computer and cybernetics tools in the field of the clinical evaluation of health products?

5.8. References

[AMA 99] AMABILE S., "De la veille stratégique à une attention réticulée. Le réseau d'attention interorganisationnel des mutuelles d'assurance automobile", *Revue Systèmes d'information et management*, vol. 4, no. 2, pp. 97–118, 1999.

[ANS 75] ANSOFF H.I., "Managing strategic surprise by response to weak signal", *California Management Review*, vol. 18, no. 2, pp. 21–33, 1975.

[ARE 13] ARENA L., ORIOL N., PASTORELLI I., "Système d'information et gestion du couple performance sécurité : trajectoires comparées de trois situations extrêmes", *Systèmes d'information* et *management*, vol. 18, no. 1, pp. 87–123, 2013.

[ARQ 94] ARQUES P.-Y., BOUCHER J.-M., HILLION A. *et al.*, "Méthodes en traitement du signal bruité", *Techniques de l'ingénieur. Informatique industrielle*, vol. 1, no. R7031, pp. R7031–R7031, 1994.

[BRO 09] BROSTEANU O., HOUBEN P., IHRIG K. *et al.*, "Risk analysis and risk adapted on-site monitoring in noncommercial clinical trials", *Clinical Trials*, vol. 6, no. 6, pp. 585–596, available at: https://www.ncbi.nlm.nih.gov/pubmed/19897532, 2009.

[COH 64] COHEN K., CYERT R.M., *Theory of the Firm*, Prentice Hall Int., New York, 1964.

[DIM 83] DiMAGGIO P.J., POWELL W.W., "The iron cage revisited: institutional isomorphism and collective rationality in organizational fields", *American Sociological Review*, vol. 48, no. 2, pp. 147–160, 1983.

[FRI 61] FRITZ C., "Disaster", in MERTON R.K., NISBET R.A. (eds), *Contemporary Social Problems*, Harcourt, Brace and World, New York, 1961.

[GIL 13] GILBERT P., RAULET-CROSET N., MOUREY D. *et al.*, "Pour une contribution de la théorie de l'activité au changement organisationnel", *@GRH*, no. 2, pp. 67–88, 2013.

[HEN 92] HENDERSON J.C., VENKATRAMAN N., "Strategic alignment: a model for organizational transformation through information technology", in KOCHAN T.A., USEEM M. (eds), *Transforming Organizations*, Oxford University Press, New York, 1992.

[JAR 08] JARDAT R., "How democratic internal law leads to low cost efficient processes: practices as a medium of interaction between institution and organization", *Society and Business Review*, vol. 3, no. 1, 2008.

[JIA 00] JIANG J.J., MUHANNAB W.A., KLEINC G., "User resistance and strategies for promoting acceptance across system types", *Information and Management*, vol. 37, no. 1, pp. 25–36, 2000.

[JOU 11] JOURNOT V., PIGNON J-P., GAULTIER C., *et al.* "Validation of a risk-assessment scale and a risk-adapted monitoring plan for academic clinical research studies: the pre-Optimon study", *Contemporary Clinical Trials*, vol. 32, no 1, p. 16–24, 2011.

[LEF 95] LE FLOCH J.-P., PERLEMUTER L., *Essais thérapeutiques et études cliniques*, Masson, 1995.

[LES 94] LESCA H., "Veille stratégique pour le management stratégique. Etat de la question et axes de recherche", *Economie et sociétés*, vol. 20, no. 5, pp. 31–50, 1994.

[LES 97] LESCA H., Veille stratégique : concepts et démarche de mise en place dans l'entreprise, Association des professionnels de l'information et de la documentation, Lyon, 1997.

[LES 00] LESCA N., "Processus de construction du sens à partir de signes d'alerte précoce : proposition d'un nouvel outil d'aide à la production de connaissance Puzzle®", *IX^{ieme} Conférence Internationale de Management Stratégique*, 2000.

[LES 11] LESCA H., LESCA N., Weak Signals for Strategic Intelligence : Anticipation Tool for Managers, ISTE Ltd, London and John Wiley & Sons, New York, 2011.

[MEY 77] MEYER J.W., ROWAN B., "Institutionalized organizations: formal structure as myth and ceremony", *American Journal of Sociology*, vol. 83, no. 2, pp. 340–363, 1977.

[MIG 09] MIGNERAT M., RIVARD S., "Positioning the institutional perspective in information systems research", *Journal of Information Technology*, vol. 24, no. 4, pp. 369–391, 2009.

[QUE 12] QUENTIN I. "Le système général de l'activité d'Engeström", available at: https://isabellequentin.wordpress.com/2012/09/16/le-systeme-general-de-lactivite-dengestrom/, 2012.

[RAS 97] RASMUSSEN J., "Risk Management in a Dynamic Society: A Modelling Problem", *Safety Science*, vol. 27, nos 2–3, pp. 183–213, 1997.

[SCO 13] SCOTT W.R., "Institutions and organizations. Ideas, interests and identities", *Sage Publications*, vol. 17, no. 2, 2013.

[SIM 57] SIMON H.A., *Administrative Behavior: A Study of Decision-making Processes in Administrative Organizations*, Macmillan Co., New York, 1957.

[THA 10] THALABARD J.-C., "Enjeux éthiques de la méthodologie des essais cliniques", *Traité de Bioéthique*, ERES, pp. 742–757, 2010.

6

An Ontologically-based Trajectory Modeling Approach for an Early Warning System

6.1. Introduction

Thanks to advances in scientific research, communication and information studies, and sensor technologies, considerable progress has been made in the field of early warning systems, especially for animal zone tracking. A global early warning system is needed to inform us of pending threats. The basic idea behind early warning is that the earlier and more accurately we are able to predict short- and long-term potential risks associated with natural and human-induced hazards, the more likely we will be able to manage and mitigate a disaster's impact on society, economies and the environment. Early warning is "the provision of timely and effective information, through identified institutions, that allows individuals exposed to hazard to take action to avoid or reduce their risk and prepare for effective response" [UNE 12].

Scientific research has focused on biological early warning systems over the last few decades [BUT 01, GRE 03]. In order to adapt the system to various regional environmental conditions and achieve different monitoring aims, biological early warning systems have been diversified using various test organisms such as water fleas, mussels, algae and fish [BAL 94, BEN 82, BOR 97, HEN 93]. Within the framework of defining and building a

---

Chapter written by Jamal MALKI and Alain BOUJU.

biological warning information system, several animals are used: mammal, bird, herp, invert, etc. Raw trajectories of these species are captured and analyzed over long periods.

Using collected data and other external data sources, we are now able to identify precise states of these animals in their natural environment. Different types of behavioral parameters have been developed for various kinds of monitoring systems related to their state.

This work presents an approach for integrating trajectories of marine mammal, namely seals, into an early warning tracking system. The raw data captured, commonly called a trajectory, traces an animal from a departure point to a destination point as a data sequence (sample points captured, time of the capture). Trajectory data are captured by sensors included in a tag glued to the fur of the animal behind the head (Figure 6.1). Captured trajectories consist of spatial, temporal and spatiotemporal data. Trajectory data can also contain some extra data. These datasets are organized into sequences. Every sequence, mapped to a temporal interval, characterizes a defined state of the animal. In our application, we consider three main states of a seal: *hauling out, diving* and *cruising*. Every state is related to a seal's activity. For example, a foraging activity occurs during the diving state.

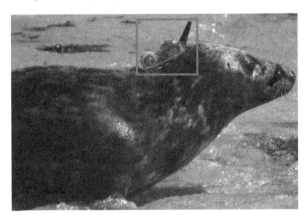

Figure 6.1. *Seal equiped with the sensor*

To detect the appropriate or protected zone used by a seal, this study develops an early warning system that integrates an alarm rule into the seal trajectory model. For that, we detect the seals' foraging areas in order to assess the interactions with human fisheries activities. Our aim is to quickly and automatically identify those important (foraging) areas from the seals trajectories. First of all, we need a trajectory model. In our previous work [WAN 13b], we defined a trajectory ontology model taking into account domain, spatial and temporal data. Using the ontological rules associated with this model, we compute the inference over these data. The experimental results addressed time computation and space storage problems of the ontology inference. Then, we proposed some solutions to reduce the inference complexity by defining time restrictions in the inference passes refinements in [WAN 13a]. This later study focused mainly on the term of time computation.

In the present work, we continue studying the ontological inference complexity, especially in terms of inference space storage complexity. We propose two-tier inference filters on trajectory data. In other words, two distinct operations are performed to enhance the inference: primary and secondary filter operations. The primary filter is applied to the captured data with the consideration of domain constraints. This filter allows fast selection of the analyzed data to pass along to the secondary filter. The latter computes the inference over the data output of the primary filter.

This chapter is organized as follows. Section 6.2 summarizes recent work related to early warning and monitoring systems with a focus on those based on trajectory data. In this context, we focus on approaches that define data models taking into account low level and semantic aspects. Section 6.3 introduces our approach and illustrates an overview of our domain data model called "trajectory ontology" and the "semantic trajectory ontology". Section 6.4 gives an overview of the "domain trajectory model". In sections 6.5 and 6.6, we show that the trajectory ontology defines temporal concepts mapped to the W3C OWL-Time ontology. Section 6.7 details the trajectory ontology inference framework and the integrated knowledge. In section 6.8, we implement the trajectory, the domain and the time ontologies rules. Section 6.9 addresses the complexity of the ontology inference over the domain and temporal rules. Section 6.10 introduces an application domain inference refinement. Section 6.11 evaluates the ontology inference over the proposed refinement and presents some results about seal zone tracking for the early warning system. Finally, section 6.12 concludes this work and presents some prospects.

6.2. Related work

In 2012, the United Nations Environment Programme (UNEP) published an analysis of the state of the art and future directions of early warning systems [UNE 12]. Divided into 4 parts, this study introduces the basic concepts of early warning systems and the role of earth observation systems for disasters and environmental change, focusing on existing early warning/ monitoring systems, and presents a global multihazard approach to early warning. The aim of this report is to identify current gaps and future needs of early warning systems through the analysis of the state of the art on existing early warning and monitoring systems for environmental hazards. The report gives interesting guidelines for developing early warning systems.

In [DOO 12], the authors present a study for developing a coastal flooding early warning system (CoFEWs) by integrating existing sea-state monitoring technology, numerical ocean forecasting models, historical databases and experiences, as well as computer science. A warning signal is presented when the storm water level that accumulated from astronomical tides, storm surge and wave-induced run-up exceeds the alarm sea level. A biological early warning and emergency management support system is given for water pollution accidents [YUA 09]. This research presents a system that integrates an online water quality monitoring device with a water quality model. The system has been instantiated in Douhe Reservoir. The monitoring device is based on water quality probes and biological sensors, which use fish motion as an indicator. Another biological early warning system is developed by [JEO 14] from the swimming behavior of Daphnia magna.

The point of view shared by these works, and certainly others not cited, lies in the fact that the system is based on data considered only in their raw states. The data are available through flat files or databases, often relational.

Based on captured data, early warning systems need a modeling approach to understand and analyze these data that we also call trajectories. Recently, several approaches have been developed because the access to the captured data became real and easy, especially with the advent of open data sharing platforms, like Movebank Data Repository [CRO 15].

Several research projects on semantic trajectory modeling started from the GeoPKDD project [GEO 05]. The GeoPKDD project emphasized the need to address and to use semantic data about moving objects for efficient trajectory analysis. To continue the investigation on the discovery of knowledge and the exploitation of moving object data, GeoPKDD has been followed first by MODAP [MOD 12] and more recently by SEEK [SEE 15]. The same community has recently presented an interesting research report in this area in [PAR 13]. Among the active initiatives aiming at boosting the research on moving object modeling, analysis and visualization, a notable contribution includes the COST action MOVE [MOV 13].

Parent *et al.* [SPA 08] introduced the first conceptual model for trajectories. This model is an evolution of the spatiotemporal MADS model to support trajectories [PAR 06]. They addressed trajectories as movements corresponding to semantically meaningful travels of humans, animals, objects and phenomena. Components of a trajectory include the definition of when a trajectory starts, when it ends and when it pauses. These components are fixed by the application, based on semantics given to the trajectories. Therefore, the conceptual model for trajectories supports these components and provides constructs and rules to use movement data as sets of identifiable trajectories traveled by application objects. A trajectory is a segment of a spatiotemporal path where alternatively the moving object position changes and stays fixed. They called the former move and the latter stop. A stop is an interesting place in which a moving entity has stopped or significantly reduced its speed for a sufficient amount of time, likely to accomplish some activity. A move is any subset of an object trajectory between consecutive stops. Thus, a trajectory is a sequence of moves going from one stop to the next one (or as a sequence of stops separating the moves). Identifying stops (and moves) within a trajectory is the responsibility of the application.

Based on this conceptual model, several studies have been proposed. Alvares *et al.* [ALV 07] adopted the conceptual model [SPA 08] for enriching trajectories with semantic geographical information. They applied spatial joins between trajectories and a given set of regions of interest (ROIs), computing frequent moves between stops and two important trajectory episodes. Episode is a maximal subsequence of a trajectory such that all its spatiotemporal positions comply with a given predicate that bears on the spatiotemporal positions and/or their annotations. Thus, a trajectory is segmented into a list of episodes. The scope of Alvares *et al.*'s [ALV 07] paper is limited to the formal definition of semantic trajectories. Based on the notion of an episodes model, Guc *et al.* [GUC 08] introduced an extensible trajectory annotation model. Their model provides two kinds of annotation element: episodes and trips. Episodes partition a trajectory and describe semantically homogeneous sections of the trajectory. Trips are defined as groups of episodes on a higher semantic level that pertain to a common aim. Parent *et al.* [PAR 13] proposed a survey focused on semantic trajectories about mobility. They extended this initial task to cover moving objects' behaviors, whose discovery represents one of the most popular uses of mobility data and possibly the ultimate goal of trajectory analyses.

Researchers in [YAN 10] proposed a trajectory computing platform that exploits a spatiosemantic trajectory model. One of the layers of the presented platform is a data preprocessing layer, which cleanses the raw GPS feed, in terms of preliminary tasks such as outliers removal and regression-based smoothing. A difference is made between the semantic and spatial dimensions in order to provide a data model representation that supports different abstraction levels. Authors present a solution for extracting semantic trajectories from raw data. However, this work did not discuss the computation complexity of the platform going from the raw data step processing to knowledge extraction and finally decision making.

Based on a space–time ontology and events approach, Boulmakoul *et al.* [BOU 12] proposed a trajectory pattern of moving objects. Important packages of the trajectory patterns are "Space Time Path Domain", "Activity Domain", "Observation and Measure Domains" and "Region Of Interest". These packages are then transformed onto unified moving object trajectory queries expressed in SQL-like relational database language. Queries operations on space and time are performed using simple relational entities and functions so they seem to rely on a pure SQL-based approach, not on semantic queries. This work also did not discuss the evaluation of the proposed approach on real data sets.

In [BOU 13], the authors gave a brief outline of a scalable data collection framework for the unified moving object trajectories meta-model. They gathered different kinds of geographical data based on the unified moving object trajectories' meta-model. The collection framework offers components to collect spatiotemporal data. They test the scalability of the proposed system by a vehicle tracking simulator that generates and simulates spatiotemporal data of different moving objects. Recently, Boulmakoul *et al.* [BOU 15] proposed a trajectory's data model, which has advantages in terms of both conceptual and ontological space–time. So they extend the model with new patterns as the space–time path to describe the activities of the moving object and the composite region of interest. The case study presented concerns tracking travelers at the airport.

Recently, much research focuses on moving objects database (MOD) technologies, such as the discrete spatiotemporal trajectory based moving object database (DSTTMOD) system [MEN 03], and moving objects spatiotemporal (MOST) [WOL 98, OUR 99]. The database representation of spatiotemporal trajectories still requires integration of semantic-based approaches necessary for a successful application to many scientific-oriented domains to study moving objects' activities in space and time. For representation and modeling of semantic trajectories in the MOD approach, we can distinguish two different visions: a traditional one that includes moving object semantics since the phase of data design [ZHE 09] and a posteriori approach in which trajectories are annotated by analyzing their raw features [ALV 07, YAN 10].

Most of the research advances in trajectories and semantics may be broadly classified among three research areas: spatiotemporal data modeling for the representation of semantic trajectories; knowledge discovery from data for semantic trajectory mining and geographic visualization; and visual analytics for semantic trajectory visualization.

6.3. Modeling approach

6.3.1. *Design and methodology*

Our work is based on moving object trajectories. This requires a trajectory data model and a moving object model. Moreover, to enrich data with knowledge, a semantic model should be taken into consideration. Therefore, we need a generic model to consider the trajectory, moving object and semantic models simultaneously as shown in Figure 6.2.

The semantic trajectory model can consume captured data of trajectories and other external data as shown in Figure 6.2 (link (1)). These data are related to an application domain. As a result, this requires an application domain trajectory model that consists of a domain model, as shown in Figure 6.2 (link (2)). The latter will support semantics related to users' needs.

In the domain model, we also find the necessary semantics related to the real moving object, its trajectories, its activities and others. This semantics is often designed by a domain expert. In general, considering various facets of data requires that the semantic trajectory model be extended by other models: application domain, temporal and spatial models. Then, the main issue is to build and design the semantic trajectory model with its required components.

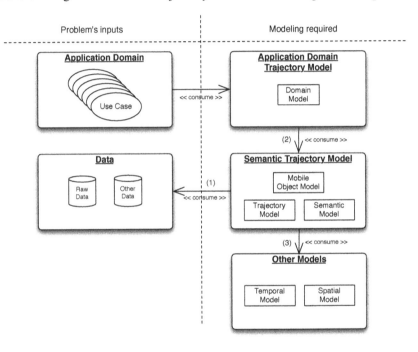

Figure 6.2. *Problem and the modeling required*

The semantic trajectory modeling approach is tightly related to the problem of a semantic gap between this model and raw data. Link (1) in Figure 6.2 presents this gap. Moreover, our approach involves multiple models and then must establish semantic mappings among them to ensure interoperability. In Figure 6.2, links (2) and (3) match the domain, temporal and spatial models with the semantic trajectory model. This matching extends the capabilities of our approach. For more efficient semantic capabilities, we want to annotate the data with domain, temporal and spatial knowledge. This knowledge is defined by experts representing users' needs. Annotating data with this knowledge could be done automatically or manually. We cannot use a manual annotation over huge data. Therefore, we choose an automatic annotation that can be accomplished by an ontology inference mechanism. This inference mechanism derives new semantics from existing information using additional knowledge. Later in this work, we will present this inference mechanism as sets of rules.

6.3.2. Semantic trajectory ontology

In [MAL 12a, WAN 14], we proposed a methodology for modeling trajectory data. This methodology focused on several real cases. For each case, we define a context, data capture, an analysis process of these data and a domain model. From these models, we define a "Semantic Trajectory Domain" based on a unified trajectory pattern, "Trajectory Domain", also called a generic trajectory model in other works, as shown in Figure 6.3.

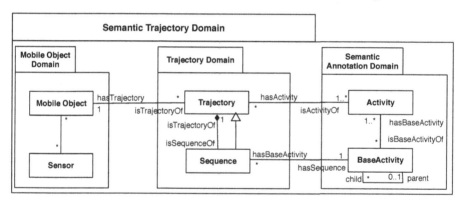

Figure 6.3. *Semantic trajectory modeling approach*

The "Semantic Trajectory Domain" as shown in Figure 6.3 is based on three domains:

1) mobile object domain model: a mobile object is considered as a series of moving points in a form of 3D dimensions. It is equipped with one or more Sensor objects. The Deployment describes the spatiotemporal relationships between the sensor and the mobile object;

2) trajectory domain model: defines the trajectory components independently of any application domain. This high-level data model

can be adapted to maintain additional requirements and can be used in many moving object applications. A trajectory is therefore formed by spatial, temporal and spatiotemporal components. More precisely, a trajectory consists of a series of spatiotemporal points, instances of a `Sequence`, representing an object's movements;

3) semantic annotation model: defines semantic annotations that are organized as general activities and a hierarchy of basic activities.

To build the trajectory ontology, we use model transformation techniques introduced by the model-driven engineering (MDE) community. For this, we choose an automatic transformation from a UML model into a formal OWL ontology. We use a transformer tool called uml2owl[1] [HIL 07]. This transformer, based on the meta-model eCore Eclipse, takes as input a UML model and turns it into OWL-DL ontology. So, we transform the trajectory data model (Figure 6.3) to an OWL ontology, named `owlSemanticTrajectory`. Figure 6.4 presents the declarative part of this ontology. It contains three parts: mobile object, trajectory and semantic ontologies. By definition, a trajectory is a set of spatiotemporal concepts. Spatial and temporal models can be reused to enrich description of the concepts in the trajectory ontology to represent their spatial and temporal properties. Table 6.1 gives definitions of the main concepts of the sematic trajectory ontology. Table 6.2 explains the relationships between concepts in the semantic trajectory ontology.

Concept	Definition
Trajectory	Logical form to represent sets of sequences
Sequence	Spatiotemporal interval representing a capture
GeoSequence	Spatial part of a sequence
Specific sequence	Metadata part of a sequence
Activity	Mobile object's activity in a sequence
Mobile object	The moving object equipped with a sensor

Table 6.1. *Dictionary classes of the trajectory domain*

---

1 http://perso.univ-lr.fr/ghillair/projects.html.

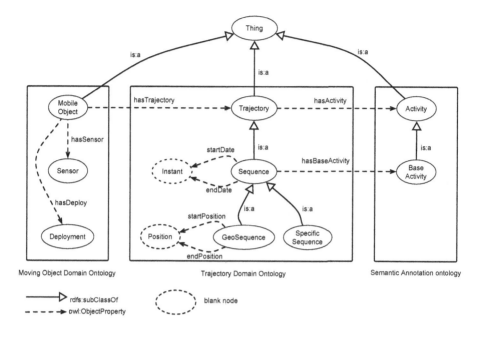

Figure 6.4. *A view of the semantic trajectory ontology*
owlSemanticTrajectory

Concept	Definition
hasActivity/hasBaseActivity	An object property to the activity of a trajectory/sequence
startPosition, endPosition	The capture position of a geosequence
startDate, endDatee	The capture time of a sequence
hasTrajectory	The trajectory of a mobile object

Table 6.2. *Relationships between concepts in the semantic trajectory domain*

6.4. Domain trajectory ontology

Our application domain is seals' trajectories, where a seal is considered as a mobile object. Trajectories of seals between their haul-out sites along the coasts of the English Channel or in the Celtic and Irish seas are captured using GNSS systems. The captured data comes from the LIENSs laboratory[2] in collaboration with SMRU[3].

We consider three main states of a seal: Haulout, Cruise and Dive. Figure 6.5 shows the three states, the transitions and their guard conditions. Every state is related to a seal's activity, such as Resting, Traveling and Foraging. The captured data can also contain some meta-data called conductivity-temperature-depth (CTD) about the marine environment such as water conductivity, temperature and pressure. From the analysis of the captured data, we define a seal's trajectory model (Figure 6.6).

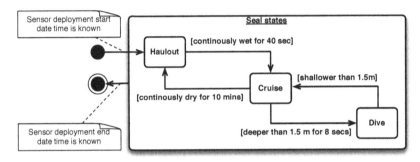

Figure 6.5. *The three states of seal trajectory*

In this work, we consider the seal's activity performed during its dives. The instances of the concepts Haulout and Cruise are mainly related to the concept of travel and are actually not taken into account in this work. According to the domain expert, instances of the Dive concept are associated with three main activities: resting, traveling, foraging and a mixed activity traveling-foraging. Starting from our semantic trajectory ontology owlSemanticTrajectory (Figure 6.4), we define the seal trajectory ontology, named owlSealTrajectory (Figure 6.7).

---

2 University of La Rochelle/CNRS – http://lienss.univ-larochelle.fr.
3 SMRU: Sea Mammal Research Unit – http://www.smru.st-and.ac.uk.

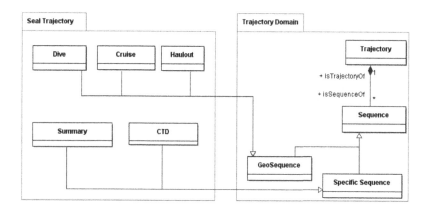

Figure 6.6. *Seal trajectory connected to trajectory domain*

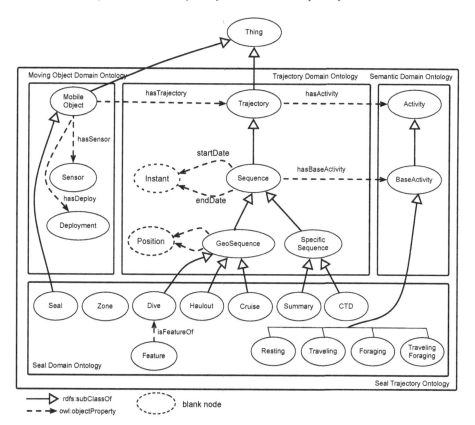

Figure 6.7. *Overview of the seal trajectory ontology*

6.5. Time ontology

The seal trajectory ontology includes concepts that can be considered as temporal. The concept `Sequence` is a temporal interval. Representation of temporal concepts and temporal relationships is a well-known research topic. In this work, we choose the reuse of `OWL-Time` ontology[4] [HOB 06]. The latter is developed by the World Wide Web Consortium (W3C) and describes the temporal concepts and relationships. An extract of the declarative part of this ontology is shown in Figure 6.8 described in detail in [JER 04]. The needed temporal relationships lead to Allen temporal algebra [ALL 83].

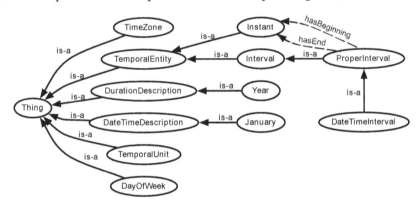

Figure 6.8. *A view of the OWL-time ontology*

6.6. Mapping trajectory and time ontologies

From `OWL-Time` ontology, as shown Figure 6.8, we are mainly interested in the `ProperInterval` and `Instant` concepts and the two properties `hasBeginning` and `hasEnd` between them. We defined a trajectory ontology (Figure 6.7) where a `Sequence` is a temporal interval having beginning and ending time. To meet these requirements, we need to connect trajectory and time ontologies by finding the alignment between them. Table 6.6 presents the alignment concepts and relationships between trajectory domain ontology and OWL-time ontology.

---

4 http://www.w3.org/2006/time.

Trajectory ontology	OWL-time ontology
Sequence	ProperInterval
startDate	hasBeginning
endDate	hasEnd

Table 6.3. *Matching trajectory and time ontologies*

According to Table 6.6, the mapping process, as shown in Figure 6.9, can be written as follows:

1) `owlSealTrajectory:Sequence` is mapped to `time:ProperInterval` by the OWL construct `owl:equivalentClass`;

2) `owlSealTrajectory:startDate` is mapped to `owlTime:hasBeginning` by the OWL construct `owl:equivalentProperty`;

3) `owlSealTrajectory:endDate` is mapped to `owlTime:hasEnd` by the OWL construct `owl:equivalentProperty`.

The concept `Sequence` from the trajectory domain ontology is connected to `ProperInterval` from OWL-Time ontology. Then, the properties of the latter are visible and available for the former [WAN 13b].

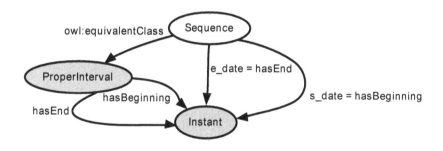

Figure 6.9. *Mapping* `owlSealTrajectory` *and* `owlTime`

6.7. Trajectory ontology inference framework

Inference is the ability to make logical deductions based on ontologies, rules and optionally individuals. It derives new knowledge based on rules.

A rule's definition, Figure 6.10, has an antecedent, filters and a consequent. If knowledge is represented using RDF triples, then the antecedent is a set of triples, filters apply restrictions and finally the consequent is a new derived triple.

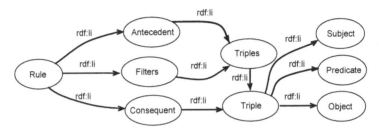

Figure 6.10. *Rule's definition*

In the present work, we consider three kinds of inference:

1) inference using standard rules: our semantic trajectory ontology is based on RDF, RDFS and OWL constructs. The inference mechanism associates with each construct a rule. The resulting sets are called standard rules. An example of standard rules is OWLPrime in Oracle RDF triple store [ORA 09];

2) inference using temporal rules: our semantic trajectory ontology uses temporal relationships as defined by Allen's algebra [ALL 83]. Each relationship is defined as a rule such as: `intervalAfter`, `intervalBefore`, `intervalDuring`, etc. In [MAL 12b], we present the inference using temporal rules and we give more details about its implementation and the related computation complexity;

3) inference using domain rules: the seal trajectory ontology, Figure 6.7, takes into account several seal's activities from the "Seal Domain Ontology". In this declarative part of the ontology, each seal activity is related to the activity concept of the upper model "Seal Domain Ontology". The imperative part of the set of these concepts and their relationships defines the inference using domain rules. Section 6.8 details this inference.

6.8. Trajectory ontology inference framework implementation

Our implementation framework uses Oracle RDF triple store [ORA 09]. Based on a graph data model, RDF triples are persisted, indexed and queried, like other object relational data. As previously presented, this framework must first declare the three ontologies:

– owlSemanticTrajectory: declarative part of the semantic trajectory ontology (Figure 6.4);

– owlSealTrajectory: declarative part of the seal trajectory ontology (Figure 6.7);

– owlTime: declarative part of the time ontology (Figure 6.8).

The basic components of an ontology declaration are concepts, attributes and relationships between concepts. Each relationship has a declarative part as an RDF ObjectProperty and an imperative part, formally, an associated rule as an IF-THEN pattern (Figure 6.10). In the implementation of this framework, we have chosen to create homogeneous sets of rules, called a rule base, to promote their reuse in the context of different applications. In practice, we create:

– Standard_Rules: a rule base of the standard rules containing all RDFS constructs (2 RDF and 14 RDFS standard-defined rules) and a subset of OWLPrime rules [WU 13], particularly equivalentProperty and equivalentClass that are used in the mapping implementation;

– Time_Rules: we implement this rule base to hold the interval temporal relationships. Section 6.8.1 gives relevant details about Time_Rules' implementation;

– Seal_Rules: we implement this rule base to hold the domain's rules, especially, the seal's activities. Section 6.8.2 gives relevant details about Seal_Rules's implementation.

6.8.1. *Temporal inference implementation*

The rule base Time_Rules implements the set of temporal relationships: intervalEquals, intervalBefore, intervalDuring, intervalOverlaps, intervalOverlappedBy, intervalStartedBy, intervalFinishedBy, intervalFinishes, intervalContains, intervalMetBy, intervalMeets, intervalStarts and intervalAfter. As an example, Figure 6.11 shows the declarative part of the intervalAfter_rule. The imperative parts of Time_Rules are based on operations defined in the table TM_RelativePosition of the ISO/TC 211 specification about temporal schema [ISO 02]. In [MAL 12b], we gave more technical details about the imperative of the implementations of Time_Rules.

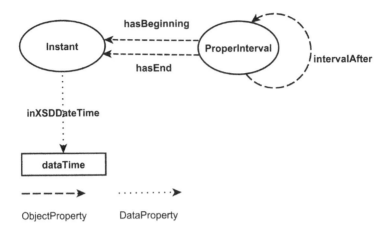

Figure 6.11. *Declarative part of* intervalAfter *rule*

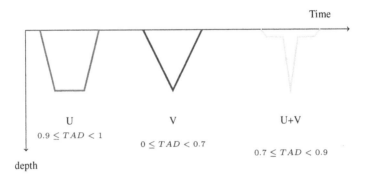

Figure 6.12. *Dive shape according to* TAD *values*

6.8.2. *Domain inference implementation*

The rule base Seal_Rules defines the seal rules associated with activities. According to the domain expert, there is a correlation between the geometrical shape of dives and activities. To classify geometric shapes of dives, the TAD index [FED 01] is computed over a training dataset. For this classification, we can distinguish three patterns (Figure 6.12):

– dive shaped U: if $0.9 <= TAD < 1$;

– dive shaped U+V: if $0.7 <= TAD < 0.9$;

– dive shaped V: if $0 <= TAD < 0.7$.

To define the seal activities, and according to the domain expert, we take into consideration three parameters:

– the geometrical shape of dives (TAD) (Figure 6.12);

– the maximum dive depth;

– the surface ratio, which is the ratio between surface duration and dive duration.

Figure 6.13 shows the declarative part definition of the concept Dive with its considered parameters as attributes, and as an example, the concept Foraging associated with the foraging_rule in the owlSealTrajectory ontology. For the imperative definition parts of rules, the decision Table 6.4 summarizes conditions of the IF parts of rules associated with activities as follows:

– Resting is when a seal is sleeping at the sea bottom with the TAD higher than 0.9. The surface duration after the dive state should be quite high so that seals have enough time to breath before another sleep under water;

– Traveling could be in any dive depth deeper than 3 m, but the TAD should be lower than 0.7 because the seal does not need to spend a lot of time at the maximum depth. The surface duration does not make any difference in this case;

– Foraging is when the dive depth is deeper than 3 m. The TAD however should be high (>0.9) because the gray seal is a benthic forager, which means it is feeding on fish located on or close to the sea bottom (i.e. at the maximum depth available). Also the surface duration is short because the seal wants to go back quickly to look for more fish;

– TravelingForaging is when the dive depth is deeper than 3 m. The TAD however should be higher than 0.7 and smaller than 0.9. Also the surface duration is short because the seal wants to go back quickly to look for more fish.

6.8.3. Trajectory ontology inference entailment

In our framework, an inference mechanism creates a rule index, as shown in Figure 6.14. A rule index, also named an entailment, is an object containing pre-computed triples from applying a specified set of rulebases to a specified set of models. If a graph query refers to any rule bases, a rule index must exist and be complete for each rule base-model combination in the query. The USER_RULES=T option is required while applying user-defined rules. The parameter Passes is the number of rounds that the inference engine should run. Its default value is REACH_CLOSURE, which means the inference engine will run till a closure is reached. If the number of rounds specified is less than the number of actual rounds needed to reach a closure, the status of the rules index will then be set to INCOMPLETE.

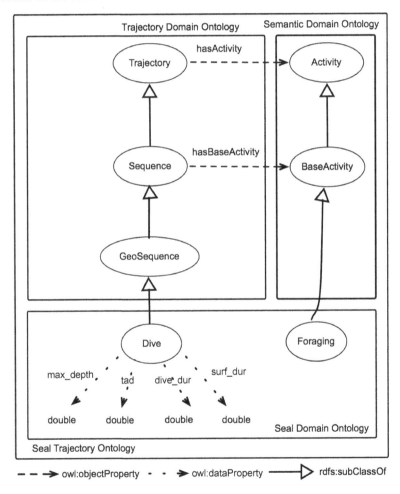

Figure 6.13. *Main declarative parts needed by the* foraging_rule

Rules	Max dive depth (m)	Dive shape or TAD	Surface ratio = surface dur/dive dur
Resting	<10	>0.9	>0.5
Travelling	>3	<0.7	All
Foraging	>3	>0.9	<0.5
Traveling Foraging	>3	>0.7 and <0.9	<0.5

Table 6.4. *Decision table of IF parts of seal activities*

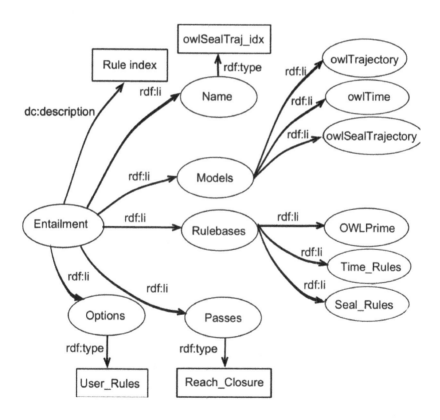

Figure 6.14. *Seal ontology inference entailment*

6.9. Experiments

Experiments are performed on a virtual machine server running Linux 2.6.18 and Java 1.6 on an Intel (R) Xeon X7560 CPU at 2.27GHz with a maximum of 40 GB disk space and 4 GB of RAM.

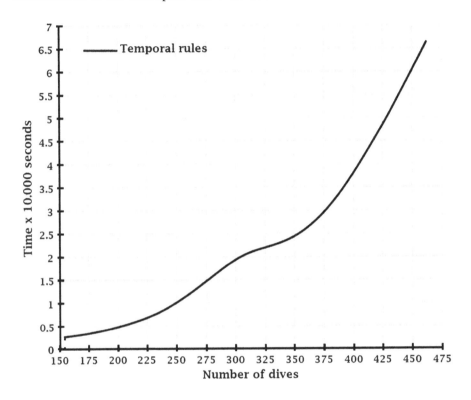

Figure 6.15. *Entailment computation time over the temporal rules*

In our experiment, we measure the time needed to compute the entailment for different sets of real trajectory data. We consider one seal's trajectory data captured from June 16 until July 18, 2011. We have 10,000 captured data. In this experiment, the seal rulebase contains only the foraging rule. The input data type for this entailment are dives. Figure 6.15 shows the experiment results for the computation time in seconds needed by the entailment. For example, for 450 dives, the inference takes around 60,000 seconds ($\simeq$16.6 h). Figure 6.16 shows the experiment results for the number of the triples inferred by the inference mechanism. For example, for 450 dives, the inference generates around two 200,000 triples.

We noticed that the inference time increases seemingly out of proportion when using user-defined rules. This is because the Oracle inference engine does not integrate OWL rules and user-defined rule inference components similarly. As conclusion, we have to define conditions over the inference computation. For this reason, we introduce an inference refinement process to reduce computational complexity.

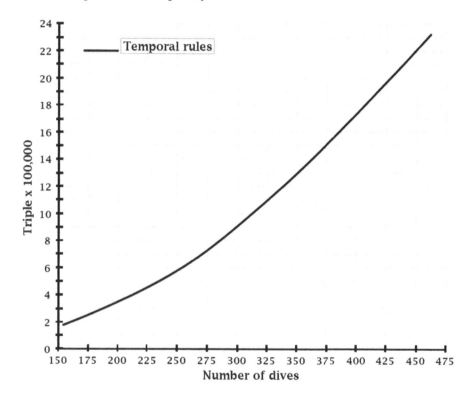

Figure 6.16. *Triples inferred over the temporal rules*

6.10. Application domain inference refinement

We introduce a two-tier inference refinement on trajectory data. In other words, two distinct operations are performed to enhance the inference: primary and secondary inference operations. Figure 6.17 shows the two-tier inference filter refinement. The primary filter is applied to the captured data to classify them into a set of interesting places. It allows fast selection of the classified data to pass along to the secondary inference. The latter computes the inference mechanism considering the resulting places. Then, instead of annotating each sequence in the model, we annotate each place with the expert knowledge. The secondary inference yields the final knowledge data that the user can query.

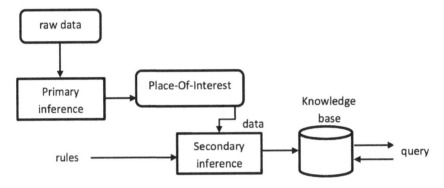

Figure 6.17. *A two-tier inference filter refinement*

Our proposal is to analyze the captured data before computing the ontology inference. This analysis is achieved because of our primary filter. This filter considers trajectories that are segmented by the object positions. These positions change and remain fixed. Spaccapietra [SPA 08] named the former moves (Definition 6.1) and the latter stops (Definition 6.2). For this reason, a trajectory is seen as a sequence of moves going from one stop to the next one.

DEFINITION 6.1.– *A move is a part of a trajectory represented as a spatiotemporal line.*

DEFINITION 6.2.– *A stop is a part of a trajectory having a time interval and represented as a single point.*

The interesting places are related to where the moving object stays and visits more often. The definition of a place of interest is based on a neighbor of points notion (Definition 6.3).

DEFINITION 6.3.– *Neighbors of a point (p_i) are a list of points from the Move data where the distance between p_i and any neighbor point is smaller than a fixed radius:*

$$Neighbor(p_i) = \{(p_j)_{j=1}^n : p_i, p_j \in Move, \ distance(p_i, p_j) < radius\}$$

To define the places of interest, we introduce some necessary definitions used in the calculation process given by Algorithm 6.1.

DEFINITION 6.4.– *For a given point (p), a peak is the cardinality of the list $Neighbor(p)$.*

DEFINITION 6.5.– *Points_Neighbors are a list of points and their neighbors:*

$$Points\_Neighbors = \{(p_i, Neighbors_i)_{i=1}^n : p_i, Neighbors_i \in Move\}$$

DEFINITION 6.6.– *Place$_i$ is an interesting place that contains at least a $Neighbor_i$ and the number of the moving object's visits $nVisits$:*

$$Places = \{(Neighbors_i, nVisits_i)_{i=1}^n : Neighbors_i \in Move\}$$

The place of interest process is given by Algorithm 6.1. Lines 5–9 gather move data into groups of neighbors, named $Points\_Neighbors$. These groups are defined with respect to a $radius$. This radius is a fixed distance between two points to calculate the neighbors. It is application dependent. Lines 10–24 build the interesting places, named $Places$. In line 10, we consider each neighbor in the preceding calculated $Points\_Neighbors$. In line 11, we consider a threshold related to the cardinality of the current neighbor. This threshold is application dependent. In lines 12–14, every point of the current neighbor that belongs to a place should be far from the stop data more than the fixed radius. According to the value of the distance between the current point and the current place, we distinguish two cases. In lines 15 and 16, the point is far from the place, so we create a new place holding the current neighbor. Else, lines 18 and 19 add the current neighbor to the current place and increase the number of visits of this place.

input : $Move$
input : $Stop$
input : $radius$
output: $Places$
1 initialization;
2 $Neighbor \leftarrow \phi$;
3 $Points\_Neighbors \leftarrow \phi$;
4 $Places \leftarrow \phi$;
5 **for** *each* $p_i \in Move$ **do**
6 | calculate $Neighbor(p_i)$;
7 | $Points\_Neighbors \leftarrow (p_i, Neighbors(p_i))$;
8 | $Move \leftarrow Move - Neighbor(p_i)$;
9 **end**
10 **for** *each* $pn \in Points\_Neighbors$ *AND*
11 | *condition(peaks$_{pn}$)* **do**
12 | **for** *each* $p_i \in pn$ **do**
13 | | **for** *each place* $\in Places$ *AND*
14 | | | *condition(distance($p_i, Stop$) > radius)* **do**
15 | | | **if** $distance(p_i, place) > radius$ **then**
16 | | | | $new\_place = new\ Place(pn, 1)$;
17 | | | **else**
18 | | | | $place.Neighbors\ + = pn$;
19 | | | | $place.nVisits\qquad + = 1$;
20 | | | **end**
21 | | | $break$;
22 | | **end**
23 | **end**
24 **end**

25 **Algorithm 6.1.** *The Place of Interest algorithm*

6.11. Research results

To analyze our trajectory data, we pass them to the Place Of Interest algorithm. This algorithm analyzes the data and gives as output interesting places, as shown in Figure 6.18. Figure 6.19 shows the evaluation of the two-tier inference refinement over data. We evaluate the space storage consumed by the inference. For that purpose, this experiment gives a number of triples generated by the temporal inference on different sets of dives. The results show its impact by the following experiments:

1) temporal rules: this experiment analyzes the inference on real data taking into account standard temporal rules;

2) refined temporal rules – real data: this experiment analyzes the inference on real data considering optimized temporal rules;

3) refined temporal rules – generated data: this experiment analyzes the inference on generated data as in the previous experiment;

4) refined temporal rules + two-tier refinement – real data: this experiment analyzes the inference on real data using optimized temporal rules and the two-tier refinement algorithm.

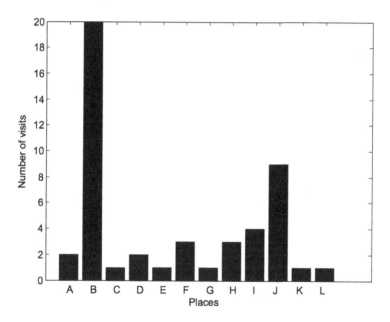

Figure 6.18. *Calculated interesting places over trajectory data*

This experiment, as shown in Figure 6.19, shows that the inference generates far less triples with the two-tier refinement, result 4, than the conventional inference, results 1–3. The reason is that result 4 is achieved with filtered data. However, the filtered data should maintain the main properties of the data. So, we conclude that it is not interesting to consider all the trajectory data in the inference mechanism. In this work, the filtered data are obtained because of the Place Of Interest algorithm. This solution entails two main challenges as follows:

1) the inference process on temporal intervals must be adapted for the case of the places of interest that are temporal regions in our work;

2) the definition of the places of interest is often domain dependent. It means that it is necessary to take into account the domain's requirements to build the places of interest without altering data quality.

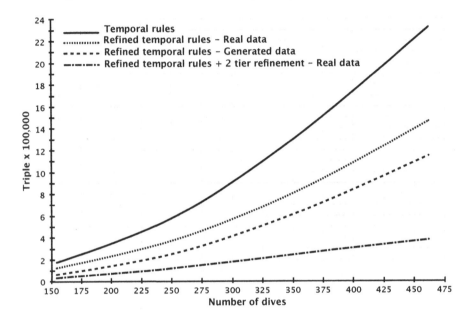

Figure 6.19. *Enhancement over the two-tier inference refinement*

To confirm the quality of the interesting places, we query the resulting semantic data to find all the foraging places, as shown in Figure 6.20. Figure 6.21 is a map showing these foraging places. These obtained foraging places overlap with the majority of the fishing zones known by the biologists in this geographical zone.

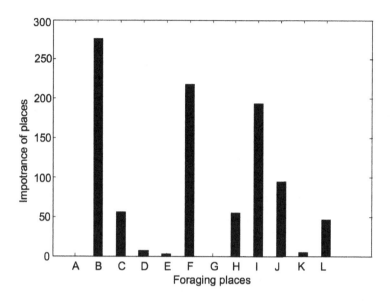

Figure 6.20. *Interesting places to foraging places*

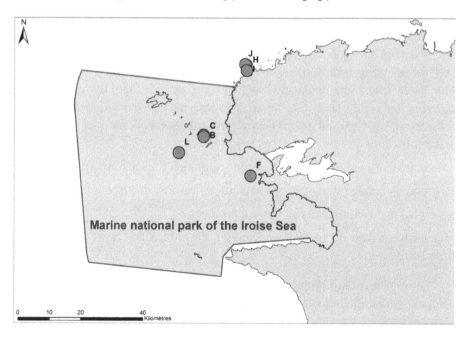

Figure 6.21. *Marine park in western Brittany with the evaluated foraging places*

6.12. Conclusion and future work

In this work, we proposed an approach based on the trajectories of a marine mammal animal as part of an early warning system. Using this approach, the system can construct predictions based on past observations. The example of the natural foraging places of this animal shows that the system can provide comparisons between known facts and ground truths observed after the capture of new trajectories.

The proposed approach modeling is based on ontologies to build a semantic trajectory ontology. We consider three separated ontological models: a general trajectory domain model, a domain knowledge or semantic model and a temporal domain model. To implement the declarative and imperative parts of the ontologies, we consider the framework of Oracle Semantic Triples Store. To define the domain and temporal reasoning, we implement rules related to the considered models. The domain rules consider seals activities and the temporal rules are based on Allen relationships. Then, we define an application domain inference refinement, called two-tier inference filters. In other words, two distinct operations are performed to enhance the inference: primary and secondary filter operations. The primary filter analyzes the trajectory data into places of interest. The secondary filter computes the ontology inference over the semantic trajectories using the ontology domain and temporal rules. The latter filters the interesting places into domain activity places. The experimental results show that we are able with the two-tier inference filters to consider all the captured data. The main contributions of this work are related to the following:

– how to use an ontological modeling approach for semantic trajectories;

– how to define inferences on semantic trajectories to answer user queries;

– what is the complexity of these inferences;

– what we can do to face and reduce the inferences costs of inference complexity.

The implementation framework for our approach presents all the required components for the trajectory ontology inference based on a RDF triple store. Many experiments were carried out to evaluate the approach in the context of seal trajectories. The continuation of this work will be dedicated to comparing our results with the results of existing studies, in particular those interested in trajectories using ontologies. At present, we are in the phase of collecting the implementation solutions of some cited approaches. This step is rather complex, and the adaptation of these implementations in our domain will certainly be an interesting work. Other directions for our perspectives include:

– studying the possibility of generalizing our Place Of Interest algorithm. This is to ensure that the filtered data maintain the main properties of the data without altering their quality;

– extending the inference mechanism to take into account domain, time and spatial rules;

– studying ontology-assisted use queries using ontologies to help end users to formulate complex queries on trajectory data;

– studying the inference complexity using different inferences engine.

Technological advances in conceptual models, especially those based on ontologies, could bring immense benefits to early warning systems if these models have effective translation mechanisms for all that is happening in the environment. Bridging the gap between scientific research and decision-making will fully exploit the capabilities of early warning technologies to help us understand our environment and act accordingly.

The major challenge is to ensure that early warnings lead to quick reactions. This requires data to be processed efficiently and quickly through processing. As we have shown in this work, the ontological models applied in the framework of an early warning system are far from revealing all their capacities due in particular to the complexity underlying these models.

6.13. References

[ALL 83] ALLEN J.F., "Maintaining knowledge about temporal intervals", *Communication of the Association for Computing Machinery (ACM)*, vol. 26, no. 11, pp. 832–843, 1983.

[ALV 07] ALVARES L.O., BOGORNY V., KUIJPERS B. *et al.*, "A model for enriching trajectories with semantic geographical information", *Proceedings of the 15th annual ACM international symposium on Advances in geographic information systems*, ACM, pp. 22:1–22:8, 2007.

[BAL 94] BALDWIN I.G., HARMAN M.M.I., NEVILLE D.A., "Performance characteristics of a fish monitor for detection of toxic substances–I. Laboratory trials", *Water Research*, vol. 28, no. 10, pp. 2191–2199, 1994.

[BEN 82] BENECKE G., FALKE W., SCHMIDT C., "Use of algal fluorescence for an automated biological monitoring system", *Bulletin of Environmental Contamination and Toxicology*, no. 28, pp. 385–395, 1982.

[BOR 97] BORCHERDING J., JANTZ B., "Valve movement response of the mussel Dreissena polymorpha – the influence of pH and turbidity on the acute toxicity of pentachlorophenol under laboratory and field conditions", *Ecotoxicology*, no. 6, pp. 153–165, 1997.

[BOU 12] BOULMAKOUL A., KARIM L., LBATH A., "Moving Object Trajectories Meta-Model and Spatio-Temporal Queries", *International Journal of Database Management Systems (IJDMS)*, https://hal.inria.fr/hal-00996854, vol. 4, no. 2, pp. 35–54, 2012.

[BOU 13] BOULMAKOUL A., KARIM L., LBATH A., "Article: a high performance scalable data collection system for moving objects", *International Journal of Computer Applications*, vol. 67, no. 9, pp. 36–43, 2013.

[BOU 15] BOULMAKOUL A., KARIM L., BOUZIRI A.E. *et al.*, "A system architecture for heterogeneous moving-object trajectory metamodel using generic sensors: tracking airport security case study", *IEEE Systems Journal*, vol. 9, no. 1, pp. 283–291, 2015.

[BUT 01] BUTTERWORTH F.M., GUNATILAKA A., GONSEBATT M.E., *Biomonitors and Biomarkers as Indicators of Environmental Change 2: A Handbook*, Plenum Publishers, New York, 2001.

[CRO 15] CROFOOT M.C., KAYS R.W., WIKELSKI M., "Shared decision-making drives collective movement in wild baboons", *Science*, vol. 348, and Movebank Data Repository, 2015.

[DOO 12] DOONG D.J., CHUANG L.Z.H., WU L.C. *et al.*, "Development of an operational coastal flooding early warning system", *Natural Hazards and Earth System Sciences*, no. 2, pp. 379–390, 2012.

[FED 01] FEDAK M.A., LOVELL P., GRANT S.M., "Two approaches to compressing and interpreting time-depth information as collected by time-depth recorders and satellite-linked data recorders", *Marine Mammal Science*, vol. 17, no. 1, pp. 94–110, 2001.

[GEO 05] GEOPKDD, Geographic privacy-aware knowledge discovery and delivery, KDDLAB, Knowledge Discovery and Delivery Laboratory, ISTI-CNR and University of Pisa, 2005.

[GRE 03] GREEN U., KREMER J.H., ZILLMER M. *et al.*, "Detection of chemical threat agents in drinking water by an early warning real-time biomonitor", *Environmental Toxicology*, vol. 18, no. 6, pp. 368–374, 2003.

[GUC 08] GUC B., MAY M., SAYGIN Y. *et al.*, "Semantic annotation of GPS trajectories", *11th AGILE International Conference on Geographic Information Science,* Girona, Spain, 2008.

[HEN 93] HENDRIKS A.J., STOUTEN M.D.A., "Monitoring the response of microcontaminants by dynamic Daphnia magna and Leuciscus idus assays in the Rhine delta: biological early warning as a useful supplement", *Ecotoxicology and Environmental Safety*, vol. 26, no. 3, pp. 265–279, 1993.

[HIL 07] HILLAIRET G., ATL use case – ODM implementation: bridging UML and OWL, Technical Report, 2007.

[HOB 06] HOBBS J.R., FANG P., Time ontology in OWL, W3C recommendation, W3C, 2006.

[ISO 02] ISO/TC_211, Geographic Information – Temporal Schema, ISO 19108, International Organization for Standardization, 2002.

[JEO 14] JEONG T.Y., JEON J., KIM S.D., "Development and evaluation of new behavioral indexes for a biological early warning system using Daphnia magna", *Drinking Water Engineering and Science*, no. 1, pp. 1–9, 2014.

[JER 04] JERRY R.H., FENG P., "An ontology of time for the semantic web", *ACM Transactions on Asian Language Information Processing*, vol. 3, pp. 66–85, 2004.

[MAL 12a] MALKI J., BOUJU A., MEFTEH W., "An ontological approach modeling and reasoning on trajectories. Taking into account thematic, temporal and spatial rules", *Technique et Science Informatiques*, vol. 31/1-2012, pp. 71–96, 2012.

[MAL 12b] MALKI J., WANNOUS R., BOUJU A. *et al.*, "Temporal reasoning in trajectories using an ontological modelling approach", *Control and Cybernetics*, vol. 41, no. 4, pp. 1–16, 2012.

[MEN 03] MENG X., DING Z., "DSTTMOD: a Discrete Spatio-Temporal Trajectory Based Moving Object Database System", *In Proceedings of 14th International Conference on Database and Expert Systems Applications (DEXA 2003)*, Prague, Czech Republic, pp. 444–453, 2003.

[MOD 12] MODAP, Mobility, Data Mining and Privacy, http://www.modap.org, FP7/ICT FET OPEN, 2009–2012.

[MOV 13] MOVE, European Science Foundation, European Cooperation in Science and Technologies (COST) Action IC0903: Knowledge Discovery from Moving Objects (MOVE), 2009–2013.

[ORA 09] ORACLE, Oracle Database Semantic Technologies, version 10gR2, 2009.

[OUR 99] OURI W., PRASAD S., BO X. *et al.*, "DOMINO: Databases fOr MovINg Objects tracking", *ACM SIGMOD International Conference on Management of Data (SIGMod-99)*, pp. 547–549, 1999.

[PAR 06] PARENT C., SPACCAPIETRA S., ZIMANYI E., *Conceptual Modeling for Traditional and Spatio-Temporal Applications: The MADS Approach*, Springer-Verlag, New York, 2006.

[PAR 13] PARENT C., SPACCAPIETRA S., RENSO C. *et al.*, "Semantic trajectories modeling and analysis", ACM Computing Surveys (CSUR), vol. 45, no. 4, 2013.

[SEE 15] SEEK, EU Marie Curie Project N 295179, PEOPLE IRSES 2011 scheme, 2012-2015.

[SPA 08] SPACCAPIETRA S., PARENT C., DAMIANI M. *et al.*, "A conceptual view on trajectories", *Data and Knowledge Engineering*, vol. 65, pp. 126–146, 2008.

[UNE 12] UNEP, Early warning systems: a state of the art analysis and future directions, Report, 2012.

[WAN 13a] WANNOUS R., MALKI J., BOUJU A. *et al.*, "Modelling mobile object activities based on trajectory ontology rules considering spatial relationship rules", *Modeling Approaches and Algorithms for Advanced Computer Applications, Studies in Computational Intelligence*, vol. 488, pp. 249–258, 2013.

[WAN 13b] WANNOUS R., MALKI J., BOUJU A. *et al.*, "Time integration in semantic trajectories using an ontological modelling approach", in PECHENIZKLY M., WOJCIECH-OWSKI M. (eds), *New Trends in Databases and Information Systems*, Springer, Berlin, 2013.

[WAN 14] WANNOUS R., Computational inference of conceptual trajectory model: considering domain temporal and spatial dimensions, PhD thesis, University of La Rochelle, 2014.

[WOL 98] WOLFSON O., XU B., CHAMBERLAIN S. *et al.*, "Moving objects databases: issues and solutions", *Proceedings of the 10th International Conference on Scientific and Statistical Database Management*, SSDBM '98, IEEE Computer Society, 1998.

[WU 13] WU Z., EADON G., DAS S. *et al.*, Database-based inference engine for RDFS/OWL constructs, US Patent 8,401,991, 2013.

[YAN 10] YAN Z., PARENT C., SPACCAPIETRA S. *et al.*, "A hybrid model and computing platform for spatio-semantic trajectories", SIMPERL E., CIMIANO P., POLLERES A. *et al.* (eds), *The Semantic Web: Research and Applications*, Springer, Berlin, 2010.

[YUA 09] YUAN X., WU Y., LIANG S. *et al.*, "Early warning and emergency response system for water pollution accidents in Wuhan City, China", *Proceedings of the 2009 International Conference on Environmental Science and Information Application Technology*, ESIAT '09, vol. 2, pp. 171–174, 2009.

[ZHE 09] ZHENI D., FRIHIDA A., GHEZALA H. *et al.*, "A semantic approach for the modeling of trajectories in space and time", in HEUSER C.A., PERNUL G. (eds), *Advances in Conceptual Modeling – Challenging Perspectives*, Springer, Berlin, 2009.

7

Toward a Modeling of Population Behaviors in Crisis Situations

7.1. Introduction

At present, many indicators and sensor systems are designed to produce alerts and reduce disaster risks. In this chapter, we describe the context of these systems, where these systems are developed, and the objectives of our study.

7.1.1. *Context*

The insertion into intelligent systems of cognitive elements and realistic human behaviors making possible the reproduction or prediction of events or actions is an important issue for developers. Understanding human behavior in a way that could be integrated in intelligent systems is still a challenge today that needs the interconnection of heterogeneous elements that can be physiologic, psychological, social or even environmental.

At present, because of Information and Communication Technologies (ICTs), it is faster and more efficient to manage real time data, make maps from geolocalized data or to make assessments based on scenarios that integrate data from different sources. These developments enable the improvement of crisis management systems, developed to support those who

Chapter written by Elsa NEGRE, Maude ARRU and Camille ROSENTHAL-SABROUX.

respond to disasters that can be humanitarian, economic, ecological or social for example, and which are becoming more and more complex. These crisis management systems help in particular to predict as soon as possible the consequences of a crisis and its evolution in a given territory. Despite knowledge and techniques developed in order to minimize or avoid disastrous consequences that crises can produce, they remain, by definition, determined by uncertain phenomena, which are not always considered in these crisis management systems. The vulnerability of territories, the need for coordination among services and the probable behaviors of populations-in-danger, for example, are sometimes neglected.

7.1.2. *Objectives of the study*

Before and during a crisis, people act according to their own knowledge and interpretation schemes [MIL 90]. These schemes do not always allow people to react in an appropriate way to risky situations and can lead to dangerous reactions. To respond to these problems, crisis management programs usually include early warning systems that permit recipients to (1) know risks and define indicators to be monitored to anticipate crisis, (2) monitor these indicators in order to be able to (3) trigger warnings and broadcast them as quickly as possible to populations at risk, and finally (4) bring up and raise awareness among populations exposed to risks. ICTs are keys elements in these early warning systems. They allow people to orient their behaviors when a crisis is announced by providing them with information before the crisis, and orienting them in the perception and interpretation of the signals perceived during the crisis.

Several actors gravitate around these early warning systems with different roles. The main actors are the crisis management specialists and experts who build and develop the warning system, the decision makers who act for crisis resolution, the operational actors who apply the decisions taken in crisis cells and finally the populations. This chapter focuses only on the last category of actors, the populations, by proposing an analysis based on their behaviors during a crisis.

The consideration of laws and phenomena that influence human behaviors in crisis situations seems for us an important area of research and reflection on the improvement of the warning systems: in warnings broadcasts, crisis communication and in the development of educational policies and targeted awareness. Indeed, many recommendations advocate orienting warning systems toward more people-centered aspects, mainly through the participation of populations in decision-making processes [BAS 06]. It seems to us complementary to this approach to integrate human considerations in the risk knowledge and the awareness made through the knowledge of population behaviors. Then, in this chapter, we are interested in the following issue: understand how and according to what factors people react in crisis situations and adapt their behaviors.

Thus, at first, to lead this study, we present our definition of the general concept of behavior based on a state of the art and specify in this part the stakes of behavior in crisis situations and the most commonly observed reactions. We then list the factors we identify as having an impact on behavior in a crisis situation. Each of these factors is detailed and associated with a list of indicators. Finally, we propose our research perspective with different modeling choices that we wish to implement to represent behaviors and to analyze data that will be provided for the identified indicators.

7.2. What is behavior?

We focus in this section on the key concept of behavior. We define the concept before providing an overview of the specifics of behavior in crisis situations and how we can approach this concept according to the factors that have an influence on it.

7.2.1. Definition

Behavior is a concept that needs to be examined and well defined; it can be approached very differently in the scientific world. Some speak of a "nomadic" concept that can take several meanings according to the disciplines [TON 09]. In philosophy, for example, definitions rely mainly on notions of consciousness and experience [MER 42], whereas in cognitive sciences it can be approached as a logical sequence of actions [SKI 05]. The most important number of works on the subject is provided by the human sciences, especially in the fields of ethology and psychology [ALC 89, COO 07]. In this chapter, we detail the definition proposed by Sillamy [SIL 83], for whom behavior corresponds to the "reactions of a person, considered in a milieu and in a given unit of time to an excitation or a set of stimuli". This definition permits to to clearly situate behavior, considering time and space, as a response to a set of excitations or stimuli. In this chapter, we limit the study of behaviors to observable reactions by an external entity.

We propose here an approach based on cognitive and environmental factors that can be modeled in a computable way. Several models already exist in the computer science literature, in multiagent systems (MAS) notably. We can cite the example of Müller and Pischel [MUL 11], with the inteRRaP architecture, or Ferguson's [FER 92] architecture, with his TouringMachine architecture. This type of representation takes into account only to a weak extent the motivations and interactions between individuals [GOL 05] and cognitive phenomena; in crisis situations, they are generally targeted at a few sequences of actions that have been defined in advance according to simplified scenarios [ZOU 10, ADA 10].

Human behavior is also integrated in artificial intelligence research where the idea is to transpose into a virtual reality elements of knowledge and the processing of this knowledge that make if possible for virtual individuals to make strategic choices. We find this type of research in domains such as the automatic production of explanations or mathematical problem-solving for example [BAL 94], but it is still difficult to integrate the cognitive or emotional dimensions of behavior to these computer science representations.

7.2.2. *Behaviors in crisis situations*

Individual behaviors in crisis situations do not correspond to the behaviors of everyday life. It is difficult to represent these behaviors with the information that has been obtained after a crisis as this information is always static and contextual, and it is difficult to integrate the diversity of human reactions that can appear in these situations [DAU 13]. Nevertheless, we can work to establish tendencies or correlations of factors that orient particular behaviors. The behaviors frequently observed in crisis situations are as follows [DAU 13]: evacuation, escape; panic, escape; stupor, shock; immobility; confinement, sheltering; struggle against disaster effects; search for relatives; assistance, emergency relief; "antisocial" behavior; curiosity; return to the habitation or work place. We distinguish three types of behaviors: (1) reflex or instinctive behaviors that permit rapid action through struggle, stupefaction or evasion; (2) panic behavior or crowd phenomena that can emerge from imitation or contagion mechanisms; and (3) controlled behaviors that are reasoned reactions [PRO 15].

It is important to take into account as many elements as possible to study behaviors in crisis situation; two events that seem similar can lead to very different reactions. Between the tsunami that occurred in Fukushima on March 11, 2011, and the other one that occurred 5 years later on November 22, 2016, authorities' and inhabitants' reactions have significantly evolved. In 2016, the Prime Minister ordered the government to give precise and reliable information to people on evacuation procedures and the appeals to evacuate were more much numerous. Reactions have generally been strongly influenced by the experience lived five years earlier.

Emotions such as fear or surprise can also have a strong influence on crowd movements as in the Nice attacks on July 14, 2016, which was Bastille Day in France. After the attacks, people began to run without knowing where to go and several rumors spread in streets. These panic movements are related to the perception of danger and the perception of the means that people have to escape; they can aggravate crisis consequences.

7.2.3. *Understanding behavioral factors*

An approach to the crisis through the analysis of human behavior is relatively complex and requires a good understanding of the mechanisms underlying collective movements. Behavioral mechanisms in crisis situations are still little studied [HEL 00, PRO 15] or poorly represented [QUA 08], especially in computer science. They are often limited to observation and analysis of the reactions produced during a specific event [RIP 09, RUI 10] for which data has been collected. They can also focus on the analysis of a specific behavior such as pillaging or panic [QUA 08, HAG 11, CRO 13]. We focus here on individual behaviors, without including interactions between individuals and considering the collective as a separate entity with its own mechanisms. A distant objective of this study is to be able to propose thereafter an approach to collective movements in crisis situations.

7.3. Impact factors on behaviors

Before being able to propose a computer science model and analyzing the influences of the different behavioral factors on the global responses of populations in crisis situations, we have to describe individual behaviors by decomposing as finely as possible their different factors. The base components are indicators, measurable elements that can be aggregated with different methods to describe a multitude of observations on the same parameter using a single indicator.

Figure 7.1 represents the indicators, or data, that are the constituents of behavioral factors, and the base of a structure that leads to behaviors themselves. An example of an application of this kind of structure is the one which has been proposed to rank Smart Cities [GIF 07]: it facilitates a description of the smart level of cities according to different factors. In this representation, indicators of health status, for example, are life expectancy, number of hospital beds, number of doctors per inhabitant and satisfaction level with the health system quality.

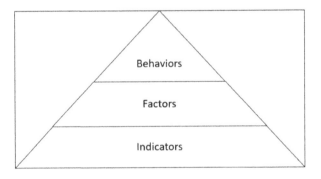

Figure 7.1. *From indicators to behaviors*

7.3.1. *Existing models for the representation of behavioral factors*

Several models in the literature propose to structure the constitutive elements of behavior as we will present in the following section. We use these models to characterize our proposition of behavioral factors, in particular for their representation of emotions, intentions and human personality. The most frequently used models are briefly described here.

7.3.1.1. *Emotions: OCC and Roseman models*

Most existing models representing emotions are based on the OCC model (Orthony, Clore and Collins) or on the Roseman model. The OCC model, proposed in the book *The Cognitive Structure of Emotions* [ORT 90], was developed by cognitive scientists but has quickly been used in computer applications. It is based on three types of conceptual object: events, actions and perceptions that will trigger emotions [BAR 02].

The second model, developed by Roseman, psychologist at the University of Rutgers [ROS 96], defines five evaluation criteria that are able to represent the mental states of 13 distinct emotions. For example, hope corresponds to the mental state where an event is evaluated as uncertain and consistent with the goals of the agent [OCH 05].

7.3.1.2. *Rationality: the BDI model*

BDI (Beliefs, Desires, Intentions) models were developed in the 1980s to be integrated into MAS [BRA 87] and they allow the construction of rational agents. In a BDI architecture, an agent is characterized by a set of beliefs B, a set of desires D and a set of intentions I. These three sets represented in Figure 7.2 are involved in decision processes that enable a choice of actions to realize from a base of plans (defining the possible strategies of the agents) [TAI 12].

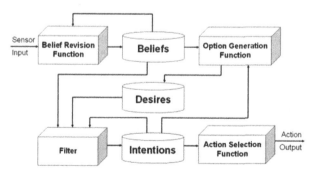

Figure 7.2. *BDI architecture*

This type of approach, relatively complex, in multiagent architectures allows the structuring of so-called rational behavior based on constructed and identified decisions.

7.3.1.3. *Personality: the FFM model*

The five factor model (FFM) is based on five personality factors, often referred to by the acronym OCEAN for Openness, Conscientiousness, Extraversion, Agreeableness and Neutroticism. It enables the analysis of human personality based on observations carried out from clinical practices. The model is well recognized in the scientific community and has been built in several stages over the past 60 years [DIG 90].

These four models remain theoretical and difficult to instantiate with regard to validating hypotheses based on data corresponding to their constituent elements. We were mainly inspired by them to define our behavioral factors. The BDI model, which allows a greater freedom of options in the models of knowledge representation, could be integrated into our modeling choices.

7.3.2. **Proposition of 20 factors**

We choose here to take over the behavior formalization of Kurt Lewin [LEW 36], who conceptualizes a behavior B as a function of a person P and their environment E: B=f(P,E). Twenty behavioral factors presented below have been selected to have an influence on human behaviors in crisis situations from research in literature. We assembled them in two categories, according to the objects they refer to, individual and environmental, and to the types of information sources that allow to characterize them. We present here these factors with a list of indicators associated with each of them.

7.3.2.1. *Factors linked to the individual*

1) *Civil status*: individual characteristics have an obvious statistical influence on the reactions that individuals may display in a given situation. We retain the following indicators as main elements, which are commonly found in sociological studies[1]: age (F1a), gender (F1b), nationality (F1c) place of residence (F1d), level of schooling (F1e) and occupation (F1f).

---

1 https://www.insee.fr/.

2) *Personality*: we used the FFM personality model [ZOU 10] to define our five personality components: desires (F2a), moral principles (F2b), sociability (F2c), beliefs, whether religious or not (F2d) and the ability to decide (F2e), to which we added mimetic reactivity (F2f). The mimetic reaction in crisis situations is a phenomenon largely studied in financial literature. Mimicry can be defined as a set of individual behaviors that present correlations [JON 01]. We distinguish rational mimicry, when an individual acts with mimicry due to a lack of information, and irrational mimicry, when the information is known by the individual but is not taken into account in its actions.

3) *Motivation to escape defend*: evacuating the danger zone (F3a) and defending oneself by fighting against the danger (F3b) are two great reactions expected in crisis situation. These reactions depend on several other factors: the risk assessment, for instance, and the geographical area, but also on the resources that the person may have to protect the survival of their family or their harvest for example [ADA 16].

4) *Responsibility*: in cases of crises in an organization, control and management of the situation are naturally expected by the leaders, the people in charge of a group due to their status or their competences [WOO 08]. In a situation such as a fire alarm in a school for example, a teacher may have a different reaction depending on whether they are alone, in their office, or in the classroom teaching to a student group. As much as they can evaluate the danger as insufficient and not react by continuing their activities if they are alone in their office, it will seem essential to them to evacuate their students under good conditions if they are teaching. They are responsible for their students and have to set an example for them to follow. Let us take an example closer to everyday life: an adult who wants to cross the road on a pedestrian crossing when the pedestrian light is red. There is a much greater probability that this adult will go through if they are alone compared to if they are accompanied by one or more children, or even if one or more children are in their entourage. The responsibility level of a person (F4) permits us to measure this factor.

5) *Emotions*: the previously mentioned OCC model [VAN 06] offers a classification into 10 primary emotions: joy, hope, pride, admiration, contentedness, sadness, fear, shame, reproach, pity. Other classifications can be found, especially in works on the detection of emotions in social networks, with the categories of pleasure, appeasement, love, surprise, displeasure, derangement, contempt, sadness, anger, boredom and negative surprise [HAM 15]. In our choice of representation, we classify emotions more

simply in the six universal categories that can be read on faces [EKM 71]: joy (F5a), sadness (F5b), anger (F5c), disgust (F5e) and surprise (F5f).

6) *Experience*: a person's personal story can have a great influence on their reactions, depending on their experience of another crisis in the past (F6a), their objective (physical and intellectual) to evacuate and to defend themself (F6b) and their subjective ability to evacuate and defend themself (F6c). Subjective capacities evolve according to the successes or the failures of evacuating and defending oneself in similar situations and in the situation in progress (subjective capacities to defend oneself, for example, diminish gradually during a failure to stop the progression of a fire) [ADA 16].

7) *Explicit knowledge*: explicit knowledge of people can play a major role in some situations, especially in risk assessment, and save many lives [ARR 16b]. Knowledge can be categorized into three main categories: common knowledge, shared by a population on a regional or national scale (F7a), knowledge acquired during risk preparedness education (F7b), knowledge provided by access to documents (F7c) and by access to knowledge sharing tools (F7d).

8) *Risk assessment*: the subjective perception of risk may be consistent with the objective risk or not [STR 71]. We consider that risk assessment is composed of both an objective part (F8a), which highly depends on the perceptible signals of the crisis (see section 7.3.2.2), and a subjective part (F8b), which mainly depends on the personality of the individual and the emotions felt.

9) *Perception of the alert system*: we define perception as the process of collecting, organizing and interpreting stimuli that can be information or knowledge coming from different sources. The indicator corresponding to this factor (F9) can be measured through responses to a questionnaire [ARR 16a].

10) *Current action*: some components of human actions can be determined automatically from videos [NIE 08]. We differentiate here the types of actions that a person performs when a crisis occurs or is announced according to their degrees of interaction (F10a), concentration (F10b), and movement (F10c). For example, the degree of interaction of a person who is chatting with friends around a coffee is strong, and their degrees of concentration and movement are rather low. On the contrary, a person who travels alone in their car in a rainy weather will have a low degree of interaction, and their degrees of concentration and movement will be much stronger. This person could be less attentive to crisis signals.

11) *Physiological signals*: a lot of work studies the links that can be made between the physiological signals of an individual and their emotional and psychological reactions [CAC 90]. The four physiological indicators that we retained here can be measured with sensors: heart rate (F11a), blood pressure (F11b), level of sweating (F11c) and muscle contraction (F11d). They can be measured during simulations or exercises by blood pressure monitors or intelligent watches for example.

7.3.2.2. Factors linked to the environment

12) *Geographic zone characteristics*: the first elements considered in the studies of people vulnerability in crisis situations are the characteristics of the geographical areas concerned [COM 15]. They include zone extent (F12a), population density (F12b), poverty level (F12c), economic status (F12d), urban level (F12e), population pyramid (F12f) or even cultural characteristics: individual versus group orientation (F12g) and trust in government (F12h).

13) *Interaction capacity*: in terms of the ability to interact, we take into account both the physical interactions that depend on the zone attendance (F13a) and the virtual interactions that depend mainly on the smartphone number by inhabitant (F13b). Mobility capacity is represented by access to transport (F13c).

14) *Perceptible signals of the crisis*: in a decision-making and action process set up to evacuate an area in case of a fire, for example, the first step will be to identify the risk based on perceptible signals [KIN 15]. The direct perception of smoke or flames in close range by an individual has a significant impact on his decision to evacuate a building. Indicators for these signals depend directly on the type of crisis that is concerned. This is why we define three generic indicators for this factor: visual signals (F14a), sound signals (F14b) and olfactory signals (F14c).

15) *Period characteristics*: behaviors of people will be different depending on whether the crisis surprises them at day or night (F15a), and depending on the number of hours that separate them from the peak of the crisis (F15b) [PRO 15].

16) *Temporal phase of the crisis*: in this chapter, we concentrate on the behavior of people before the crisis (F16a), from beginning (F16b) to peak (F16c) and in its descending phase (F16d), as well as in the after crisis (F16e), which corresponds to a phase of return to habitual behaviors [PRO 15].

17) *Alerts/transmitted information*: we chose to characterize alerts and information transmitted according to their quantity (F17a), which must not be too low or too high, their quality (F17b) evaluated from the information and recommendations provided and according to the number of broadcasting channels (F17c) [DGS 13].

18) *Entourage characteristics*: one of the first reflexes in a crisis situation is to search for friends and to exchange with relatives [DUP 03]. We retain as characteristics of the entourage the density of persons close to the individual (F18a), the presence of authority representatives, police officers (F18b), the security level of the area (F18c) and the presence of close relations (F18d).

19) *Behaviors of the closest people*: studies on social contagion tend to demonstrate that the influence of the geographically closest people is higher than the global entourage on the actions of individuals [GOL 05]. Threshold models are used to illustrate this phenomenon. In these models, each agent owns a contagion threshold which, when it is crossed, bring them to exercise the same activity as the activity exerted by their neighbors. The contagion level of an agent varies according to the number of their neighbors who exercise a similar activity [GRA 78, SOL 00]. The indicators we choose to characterize this factor are the two dominant behaviors in the close entourage F19a and F19b that dominate by their contagion levels. They can correspond, for example, to the absence of reaction and panic, or stupor and return to the place of residence.

20) *Entourage global behavior*: this is the global dominant behavior (F20), which is adopted by the population within a wide area [DUP 03].

Figure 7.3 shows the different data and information that we can integrate into our model to take into account the information identified as having an influence on behavior. Data, or indicators (F1a, F1b etc.), represented in this figure permit us to indirectly characterize behaviors. Each of the factors contains information that can be manipulated by algorithms based on the indicators that characterize them.

The distinction between data, information and knowledge in our choice of definition is more explicitly represented in Figure 7.4 by the correspondence with the components of behavior.

Researchers in social science, sociology and psychology are able to analyze behaviors from direct or reported observations and produce research results from these observations. Unfortunately, in computer science we do not have the means to produce results from this level that explain behavior, or even behavioral factors. Behaviors are derived from difficultly explainable knowledge, and therefore by definition they are not manipulable by computer means. To produce analyses and obtain results in computer science, we have to reason at the level of data, which can be manipulated and aggregated automatically to produce information, even knowledge.

KNOWLEDGE		INFORMATION	DATA							
	Factors linked to individual	Civil status	F1a	F1b	F1c	F1d	F1e	F1f		
		Personality	F2a	F2b	F2c	F2d	F2e	F2f		
		Motivation to escape/defend	F3							
		Responsibility	F4							
		Emotions	F5a	F5b	F5c	F5d	F5e	F5f	F5g	
		Experience	F6a	F6b	F6c					
		Explicit knowledge	F7a	F7b	F7c	F7d				
		Risk assessment	F8a	F8b						
		Perception of the alert system	F9							
Behaviors		Current action	F10a	F10b	F10c					
		Physiological signals	F11a	F11b	F11c	F11d				
	Factors linked to the environment	Geographic zone characteristics	F12a	F12b	F12c	F12d	F12e	F12f	F12g	F12h
		Interaction capacity	F13a	F13b	F13c					
		Perceptible signals of the crisis	F14a	F14b	F14c					
		Period characteristics	F15a	F15b						
		Temporal phase of the crisis	F16a	F16b	F16c	F16d	F16e			
		Alerts / Transmitted information	F17a	F17b	F17c					
		Entourage characteristics	F18a	F18b	F18c	F18d				
		Behaviors of the closest people	F19a	F19b	F19c					
		Entourage global behavior	F20							

Figure 7.3. *From knowledge to data*

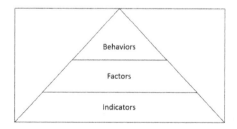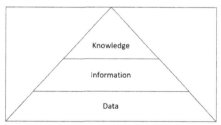

Figure 7.4. *Connection between behavior representation levels and the generic concepts of data, information and knowledge*

7.4. Perspectives

One of the reasons for researching a model that permits reasoning about behavioral factors is to provide the possibility to people responsible for crisis management systems of taking into account human reactions toward warnings and crisis in a general way. With a model of behaviors, we aim to test hypotheses on the participation of the different factors selected previously for the behaviors for a given population. We will also propose, from this model, to evaluate the importance of the factors according to the type of crisis. Results obtained from such analyses could help in prevention and preparation of crisis management programs to construct other models providing real-time predictions with the integration of new indicators into warning systems. Nevertheless, this last step needs models validated from big masses of data; we only envisage it in the medium or long term.

Several modeling possibilities are worth considering to integrate the indicators, which will then allow us to analyze data collected and, in a more advanced phase, to possibly propose predictive analyses or decision aiding for the construction of scenarios. We retain here three choices that are able to integrate behavioral factors into mathematical or semantic analysis objectives and that we will put into practice to present first results on test examples:

– key-value models for a statistical analysis: a key-value model can be directly extracted from the indicators proposed in Figure 7.3. According to the preliminary chosen analysis, we can select the indicators and correlations to be tested. The multiple correspondence analysis method could be particularly adapted to test hypotheses based on this type of model; it allows us to treat the correlation links between any number of variables. It is very often used in the analysis of responses to questionnaires. In practice, we can use this method to explain one or more indicators from another set of indicators. Unfortunately, this method does not allow us to recognize already known relationships between indicators;

– ontologies and decision rules: ontologies have already been proposed to represent behavioral strategies [SIL 01, SIL 06]. We can integrate our behavioral factors by implementing an ontology, and adding a working memory module that would allow us to take advantage of decision rules to discover information from collected data. In computer science, ontologies are defined as formal and explicit specifications of the terms of a domain and the relations between these terms [GRU 93]. Issued from knowledge engineering, they allow us to represent semantic relations with composition or inheritance links for example. Their goal is to provide a consensual, normative, coherent, shareable and reusable semantic formalism of information as it can be used by a computer;

– predictive models and correlation analyses: based on complete information on past situations or statistical studies, we could construct a Bayesian network or Markov process models that would allow us to make predictions from existing data in crisis management systems and probability tables. Today, we do not have this possibility. A Bayesian network is, in computer science and statistics, a graphic probabilistic model that represents random variables under the form of an acyclic-oriented graph. Bayesian networks at the same time are (1) models of knowledge representation, (2) conditional probability calculators and (3) a basis for decision support. Here, we could describe the causal relations between variables from this type of graph. The causal relationships between variables are not deterministic but rather probabilistic. Consequently, the observation of a cause does not systematically imply the effects that depend on it, but it modifies the probability of observing them. The advantage of using Bayesian networks is to simultaneously take into account *a priori* knowledge (represented by the graph) and the experience given by the data.

These modeling choices will have to be refined to enrich a representation which is probabilistic for at least a part, or based on fuzzy logic, which are the two theoretical bases for reasoning and decision making in uncertain situations [GAI 78]. Indeed, "Behavior cannot be reduced to a state or to a series of states such as a succession of points that would define the trajectory of a traced path. It contains uncertainty" [TON 09].

We conclude that, at first glance, a combination of the three models presented before, integrating knowledge, expertise, experience and probability engineering, could be considered to exploit information as much as possible from the data collected. This multiple approach makes it possible for the contributions of each of the models to obtain a behavior analysis as complete and realistic as possible.

7.5. Conclusion

In this chapter, we proposed a first step in the project to integrate a global vision of population behaviors in crisis management systems. We identified 20 factors that we decomposed in indicators able to be transformed in practice as manipulable elements by computer scientist systems. These indicators will be tested in the three presented models in future work. Our approach aims to take advantage of forces and weaknesses and is oriented around the interest of these models in organizational learning.

This first approach constitutes the theoretical part of a research project. The next step of our work, the collection and data exploitation phase, will permit us to acquire information and to analyze the indicators presented before. We currently collect data from responses to questionnaires proposed to populations and to operational actors in the context of crisis management exercises. These data will permit us to instantiate our models on a selection of behaviors identified as probable in the situations played during exercises. We also envisage simulating crisis situations with MAS with the insertion of the selected behaviors. Obviously, our modeling choices will be submitted to tests with probable reevaluations of the theoretical part to provide more detailed representations to be able to interpret in the most univocal manner as possible the results obtained.

7.6. References

[ADA 10] ADAM C., CANAL R., GAUDOU B. *et al.*, "Simulation of the emotion dynamics in a group of agents in an evacuation situation", *International Conference on Principles and Practice of Multi-Agent Systems*, 2010.

[ADA 16] ADAM C., GAUDOU B., "Modelling human behaviours in disasters from interviews: application to Melbourne bushfires", *Social Simulation Conference (SSC)*, Rome, Italy, 2016.

[ALC 89] ALCOCK J., *Animal Behavior*, Sinauer Associates, Sunderland, 1989.

[ARR 16a] ARRU M., MAYAG B., NEGRE E., "Early-warning system perception: a study on fire safety", *13th International Conference on Information Systems for Crisis Response and Management*, Rio de Janeiro, Brazil, May 22–25, 2016.

[ARR 16b] ARRU M., NEGRE E., ROSENTHAL-SABROUX C. *et al.*, "Towards a responsible early-warning system: knowledge implications in decision support design", *Research Challenges in Information Science (RCIS), 2016 IEEE Tenth International Conference*, Grenoble, France, pp. 1–12, 2016.

[BAL 94] BALACHEFF N., "Didactique et intelligence artificielle", *Recherches en didactique des mathématiques*, vol. 14, pp. 9–42, 1994.

[BAR 02] BARTNECK C., "Integrating the OCC model of emotions in embodied characters", *Workshop on Virtual Conversational Characters*, pp. 39–48, 2002.

[BAS 06] BASHER R., "Global early warning systems for natural hazards: systematic and people-centred", *Philosophical Transactions of the Royal Society of London A: Mathematical, Physical and Engineering Sciences*, vol. 364, no. 1845, pp. 2167–2182, 2006.

[BRA 87] BRATMAN M., *Intention, Plans, and Practical Reason*, Harvard University Press, Cambridge, 1987.

[CAC 90] CACIOPPO J.T., TASSINARY L.G., "Inferring psychological significance from physiological signals", *American Psychologist*, vol. 45, no. 1, p. 16, 1990.

[COM 15] COMES T., NEGRE E., MAYAG B., "Beyond early: decision support for improved typhoon warning systems", *12th International Conference on Information Systems for Crisis Response and Management,* ISCRAM Association, Kristiansand, Norway, 2015.

[COO 07] COOPER J.O.H., HEWARD T.E., WILLIAM L. *et al.*, *Applied Behavior Analysis*, Pearson, London, 2007.

[CRO 13] CROCQ L., *Paniques Collectives*, Odile Jacob, Paris, 2013.

[DAU 13] DAUPHINÉ A., PROVITOLO D., *Risques et catastrophes: observer, spatialiser, comprendre, gérer*, Armand Colin, Malakoff, 2013.

[DGS 13] DGSCGC, Guide ORSEC – Alerte et information des populations, Direction générale de la sécurité civile et de la gestion des crises, 2013.

[DIG 90] DIGMAN J.M., "Personality structure: emergence of the five-factor model", *Annual Review of Psychology*, vol. 41, no. 1, pp. 417–440, 1990.

[DUP 03] DUPUY J.-P., *La panique*, La Découverte, Paris, 2003.

[EKM 71] EKMAN P., FRIESEN W.V., "Constants across cultures in the face and emotion", *Journal of Personality and Social Psychology*, vol. 17, no. 2, p. 124, 1971.

[FER 92] FERGUSON I.A., TouringMachines: An architecture for dynamic, rational, mobile agents, PhD thesis, University of Cambridge, 1992.

[GAI 78] GAINES B.R., "Fuzzy and probability uncertainty logics", *Information and Control*, vol. 38, no. 2, pp. 154–169, 1978.

[GIF 07] GIFFINGER R., PICHLER-MILANOVIĆ N., *Smart Cities: Ranking of European Medium-sized Cities*, Centre of Regional Science, Vienna University of Technology, 2007.

[GOL 05] GOLDSTONE R.L., JANSSEN M.A., "Computational models of collective behavior", *Trends in Cognitive Sciences*, vol. 9, no. 9, pp. 424–430, 2005.

[GRA 78] GRANOVETTER M., "Threshold Models of Collective Behavior", *American Journal of Sociology*, vol. 83, no. 6, pp. 1420–1443, 1978.

[GRU 93] GRUBER T.R., "A translation approach to portable ontology specifications", *Knowl. Acquis.*, vol. 5, no. 2, pp. 199–220, 1993.

[HAG 11] HAGENAUER J., HELBICH M., LEITNER M., "Visualization of crime trajectories with self-organizing maps: a case study on evaluating the impact of hurricanes on spatio-temporal crime hotspots", *Proceedings of the 25th conference of the International Cartographic Association,* Paris, France, 2011.

[HAM 15] HAMON T., FRAISSE A., PAROUBEK P., *et al.*, "Analyse des émotions, sentiments et opinions exprimées dans les tweets: présentation et résultats de l'édition 2015 du défi de fouille de texte (DEFT)", 2015.

[HEL 00] HELBING D., FARKAS I., VICSEK T., "Simulating dynamical features of escape panic", *Nature*, vol. 407, no. 6803, pp. 487–490, 2000.

[JON 01] JONDEAU E., "Le comportement mimétique sur les marchés de capitaux", *Bulletin de la Banque de France*, vol. 95, pp. 85–97, 2001.

[KIN 15] KINATEDER M.T., KULIGOWSKI E.D., RENEKE P.A. *et al.*, "Risk perception in fire evacuation behavior revisited: definitions, related concepts, and empirical evidence", *Fire Science Reviews*, vol. 4, no. 1, p. 1, 2015.

[MER 42] MERLEAU-PONTY M., *La structure du comportement*, Presses Universitaires de France, Paris, 1942.

[MIL 90] MILETI D.S., SORENSEN J.H., Communication of emergency public warnings: A social science perspective and state-of-the-art assessment, Report, Oak Ridge National Lab, 1990.

[MUL 11] MULLER J.P., PISCHEL M., The agent architecture inteRRaP: Concept and application, Deutsches Forschungszentrum für Künstliche Intelligenz GmbH, FRG, 2011.

[NIE 08] NIEBLES J.C., WANG H., FEI-FEI L., "Unsupervised learning of human action categories using spatial-temporal words", *International Journal of Computer Vision*, vol. 79, no. 3, pp. 299–318, 2008.

[OCH 05] OCHS M., SADEK D., PELACHAUD C., "La représentation des émotions d'un agent rationnel", *Workshop Francophone sur les Agents Conversationnels Animés*, pp. 43–52, 2005.

[ORT 90] ORTONY A., CLORE G.L., COLLINS A., *The Cognitive Structure of Emotions*, Cambridge University Press, Cambridge, 1990.

[PRO 15] PROVITOLO D., DUBOS-PAILLARD E., VERDIÈRE N. *et al.*, "Human behaviors in the face of disasters: from observing to conceptual and mathematical modeling", *Cybergeo: Revue européenne de géographie/European journal of geography*, vol. 735, 2015.

[QUA 08] QUARANTELLI E.L., "Conventional beliefs and counterintuitive realities", *Social Research: An International Quarterly of the Social Sciences*, vol. 75, no. 3 (Fall 2008), pp. 873–904, 2008.

[RIP 09] RIPLEY A., *The Unthinkable: Who Survives when Disaster Strikes and Why*, Harmony Books, New York, 2009.

[ROS 96] ROSEMAN I.J., "Appraisal determinants of emotions: Constructing a more accurate and comprehensive theory", *Cognition & Emotion*, vol. 10, no. 3, pp. 241–278, 1996.

[RUI 10] RUIN I., "Conduite à contre-courant et crues rapides, le conflit du quotidien et de l'exceptionnel", *Annales de géographie*, no. 4, pp. 419–432, 2010.

[SIL 01] SILVERMAN B.G., More realistic human behavior models for agents in virtual worlds: emotion, stress, and value ontologies, *ACASA Technical Report*, 2001.

[SIL 06] SILVERMAN B.G., JOHNS M., CORNWELL J. *et al.*, "Human behavior models for agents in simulators and games: part I: enabling science with PMFserv", *Presence: Teleoperators and Virtual Environments*, vol. 15, no. 2, pp. 139–162, 2006.

[SKI 05] SKINNER B.F., "Science et comportement humain", *Les cahiers psychologie politique*, vol. 7, Association française de psychologie politique, 2005.

[SOL 00] SOLOMON S., WEISBUCH G., DE ARCANGELIS L., *et al.*, "Social percolation models", *Physica A: Statistical Mechanics and its Applications*, vol. 277, no. 1, pp. 239–247, 2000.

[STR 71] STREUFERT S., TAYLOR E.A., Objective risk levels and subjective risk perception, Report no. 40, Purdue University and Group Psychology Programs, Office of Naval Research, August 1971.

[TAI 12] TAILLANDIER P., THEROND O., GAUDOU B., "Une architecture d'agent BDI basée sur la théorie des fonctions de croyance: application à la simulation du comportement des agriculteurs", *Journées Francophones sur les Systèmes Multi-Agents*, pp. 107–116, 2012.

[TON 09] TONIOLO A.-M., "Le comportement: entre perception et action, un concept à réhabiliter", *L'année psychologique*, vol. 109, no. 01, pp. 155–193, 2009.

[VAN 06] VAN DYKE PARUNAK H., BISSON R., BRUECKNER S. *et al.*, "A model of emotions for situated agents", *Proceedings of the fifth international joint conference on autonomous agents and multiagent systems*, ACM, Hakodate, Japan, pp. 993–995, 2006.

[WOO 08] WOOTEN L.P., JAMES E.H., "Linking crisis management and leadership competencies: the role of human resource development", *Advances in Developing Human Resources*, vol. 10, no. 3, pp. 352–379, 2008.

[ZOU 10] ZOUMPOULAKI A., AVRADINIS N., VOSINAKIS S., "A multi-agent simulation framework for emergency evacuations incorporating personality and emotions", *Hellenic Conference on Artificial Intelligence*, Athens, Greece, pp. 423–428, 2010.

8

Online Social Network Phenomena: Buzz, Rumor and Spam

Online social networks (OSNs) provide data valuable for a tremendous range of applications such as search engines and recommendation systems. However, the easy-to-use interactive interfaces and the low barriers to publication have exposed various information quality (IQ) problems, decreasing the quality of user-generated content (UGC) in such networks. The existence of a particular kind of ill-intentioned user, who are responsible for polluting OSNs' content, imposes challenges to maintaining an acceptable level of IQ. Such kinds of users may misuse all services provided by social networks to pollute their content in an automated way. IQ problems that appear on OSNs can be categorized into three different forms, buzz, rumor and spam, where each of which has properties and goals differing from others. As a natural reaction and because of the marked failure of OSNs in uprooting these IQ problems, various detection and filtering methods have been designed by various researchers to address the three uncorrelated IQ problems. Hence, in this chapter, we discuss in detail three common negative phenomena appearing in OSNs with the main strengths and drawbacks of their detection systems. Then, we provide detailed research perspectives showing the future work of these OSN phenomena.

Chapter written by Manel MEZGHANI, Mahdi WASHHA and Florence SÈDES.

8.1. Introduction

Online social networks have become the top communication media and almost the first option for users to share links, discuss and connect with others. For example, the most popular OSNs such as Twitter and Facebook have exceeded billions of registered users and millions of daily active users. As one of many OSNs, Twitter has emerged as one of the most popular microblogging social networks, allowing users to publish, share and discuss everything from social events to news and jokes through a messaging mechanism of 140 characters. Statistics state that, in November 2015, the number of active users that use Twitter monthly is about 320 million with an average of 500 million tweets published per day.

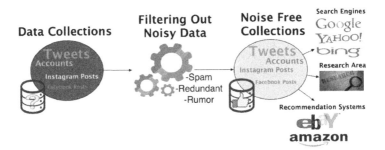

Figure 8.1. *An overview of the information quality process in social networks*

The key point of OSNs is their dependency on users as primary contributors in generating and posting information. Users' contributions might be exploited in different positive ways such as understanding users' needs and analyzing users' opinions for election purposes. OSNs' users are influenced by the information shared and propagated through the network. However, not all information flowing in OSNs is valid for consumption by users because of the presence of some ill-intentioned users aiming to spread noisy information. Mainly, this noisy information could be summarized in three different types: buzz, rumor and spam, where each of which has particular properties differing from the others. Buzz is defined as a commercial or marketing method for making noise around a particular event to improve its visibility, while rumor is simply defined as false or fake information associated with a particular event [HAS 11], where any event occurring in OSNs is characterized by a one or more keywords [SAY 09]. Spam is the content that appears in a defined context and does not have any reasonable interpretation in the given context, having an obvious difference from rumor and buzz definitions. Indeed, spammy tasks by spammers may cause major problems in different directions, such as (1) polluting search results with spam information, (2) degrading statistics accuracy obtained by mining tools, (3) consuming storage resources and (4) violating users' privacy. However, with these serious problems, OSNs' antispam mechanisms have failed to contain the spam problem, raising real concerns about the quality of "crawled" data collections.

The administrators of OSNs make great efforts to address these three negative phenomena; however, their solutions are not efficient for ultimately uprooting the three information problems. Thus, different researchers have introduced various methods to detect and filter out this noisy information in order to have a cleaned version of data. Besides the importance of OSN data for a tremendous range of areas such as search engines and the research field, filtering out noisy data to have high-quality information is the obvious and straightforward solution. Information quality processes in social networks, described in Figure 8.1, are generically summarized in three dependent steps [AGA 10]: (1) selecting the data collections (e.g. Facebook accounts, Tweets, Facebook posts) that need improvements; (2) determining the noise type (e.g. spam, rumor) to be filtered out; (3) at last, applying predesigned algorithms depending on the chosen noise type to produce noise-free data collections. Hence, in order to gain insight into these information quality problems, we discuss in detail three common negative phenomena appearing in OSNs with the main strengths and drawbacks of their detection systems. Then, we provide detailed research perspectives showing the future work of these OSN phenomenons.

The remainder of the chapter is organized as follows. An overview about the buzz concept and its detection method is given in section 8.2. Section 8.3 presents a precise definition for the rumor concept by providing an overview of all current detection methods. Section 8.4 describes the most common type of noisy information appearing on OSNs with its levels of detection. Section 8.5 discusses reseasch problems related to the three negative phenomena. Section 8.6 concludes the chapter.

8.2. Buzz: definition and detection methods

The term buzz is commonly defined as "popular information", "information spread", "viral marketing", "trends" or "event detection". Buzz could be a disaster, traffic information, an outbreak or simply news. In the social context, buzz is a commercial or marketing technique to make noise around an event in an attempt to enhance its visibility. Buzz is a popular piece of information in a specific time. This technique causes several new users to be suddenly interested in this event at a time t. Unfortunately, buzz could be used for enhancing the visibility of false or fake information.

Information spread and viral marketing: a buzz is a popular piece of information at a specific time. Maximizing the spread of this information could be used for several purposes such as to maximize the influence of a political person, to sell more products, to promote a company, etc. Handling buzz is important in order to optimize the spread of the information and then affect more suitable users. However, this notion is not very easy to manage. We can find in social media buzz that is considered as rumor and that has been spread by users without verification or often the apparition of buzz cannot be predicted in order to manage it in the right way.

In the literature, information spreading is usually associated with viral marketing. Kempe *et al.* [KEM 15] studied the different models of information spread. They consider the problem of diffusion as in viral marketing strategies in social networks: "If we can try to convince a subset of individuals to adopt a new product or innovation, and the goal is to trigger a large cascade of further adoptions, which set of individuals should we target?". They treat this problem as NP-hard.

As social networks are mainly considered as huge graphs that link users, information spread is faster since users are influenced by their relationships.

Event detection: event detection is related to finding new events from streams of social media updates. The streams are usually generated by users (user-generated content). So, event detection is more challenging because it deals with short and noisy contents, diverse and fast changing topics, and large data volumes [PET 10, LI 12].

Event detection from social media has shown its utility by detecting earthquakes from Twitter [SAK 10] using a temporal and spatial model and detecting the death of Michael Jackson [OSB 12] using a streaming model and event cross-checking. Several methods are used to detect events. A survey was proposed by [NUR 13].

Sayyadi *et al.* [SAY 09] propose an algorithm for event detection based on keywords extracted from articles in social media. They propose to represent terms in articles as a graph based on a term frequency (TF) metric. Then, they detect communities in this graph based on a betweenness centrality metric that reflects most connected nodes. Once communities are detected, they proceed to document clustering. In fact, each community of keywords may be thought of as a synthetic document, which is called a key document. Documents in the original corpus are similar; this synthetic document can be clustered, thus retrieving a cluster of topical documents. Cosine similarity is used to discover document clusters for key documents. This approach to co-occurrence keywords can then detect events but still suffers from issues like the non-consideration of the weight of each node.

More recently, Aggarwal and Subbian [AGG 12] address the problem of event detection as a clustering problem because the events can only be inferred from aggregate trend changes in the stream. They propose new methods for clustering and event detection in social streams. The results show the effectiveness of this approach.

8.3. Rumor: definition and detection methods

Rumor definition: as the detection of false information is almost a semantic content problem (i.e. one word is enough to change true information to false one), it is necessary to provide a precise definition of rumor information. According to the literature, rumor information is defined as an unverified and instrumentally relevant statement of information spread among people. Indeed, rumor information can end in three ways [DOE 12, TAN 16, ZHO 17]: (1) resolved as true (factual), (2) resolved as false (nonfactual), or (3) remain unresolved.

Rumor definition method types: rumors detection received great attention from researchers in recent years [HU 17, JIN 13, DOE 12]. Indeed, they spent huge efforts to define or find rules distinguishing true information from false on social networks. They benefited from various facts inspired by psychological and sociology studies to discover the divergence between them. For example, rumors are almost always initiated by one person or a small group, dramatically propagated in a small period and then disappearing gradually. On the other hand, non-rumor information is published by a large set of people without any dependency or correlation between them. Also, it propagates steadily and uniformly all the time. With such facts forming starting points, research has been conducted to study and detect rumors in social networks using different aspects. We categorize these researches based on what kind of information they target to detect. Hence, we found that detection is applied at two levels: (1) *topics* or (2) *individual posts*. At the topic level, they examine a set of posts associated with a particular topic to decide whether that topic is rumor or not. At the post level, they determine whether the given information inside the post is rumor or not, which is indeed much harder than the topic level from detection point of view.

Topic-based rumor detection: in [ZHA 15b], the authors have designed a technique to detect rumor topics in their early stages, applied on the Twitter social network. In order to detect a rumor topic, the authors defined a procedure with five steps. First, for incoming streams of tweets, these tweets are classified into signal tweets or non-signal tweets, where the signal tweets have inquiries such as questions related to the topic. Then, the cluster of signal tweets is identified using a metric measuring the overlap in the tweet contents. For each cluster, the system performs an analysis to determine a single statement that can represent the common text in the cluster. The system then searches for matches between non-signal tweets and cluster statements in order to classify clusters as potential rumors when they match. At last, as a set of clusters are produced, the clusters resulting from previous stage are ranked using 13 statistical features (e.g. ratio of signal tweets to all tweets in a cluster) where these clusters are used to infer about truth, a fact claim. With these steps, the authors' aim is to minimize the delay from the first appearance of rumor tweets to the detection time. In the validation, the system has been evaluated using two different datasets, known as Boston Marathon Bombing and Garden-hose, containing more than 1 billion tweets, using precision as an evaluation metric. The authors performed several experiments by including and excluding the methods that are used in identifying signal tweets and the algorithms exploited in doing statement ranking, resulting in six experiments in total. In terms of results, the best precision was obtained when using the Enquiries Corrections method for the Boston dataset with a precision of 52.1%, while the use of the corrections method has only produced the best results for the Garden-hose dataset with a precision of 52.1%. From the detection delay point of view, the best delay obtained is about 2.8 h when using the hashtag tracking method.

In [KWO 13], the authors aim at identifying rumor topics using three aspects of diffusion: temporal, structural and linguistic. For the temporal characteristic, they effectively capture the bursty temporal pattern using the Periodic External Shocks (PES) method that provides 10 features in this aspect. The structural characteristics are based on the friendship network, the largest connected component (LCC) of the friendship network and the diffusion network, resulting in 15 features in total. For linguistic characteristics, the authors studied words' semantics, using the linguistic Inquiry and Word Count (LIWC) tool to study sentiments, proposing 65 features in this area. With all of these features, the authors reduced the feature dimensionality using random forests and logic regression models by applying twofold cross-validation, selecting three temporal features, five structural features and nine linguistic features. In building an annotated dataset, the authors used websites like snopes.com and urbanlegends.about.com. They choose 130 topics (70 rumors and 60 non-rumors) that circulated during March 2006. Then, on the dataset collected, they evaluated the features proposed using Decision Tree, Random Forest and SVM classifiers. They compared the performance of their features with 15 state-of-art features forming as a baseline. The new features show a superior performance compared to the baseline in terms of accuracy, precision, recall and F-measure.

Individual post-based rumor detection: in individual post-rumor detection [ZHA 15a], the authors treated the rumor problem from a machine learning point of view by using a binary classifier to predict whether a considered message or post is rumor or not. However, as a contribution, the authors proposed a design of new features at both content and user levels, called implicit features, generated through mining deep user and content information. Their proposition is inspired by the existing features in the literature, so-called shallow features, such that those features are not able to distinguish efficiently between rumor and normal messages, since they are extracted from basic attributes at the user or content level. In the experiment session, the authors collected rumor messages from Sina Weibo Community

Management Center as a social network, having 3,229 rumor microblogs and 12,534 non-rumor microblogs. The SVM classifier has been used as a learning algorithm to build a binary rumor classified using the features proposed. As evaluation metrics, authors used precision, recall and F-measure. Two sets of experiments are performed. The first experiment evaluates each group of features individually as well as performing additional experiments combining the groups together. In terms of results, the content group features outperformed the user group features in all metrics considered, with the best results obtained when both groups were combined together. The second experiment shows a comparison between the authors' (implied) features and the state-of-the-art (shallow) features. The implied features outperformed the shallow features in all metrics considered.

8.4. Spam: definition and detection methods

Information quality: in the literature, different efforts have been made to introduce an obvious definition of information quality. Juran [JUR 99] has defined IQ as the degree of usefulness or "fitness for use" of information in a particular task or context. Wand and Wang [WAN 96] have introduced a definition of data quality as the quality of mapping between an information system state and a real world state. However, as these definitions are conceptually qualitative, researchers have introduced various dimensions to describe or measure information quality as defined in Table 8.1. These dimensions can be classified under four main categories: intrinsic, contextual, representational and accessibility. However, in order to choose the appropriate dimensions or categorizes, it is required to define the desired entity (e.g. tweet, Twitter account) and the IQ problem (e.g. social rumor and social spam). Once the IQ problem and the corresponding dimensions get determined, the next step is quantifying the selected dimensions through designing a set of metrics (or features). At last, all metrics proposed might be combined together to have a single indicator, which provides information about the quality of the entity with respect to the IQ problem. For example, rumor information is a well-known IQ problem appearing in online social networks and microblogging sites [ZUB 15]. Thus, to measure the likelihood of a tweet of being a rumor, the accuracy dimension of the intrinsic category is one of many possible dimensions that can be used. For quantifying such a dimension, checking the existence of the information in the given tweet over different online social networks is a possible metric where the positive existence is an indication of not being rumor information.

Measure	Description
Intrinsic IQ: conformance between information and real world view	
Accuracy/validity	The extent to which information is valid according to stable references such as a dictionary or set of domain norms and constraints.
Believability	The degree to which information is credible.
Objectivity	The degree to which information is unprejudiced, unbiased and impartial.
Reputation	The extent to which information is respectable.
Verifiability	The extent to which information can be checked for correctness.
Contextual IQ: the degree to which information is suitable in a given context or a task in hand	
Amount of information	The extent to which the amount of information is appropriate for use.
Relevancy	The degree to which information is applicable for a given task in hand.
Timeliness	The extent to which information is up to date for a given task in hand.
Completeness	The extent to which information matches the completeness and precision required in a given context.
Value-added	The degree to which the use of information delivers benefit to the information consumers.
Contextual understandability	The extent to which information is easily comprehended without ambiguity.
User feedback	The ability of users to provide either an implicit or explicit quality evaluation of the content.
Representational IQ: the extent to which information is well presented and usable for all users, taking into account technical aspects	
Conciseness of representation	The degree to which the structure and presentation of information is compact without being overwhelming.
Representational consistency	The extent to which the definition, format and value of information is consistent across applications and systems.
Ease of understanding	The extent to which information is comprehensible and clear.
Manipulability	The degree to which information can be updated, modified, transferred, reproduced, integrated and customized.
Accessibility IQ: the extent to which information is accessible and secure	
Access	The extent to which information is retrievable and available.
Security	The degree to which information is protected from an unauthorized access.

Table 8.1. *A definition of the four IQ categories with their dimensions [AGA 10]*

Social spam and information quality: social spam is defined as non-sensical or gibberish text content appearing on OSNs and any website dealing with user-generated content such as chats and comments [AGA 10]. Social spam may take a tremendous range of forms, including profanity, insults, hate speeches, fraudulent reviews, personally identifiable information, fake friends, bulk messages, phishing and malicious links, and porn materials. One might view social spam as irrelevant information; however, this interpretation is not quite accurate. We justify this misinterpretation through the definition of information retrieval (IR) systems [MAN 08] in which the relevancy of documents in IR systems is dependent on the input search query. Thus, irrelevant documents with respect to an input query are not necessarily spam content. Hence, as an additional definition, social spam might be defined as irrelevant information that does not have an interpretation in any context, as long as the input query is not a spam content. Since social spam is a pure IQ problem, we project the problem on to five IQ dimensions including accuracy, believability, reputation, value added and relevancy. Indeed, spam content does not represent real world data and thus it has a low degree in accuracy and believability dimensions. Also, the reputation of spam is also low because normal users tend to circulate accurate information in general. Finally, spam content does not deliver any benefit for OSN users, leading to a low degree in terms of value added and relevancy dimensions. Although projecting the social spam problem onto the IQ world provides insights regarding the efficient handling of the problem, social spammers expend great efforts to increase the degree of IQ dimensions. Therefore, understanding and knowing facts about social spammers and their behaviors can contribute in providing effective solutions to the social spam problem.

Social spammers exploit the flexibility of using OSNs to misuse all legal and possible services supported by OSNs to spread their spam content. Regardless of the type of OSN site targeted, social spammers adopt same facts or principles in their goals and behaviors, summarized as follows [WAS 16]:

– social spammers are goal-oriented persons aiming to achieve unethical goals (e.g. promote products), and thus they use their smartness to accomplish their spammy tasks in an effective and quick way;

– social spammers exploit trending topics to launch their spammy content;

– social spammers often create and launch a campaign of spam accounts in a short period (e.g. one day) to maximize their monetary profits and speedup their spamming behavior;

– as a set of APIs is provided by social networks, social spammers leverage them to automate their spamming tasks in a systematic way (e.g. tweeting every 10 min). The random posting behavior is avoided and not a preferable solution for social spammers because it may decrease the target profit and decelerate their spamming behavior.

In Twitter, social spammers leverage different sets of provided services to launch their spam attacks through (1) URL, (2) hashtag and (3) mention services. As the tweet size is restricted to 140 characters, URL shortening services (e.g. Bitly and TinyURL) are allowed in Twitter to convert long URLs to small ones. This option allows social spammers to abuse this service through posting spam websites by shortening the desired URL to hide the domain. Hashtags are widely used in OSNs as a service to group tweets by their topic, facilitating the search process. This service is misused by social spammers through tagging hashtags in their spam tweets that may also contain URLs to increase the chance of being searched by the users. The mention service provides a mechanism to send a direct message to a particular user through using the @ symbol followed by the screen name of the desired user. Differently from URLs and hashtags, social spammers misuse this service to send their tweets to a defined list of users. Besides these services, Twitter provides APIs for developers to be used in their third party applications. Social spammers exploit this distinctive service as an opportunity to automate their spamming behavior.

Twitter gives the opportunity for the users to report spam accounts through clicking on the "Report: they are posting spam" option available in all accounts. When an account is being reported, Twitter's administrators manually review and deeply analyze that account to make a suspension decision. However, such a reporting mechanism is inefficient for fighting and bringing down social spammers because it needs significant efforts from both users and administrators. Moreover, many users may provide fake reports and thus not all reports are necessarily trustworthy. As an additional attempt to reduce the spam problem, Twitter has set general rules (e.g. posting porn materials is prohibited) and permanently suspends the accounts that violate those rules [TWI 16]. Unfortunately, social spammers are smart enough to bypass Twitter's rules. For instance, social spammers may coordinate multiple accounts and distribute the desired workload among these accounts to mislead the detection. Consequently, Twitter's approaches are ineffective for real-time spam filtering.

The shortcomings in Twitter's anti-spam mechanism have motivated researchers to introduce more robust methods to increase the incoming data quality for the applications that use Twitter as a main source of information. After deepening our insights into a wide range of scientific research related to the spam detection methods in Twitter, we built a detailed taxonomy for these methods, as shown in Figure 8.2, based on different criteria, including (1) type of detection approach (Machine Learning or Honeypot), (2) level of detection (Tweet, Account and Campaign), and (3) type of features (User, Content, Link, Automation, Graph and Timing) exploited in the detection methods. Table 8.2 provides a description of these terminologies. The machine learning axis focuses on detecting social spam in an automated way, while the social honeypot approach requires an intervention from systems' administrators.

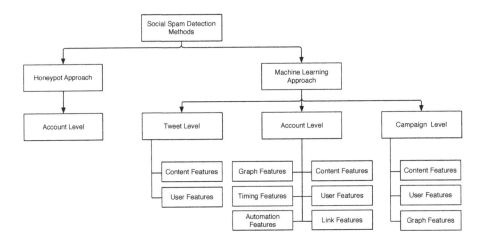

Figure 8.2. *A taxonomy for social spam detection methods in Twitter. The descriptions of some terminologies are provided in Table 8.2*

Terminology	Description
Tweet-level detection	This level is concerned with predicting the class label of a tweet, i.e. whether it is spam or non-spam.
Account-level detection	This level of detection focuses on deeply analyzing the user's profile or account to predict whether the user of the account is a spammer or legitimate user.
Campaign-level detection	This level of detection takes the collective perspective so that a group of accounts is examined to judge whether it is a spam campaign or not.
User features	Features extracted from attributes (e.g. username, screen name) existing in the user object, such as account's age and number of tweets posted by the user.
Content features	Features extracted from the content of one or more tweets, such as number of hashtags and number of URLs.
Graph features	Features required to build a bidirectional graph containing user's neighbors to extract features such as local clustering and node betweenness.
Timing features	Features extracted by analyzing the posting time of a group of tweets posted by a user, such as tweeting frequency.
Automation features	Features related to the use of external APIs supported by external websites.
Link features	Features extracted from analyzing URLs posted in user's tweets, such as tweet and URL content similarity.

Table 8.2. *A description of different terminologies used in the social spam detection taxonomy*

Machine learning approach: most of the spam detection methods employ supervised machine learning algorithms at three levels of detection, distributed between tweet-level detection, account-level detection and campaign-level detection:

– *Account Level:* the research introduced in [BEN 10, WAS 16, WU 17, WAN 10, MCC 11, STR 10, MED 16, BAR 15, HU 14, HU 13] focus on extracting features (e.g. the number of friends, number of followers, similarity between tweets and ratio of URLs in tweets) from users' accounts. In more dedicated studies, such as the research presented in [CAO 15, WAN 15], spam URLs are identified through analyzing the behavior of shortened URLs such as the number of clicks and the length of the redirection chain. However, the ease of manipulation with this type of feature by social spammers has motivated researchers to leverage graph theory to extract more complex features. For instance, the studies presented in [YAN 11, YAN 12, ALM 16] have examined the relation among users through using graph theories and metrics to measure three features including node betweenness, local clustering and bidirectional relation ratio. Leveraging such complex features gives high spam accounts detection rates; however, they are not suitable for real-time Twitter-based applications because of the huge volume of data that must be retrieved from Twitter's servers as well as the fact that graph operations mainly require exponential time at the computational level.

– *Campaign Level:* Chu *et al.* [CHU 12b] have treated the spam problem from a collective perspective view. They have clustered a set of desired accounts according to the URLs available in the posted tweets. Then, a defined set of features from the accounts clustered is designed to build a binary classification model using machine learning algorithms to identify the spam campaign. Chu *et al.* [CHU 12a] have proposed a classification model to capture the difference among bot, human and cyborg by taking into consideration the content of tweets and the tweeting behavior. Indeed, methods belonging to this detection level have a major drawback since these methods employ a set of features requiring a great number of REST API calls to get information such as users' tweets and followers. Consequently, exploiting the current version of campaign level detection methods is not appropriate for real-time filtering due to the high volume of data required from Twitter's servers.

– *Tweet Level:* Martinez-Romo and Araujo [MAR 13] have designed a language-model-based method to detect spam tweets existing in Twitter trending topics. In this method, a uni-gram language model is built for each tweet and another uni-gram model for the all the tweets posted in the trending topic. Then, the Kullback-Leibler divergence is computed between the language model of a given tweet and the language model of the topic itself. In addition, if the given tweet contains a URL, the authors have used the same concept, but also built a uni-gram language model for the URL and compared it with the language model of the tweet itself using the same divergence metric. However, this method is not suitable for real-time filtering because it needs the tweets that have been posted in the same topic from Twitter's servers. Moreover, parsing the HTML content of a URL takes a significant time, making such a feature unsuitable for real-time filtering. In a more general approach, supervised machine learning methods have been used to build binary classification models for detecting spam tweets in real-time Twitter streams as illustrated in Figure 8.3 [BEN 10, CHE 15b]. Building such models requires a training phase that exploits an already annotated dataset consisting of tweets labeled as spam and non-spam, and a set of features to be extracted from each tweet with a labeled feature space. Then, a particular supervised machine learning method (e.g. Random Forest, J48, Support Vector Machine) is used to produce a binary classification model. At the operational time, the learned classification model is exploited to predict the class label of each new incoming tweet into spam or non-spam, using the same features adopted in the training phase. As the tweet object has a limited amount of information, a few of the features described in Table 8.2 and categorized into user and content have been adopted in spam tweet detection. Most of these features are light and suitable for real-time filtering, except those features that require additional information from either the Web or from Twitter's servers. However, the major drawback of this approach is the need for a training set to have an updated classification model able to effectively detect spam tweets. A more dynamic method, so-called asymmetric-self learning [CHE 15a], has been proposed to overcome and reduce the problem of needing an up-to-date training set. This method adds incoming classified tweets, using an initial trained classification model, to the training dataset. Then, after a defined period (e.g. 1 or 2 days), the classification model is retrained using the old training tweets and the recent classified tweets. However, this approach is completely dependent on the learning algorithm since the algorithms that do not consider the distribution of the class labels during the learning phases, such as a neural network, will not produce a classification model differing from the previous one. Hence, there is no guarantee about its performance in effectively adapting to new social spammers' patterns.

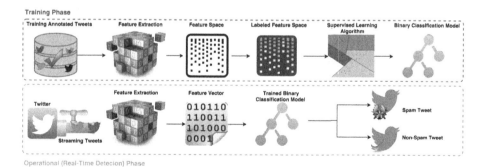

Figure 8.3. *A flowchart describing the classical real-time spam detection method consisting of two dependent phases: (1) training phase and (2) operational phase*

Honeypot approach: social honeypot is viewed as an information system resource that can monitor social spammers' behavior through logging their information such as the information of accounts and any available content [LEE 10]. In fact, there is no significant difference between Twitter's anti-spam mechanism and the social honeypot approach. Both of them need an administrative control to produce a decision about the accounts that have fallen into the honeypot trap. The necessity of administrative control is to reduce the false positive rate, as an alternative solution would be to blindly classify all users who have been dropped in the trap as spam users.

8.5. OSN-based information quality research problems

Although the existing methods have made significant achievements in addressing the three information quality problems, in some aspects further improvements are required to effectively and efficiently tackle those aspects. We summarize those aspects as two main research problems: (1) real-time noise filtering (2) and social big data filtering. Real-time noise filtering is required and mandatory in OSN-based applications such as tweet summarization since noisy data have a direct impact on the performance of those applications. The main problem in the current detection methods is relying on classification models that need extra information from ONSs' servers, making the applicability of real-time filtering quite impossible. Also, major drawbacks existing in the current real-time detection methods are the dependency on using supervised learning methods to build classification models for detecting buzz, rumor and spam. The problem of supervision-based classification models is the need for manual annotated information where such information is not always at hand and acquiring it is time consuming. Also, inspired by the nature of the problems and the dynamicity of content, the adopted features in building classification models are not too powerful to efficiently detect the noise information. Hence, this raises the need to search for new ways to efficiently and effectively detect noisy information in real time.

Working on offline social information, like a crawled dataset of tweets, may result in falling into the big data problem. Intuitively, the methods that have been designed for detecting noisy information in offline data collections are better than those that work in real-time streams. The high performance of those methods is due to the use of extra information that is not available when real-time streaming. However, the main problem of these methods is in relying too much on information required from OSNs' servers when retrieving such information needs API calls. Given the fact that OSNs constrain their APIs to a few number of calls per time window, processing a big data collection to detect and filter out the noisy data is too costly from the consumption point of view. For instance, processing 1 million Twitter accounts using features requiring API calls may take more than 3 months. Thus, the problem of big data in the context of OSNs' information quality requires new research directions to handle this problem effectively.

8.6. Conclusion

In this chapter, we presented three common negative phenomena appearing in OSNs: buzz, rumor and spam. We provided the main strengths and drawbacks of detection and filtering methods. Then, we provided detailed research perspectives showing future work concerning these OSN phenomena.

The phenomena detailed in this chapter remain the major problems in increasing the performances of systems based on social data. The research problems, addressed to improve information quality, are challenging and need a deeper understanding of the motivations of the people who diffuse information on the net. Also, treating noisy data in a big data context is considered as a very important challenge that may be useful in several applications such as recommendations (for example viral Marketing), social Internet of Things (IoT), etc.

8.7. References

[AGA 10] AGARWAL N., YILIYASI Y., "Information quality challenges in social media", *International Conference on Information Quality (ICIQ)*, Little Rock, Arkansas, 2010.

[AGG 12] AGGARWAL C., SUBBIAN K., "Event Detection in Social Streams", *Proceedings of the 2012 SIAM International Conference on Data Mining*, Anaheim, USA, 2012.

[ALM 16] ALMAATOUQ A., SHMUELI E., NOUH M. *et al.*, "If it looks like a spammer and behaves like a spammer, it must be a spammer: analysis and detection of microblogging spam accounts", *International Journal of Information Security*, vol. 15, no. 5, pp. 475–491, 2016.

[BAR 15] BARA I.-A., FUNG C.J., DINH T., "Enhancing twitter spam accounts discovery using cross-account pattern mining", *2015 IFIP/IEEE International Symposium on Integrated Network Management (IM)*, IEEE, Ottawa, Canada, pp. 491–496, 2015.

[BEN 10] BENEVENUTO F., MAGNO G., RODRIGUES T. *et al.*, "Detecting spammers on twitter", *Collaboration, Electronic messaging, Anti-Abuse and Spam Conference (CEAS)*, Redmond, USA, 2010.

[CAO 15] CAO C., CAVERLEE J., "Detecting spam URLs in social media via behavioral analysis", in HANBURY A., KAZAI G., RAUBER A. *et al.* (eds), *Advances in Information Retrieval*, Springer, Cham, 2015.

[CHE 15a] CHEN C., ZHANG J., XIANG Y. *et al.*, "Asymmetric self-learning for tackling Twitter spam drift", *2015 IEEE Conference on Computer Communications Workshops (INFOCOM WKSHPS)*, IEEE, Hong Kong, China, pp. 208–213, 2015.

[CHE 15b] CHEN C., ZHANG J., XIE Y. *et al.*, "A performance evaluation of machine learning-based streaming spam tweets detection", *IEEE Transactions on Computational Social Systems*, vol. 2, no. 3, pp. 65–76, 2015.

[CHU 12a] CHU Z., GIANVECCHIO S., WANG H. *et al.*, "Detecting automation of twitter accounts: are you a human, bot, or cyborg?", *IEEE Transactions on Dependable and Secure Computing*, vol. 9, no. 6, pp. 811–824, 2012.

[CHU 12b] CHU Z., WIDJAJA I., WANG H., "Detecting social spam campaigns on twitter", in BAO F., SAMARATI P., ZHOU J. (eds), *Applied Cryptography and Network Security*, Springer, Berlin, Heidelberg, 2012.

[DOE 12] DOERR B., FOUZ M., FRIEDRICH T., "Why rumors spread so quickly in social networks", *Communications of the ACM*, vol. 55, no. 6, pp. 70–75, 2012.

[HAS 11] HASHIMOTO T., KUBOYAMA T., SHIROTA Y., "Rumor analysis framework in social media", *TENCON 2011 – 2011 IEEE Region 10 Conference*, pp. 133–137, 2011.

[HU 13] HU X., TANG J., ZHANG Y. *et al.*, "Social spammer detection in microblogging", *IJCAI*, vol. 13, pp. 2633–2639, 2013.

[HU 14] HU X., TANG J., LIU H. "Online social spammer detection", *AAAI Conference on Artificial Intelligence*, Quebec, Canada, July 27–31, 2014.

[HU 17] HU Y., SONG R.J., CHEN M., "Modeling for Information Diffusion in Online Social Networks via Hydrodynamics", *IEEE Access*, vol. 5, pp. 128–135, 2017.

[JIN 13] JIN F., DOUGHERTY E., SARAF P. *et al.*, "Epidemiological modeling of news and rumors on Twitter", *Proceedings of the 7th Workshop on Social Network Mining and Analysis*, ACM, Chicago, USA, 2013.

[JUR 99] JURAN J., GODFREY A.B., *Juran's Quality Handbook*, McGraw-Hill, New York, 1999.

[KEM 15] KEMPE D., KLEINBERG J., TARDOS E., "Maximizing the spread of influence through a social network", *Theory of Computing*, vol. 11, no. 4, pp. 105–147, 2015.

[KWO 13] KWON S., CHA M., JUNG K. *et al.*, "Prominent features of rumor propagation in online social media", *IEEE 13th International Conference on Data Mining (ICDM)*, IEEE, Dallas, USA, 2013.

[LEE 10] LEE K., CAVERLEE J., WEBB S., "Uncovering social spammers: social honeypots + machine learning", *Proceedings of the 33rd International ACM SIGIR Conference on Research and Development in Information Retrieval*, ACM, New York, 2010.

[LI 12] LI C., SUN A., DATTA A., "Twevent: segment-based event detection from Tweets", *Proceedings of the 21st ACM International Conference on Information and Knowledge Management*, ACM, New York, 2012.

[MAN 08] MANNING C.D., RAGHAVAN P., SCHÜTZE H., *Introduction to Information Retrieval*, Cambridge University Press, New York, 2008.

[MAR 13] MARTINEZ-ROMO J., ARAUJO L., "Detecting malicious tweets in trending topics using a statistical analysis of language", *Expert Systems with Applications*, vol. 40, no. 8, pp. 2992–3000, 2013.

[MCC 11] MCCORD M., CHUAH M., "Spam detection on twitter using traditional classifiers", *Proceedings of the 8th International Conference on Autonomic and Trusted Computing*, Banff, Canada, 2011.

[MED 16] MEDA C., RAGUSA E., GIANOGLIO C. *et al.*, "Spam detection of Twitter traffic: a framework based on random forests and non-uniform feature sampling", *2016 IEEE/ACM International Conference on Advances in Social Networks Analysis and Mining (ASONAM)*, San Francisco, USA, 2016.

[NUR 13] NURWIDYANTORO A., WINARKO E., "Event detection in social media: a survey", *2013 International Conference on ICT for Smart Society (ICISS)*, Jakarta, Indonesia, 2013.

[OSB 12] OSBORNE M., PETROVIĆ S., MCCREADIE R. *et al.*, "Bieber no more: first story detection using Twitter and wikipedia", *SIGIR 2012 Workshop on Time-aware Information Access*, Portland, USA, 2012.

[PET 10] PETROVIĆ S., OSBORNE M., LAVRENKO V., "Streaming first story detection with application to Twitter", *Human Language Technologies: The 2010 Annual Conference of the North American Chapter of the Association for Computational Linguistics*, Stroudsburg, USA, 2010.

[SAK 10] SAKAKI T., OKAZAKI M., MATSUO Y., "Earthquake shakes twitter users: real-time event detection by social sensors", *Proceedings of the 19th International Conference on World Wide Web*, New York, USA, 2010.

[SAY 09] SAYYADI H., HURST M., MAYKOV A., "Event detection and tracking in social streams", *Proceedings of the International Conference on Weblogs and Social Media (ICWSM 2009)*, San Jose, USA, 2009.

[STR 10] STRINGHINI G., KRUEGEL C., VIGNA G., "Detecting spammers on social networks", *Proceedings of the 26th Annual Computer Security Applications Conference*, New York, USA, 2010.

[TAN 16] TAN Z., NING J., LIU Y. *et al.*, "ECRModel: an elastic collision-based rumor-propagation model in online social networks", *IEEE Access*, vol. 4, pp. 6105–6120, 2016.

[TWI 16] TWITTER, The twitter rules, https://support.twitter.com/articles/18311#, 2016.

[WAN 96] WAND Y., WANG R.Y., "Anchoring data quality dimensions in ontological foundations", *Communications of the ACM*, vol. 39, no. 11, pp. 86–95, 1996.

[WAN 10] WANG A.H., "Don't follow me: spam detection in Twitter", *Proceedings of the 2010 International Conference on Security and Cryptography (SECRYPT)*, Athens, Greece, 2010.

[WAN 15] WANG D., PU C., "BEAN: a BEhavior ANalysis approach of URL spam filtering in Twitter", *2015 IEEE International Conference on Information Reuse and Integration (IRI)*, New York, USA, 2015.

[WAS 16] WASHHA M., QAROUSH A., SÈDES F., "Leveraging time for spammers detection on Twitter", *Proceedings of the 8th International Conference on Management of Digital EcoSystems*, Hendaye, France, 2016.

[WU 17] WU T., LIU S., ZHANG J., XIANG Y., "Twitter spam detection based on deep learning", *Proceedings of the Australasian Computer Science Week Multiconference*, Geelong, Australia, 2017.

[YAN 11] YANG C., HARKREADER R.C., GU G., "Die free or live hard? Empirical evaluation and new design for fighting evolving twitter spammers", *Proceedings of the 14th International Conference on Recent Advances in Intrusion Detection*, Berlin, Germany, 2011.

[YAN 12] YANG C., HARKREADER R., ZHANG J. *et al.*, "Analyzing spammers' social networks for fun and profit: a case study of cyber criminal ecosystem on Twitter", *Proceedings of the 21st International Conference on World Wide Web*, New York, USA, 2012.

[ZHA 15a] ZHANG Q., ZHANG S., DONG J. *et al.*, "Automatic detection of rumor on social network", in LI J., JI H., ZHAO D., FENG Y. (eds), *Natural Language Processing and Chinese Computing*, Cham, 2015.

[ZHA 15b] ZHAO Z., RESNICK P., MEI Q., "Enquiring minds: early detection of rumors in social media from enquiry posts", *Proceedings of the 24th International Conference on World Wide Web*, Florence, Italy, 2015.

[ZHO 17] ZHOU Y., KIM D.W., ZHANG J. *et al.*, "Proguard: detecting malicious accounts in social-network-based online promotions", *IEEE Access*, vol. 5, pp. 1990–1999, 2017.

[ZUB 15] ZUBIAGA A., LIAKATA M., PROCTER R. *et al.*, "Towards detecting rumours in social media", *Artificial Intelligence for Cities, Papers from the 2015 AAAI Workshop*, Austin, USA, January 25, 2015.

9

How Can Computer Tools Improve Early Warnings for Wildlife Diseases?

9.1. Introduction

In a world where biodiversity and societal concerns are increasingly being recognized within a unified framework, monitoring the diseases that circulate in wildlife presents two main interests. First, it allows the detection of pathogenic effects (i.e. morbidity and lethality) on wildlife population dynamics and to better understand their role in the decline of endangered species. Second, since pathogens can be transmitted from wildlife to domestic animals and humans, wildlife disease surveillance ideally allows the reduction of subsequent social, economic and ecological impacts. For these promising perspectives to come true, the detection of epidemiological events in wildlife needs to be performed as early and as specifically as possible. In this perspective, the SAGIR (literally *"Surveiller pour Agir"* – "Survey to Act") network was implemented in 1986 in France as a tool to survey wildlife diseases (see Figure 9.1). The main objectives of the SAGIR network are (1) to perform the early detection of emerging diseases in wildlife and (2) to describe the epidemiological and clinical effects of emerging pathogens in wildlife.

Chapter written by Pierpaolo BRENA, Dominique GAUTHIER, Antoine HUMEAU, Florence BAURIER, Frédéric DEJ, Karin LEMBERGER, Jean-Yves CHOLLET and Anouk DECORS.

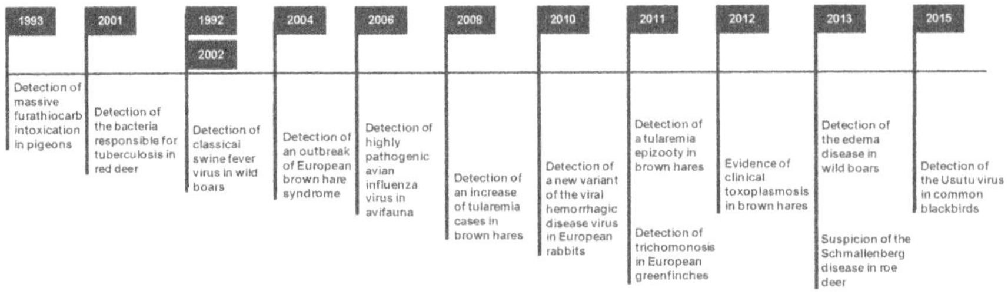

1993	2001	1992 / 2002	2004	2006	2008	2010	2011	2012	2013	2015
Detection of massive furathiocarb intoxication in pigeons	Detection of the bacteria responsible for tuberculosis in red deer	Detection of classical swine fever virus in wild boars	Detection of an outbreak of European brown hare syndrome	Detection of highly pathogenic avian influenza virus in avifauna	Detection of an increase of tularemia cases in brown hares	Detection of a new variant of the viral hemorrhagic disease virus in European rabbits	Detection of a tularemia epizooty in brown hares / Detection of trichomonosis in European greenfinches	Evidence of clinical toxoplasmosis in brown hares	Detection of the edema disease in wild boars / Suspicion of the Schmallenberg disease in roe deer	Detection of the Usutu virus in common blackbirds

Figure 9.1. *Epidemiological events detected in wildlife by the SAGIR network*

This chapter aims at illustrating the contribution of computer tools to enhance the early warning of wildlife diseases by a surveillance network composed of people and organizations operating at a national scale. First, it describes the current functioning of the SAGIR network and presents the aspects of wildlife disease surveillance that are critical to ensure the early detection of epidemiological events. We discuss the bias in the detection of such events that are incumbent on environmental factors, the human and technological resources involved and the structure of data used in the process. Then, this chapter presents the contribution of the Epifaune database and computing interface to optimize the real-time production and management of data by providing a unified data structure and standardized terminology. Finally, there will be a description of the statistical tools that are currently being investigated to enhance the sensitivity and the specificity of automated alarms for the detection of both disease outbreaks and spatiotemporal disease clusters.

9.2. Functioning of the SAGIR network

This first section describes the operational functioning of the SAGIR network as well as its guiding principles. It also highlights the main limits of the current approaches that are to be compensated by the computer tools described in the following sections.

9.2.1. *Human resources*

The SAGIR network is based on human and technical resources that involve about 190 local field correspondents from the French Hunting and Wildlife Agency (*Office National de la Chasse et de la Faune Sauvage*

(ONCFS)) and national and local Hunting Federations (*Fédérations Nationales/Départementales des Chasseurs* (FNC/FDC)). It also involves over 70 veterinary laboratories spread throughout the French metropolitan and overseas territories.

9.2.2. Generalist event-based surveillance

To achieve its objectives, the SAGIR network performs generalist event-based surveillance, namely a continuous monitoring protocol that rests on the opportunistic detection and analysis of morbidity/mortality events in wild terrestrial mammals and birds, with a main focus on game species. The identification of a pathogen by the SAGIR network is based on a diagnostic process rather than on exhaustive screening, and draws on a wide range of disciplines (e.g. anatomical pathology, microbiology, toxicology and ecology). Such an exploratory approach permits a variety of investigations such as (1) the inventory of frequent wildlife diseases, (2) the detection of emerging wildlife diseases and the monitoring of their spatiotemporal expansion, as well as (3) the characterization of the clinical and epidemiological features of a given pathogen.

9.2.3. Watching early indicators of epidemiological events

When investigating wildlife diseases, the definitive identification of the causative agent(s) can be time-consuming. In fact, the characterization of wildlife pathogens is often undermined by several factors including the alteration of carcasses, the combined action of several pathogens and the general lack of reference data for wildlife species. For management measures to be triggered as early as possible, the surveillance of wildlife diseases must therefore rely on the early indicators of potential epidemiological events.

In order to successfully detect the early stages of an epidemiological event, the SAGIR network combines generalist event-based surveillance with syndromic surveillance, namely the continuous monitoring of indicators that are not specific to a given disease but allow the rapid signaling and confirmation of epidemiological events.

9.2.3.1. *Rapid signaling*

The earliest indicator of a health problem in a given population is the increase in mortality or morbidity occurrences. Although such an indicator is not specific to a given disease, it can incite field correspondents to draw on their local knowledge, identify an abnormal situation and trigger an alarm (see Box 9.1 for the case of the 2013 Edema disease outbreak in wild boars), which is then verified and confirmed by an epidemiologist. Following this, local field correspondents collect carcasses of suspicious cases (i.e. cases that may be affected by the emerging health problem) and send them to the nearest veterinary laboratory for necropsy and complementary exams. Alternatively, when unusual clinical signs are identified in animals that are either viable or not transportable, observations can be captured on audio-visual material and forwarded to a committee of wildlife pathologists in order to produce a diagnosis [DEC 15].

Field data are critical for the characterization of the ongoing health problem. First, the age and physiological state of sampled animals and the reported clinical signs can be compared across suspicious cases. This information enables one to determine if reported cases are affected by a common health problem, which will be later confirmed by necropsy reports, and to identify the acute nature of the latter. Then, the spatial and temporal spread of suspicious cases and the variety of affected species provide additional information about the causative agent of the pathological process (i.e. whether it is infectious, traumatic of toxicological).

Context

In the first two weeks of July 2013, 12 dead and sick boars (*Sus scrofa scrofa*) were reported in the Ardèche department in south-central France, 10 of which were located in the town of Vals-les-bains. Four individuals showed neural disorders, namely shivers and convulsions. In the years 2002–2012, only seven cases were reported per year on average for the whole department. The unusually high number of cases led the local field correspondents of the SAGIR network to trigger an alarm (see Figure 9.2). The early warning of putative epidemiological events in this species is critical since wild boars can carry diseases of major concern for public health and the economy of the farming sector, including but not limited to brucellosis, tuberculosis, classical swine fever and Aujeszky's disease. Moreover, the transmission of pathogens from wild boars to domestic pigs of the same species (*Sus scrofa*) is highly probable given the sharp rise of wild boar populations [MAS 15] and the expansion of open-air pig farming [HAR 10]. Neural disorders were observed in young boars and were compatible with regulated sanitary hazards, as defined in France under *Arrêté* (decree) on July 29, 2013 and the JORF no. 0187 on August 3, 2013. In addition, wild boars are hunted for human consumption and can transmit pathogens to humans. Reinforced event-based surveillance was therefore triggered in order to confirm the outbreak of a common health problem and to identify its underlying causes.

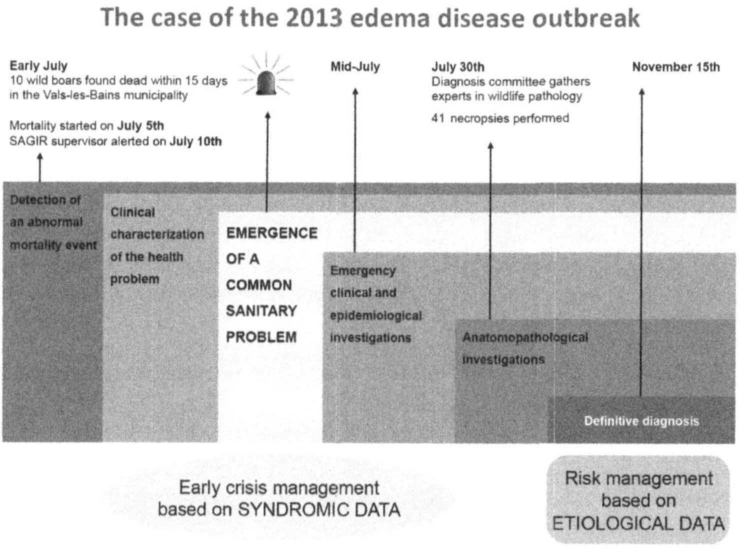

The case of the 2013 edema disease outbreak

Figure 9.2. *Sequence of main steps in the management of the 2013 edema disease outbreak in wild boars. For a color version of the figure, see www.iste.co.uk/sedes/information.zip*

Here, we present the steps of the SAGIR procedure, as well as the related data needs, from the surveillance to the management of the 2013 edema disease outbreak in wild boars.

Step 1: Identifying the emergence of an undetermined sanitary problem

Signals of abnormally high mortality in wildlife are sufficient to trigger an alarm. This alarm must then be confirmed by an epidemiologist and converted into an alert. The emergence of an undetermined common health problem can be stated when individuals of similar characteristics (e.g. age) show communal clinical and gross pathological features. Field and necropsy data are critical for characterizing the ongoing health problem. Each new case is a new source of information and has to be rapidly analyzed to provide as comprehensive a vision as possible.

For each case reported in this example, technicians from the local hunting federation (*Fédération des Chasseurs de l'Ardèche*) and the ONCFS used a standardized questionnaire to gather information about the exact geographic localization and the date of the event, the type of habitat, an estimation of the body mass of the sick/dead animal, the description of clinical signs and every other clue available on-site.

The median body mass calculated from reported cases was 20 kg (minimum 5 kg and maximum 90 kg). Given previous data on body weight gain for this species in various habitats (e.g. Markina *et al.*, [MAR 04]), reported dead individuals were aged less than 6 months. This age class corresponds to the weaning period in boars. The high proportion of juveniles in the sampled cases has to be considered with care, since it might arise either from a higher sensitivity of young individuals to the sanitary problem or from the actual demographic structure of the whole population. Indeed, the high hunting pressure in the Ardèche area suggests a rapid renewal of the wild boar population, and hence a high proportion of juveniles [SER 11]. A third of reported cases were observed alive. Seven individuals were either observed close to a water point or showed lesions that evoked a long stay in the water. Moreover, individuals that were captured alive did take the water they were given. These elements suggest that sick animals were actively searching for water. Out of the 17 animals for which their body condition was described, 77% were in good physiological shape. Three clinical pictures could be retained from the observations made by field correspondents:

1) convulsions/trembling either directly observed in live animals or deduced from marks on the ground surrounding the carcass;

2) ataxia (i.e. lack of voluntary coordination of muscle movements);

3) behavioral disorders (i.e. individuals show neither flight nor defense responses to approaching humans).

Forty-one carcasses were submitted for postmortem examinations. Complete histological examinations were performed on eight fresh carcasses. The most significant and recurrent lesions were composed of marked perivascular edema, occasional perineuronal vacuolation and rare evidence of endothelial swelling and degeneration.

Based on the necropsies and the available clinical, epidemiological and bacteriological data, the diagnostic procedure aimed at excluding the most probable causes for the reported events. Specific toxicological investigations were implemented to search toxic substances responsible for convulsions. In parallel, virus and antibody screenings were performed to identify pathogens responsible for (1) hemorrhagic syndromes, such as the classical or African swine fever virus, (2) nervous disorders, such as Aujeszky's disease virus or (3) digestive disorders, such as the Teschen disease virus. These investigations did not confirm the presence of such causative agents. Veterinarians from the SAGIR network analyzed this information and concluded with an undetermined common health problem.

Step 2: Defining a suspect case

A local management committee was set up to organize public communications and to manage potential sanitary concerns. After the emergence of a common health problem was confirmed, the next step consisted of defining the characteristics of a suspect case on the basis of field and laboratory observations. This definition is essential both to follow the space–time evolution of the ongoing morbid process and for early crisis management.

Epidemiological, clinical, lesional and bacteriological criteria contributed to define suspicious mortality events as follows:

– two wild boars dead within a 3-week time window in the same municipality;

– evidence of convulsions, ataxia or trembling;

– edema or effusion and/or lymph node necrosis and/or neuronal and/or hemorrhagic colitis.

Step 3: Mapping the risk and following its space–time evolution in near real-time

Risk assessment relies on etiological diagnoses. However, no pathogen could be identified during the first 4 months of the epizooty. Syndromic surveillance and diagnoses of exclusion were therefore essential tools of early management crisis.

Moreover, it was impossible to estimate even the qualitative risk of contamination for humans or livestock. The most significant diseases for farmed animals were excluded from the analysis. Still, the management committee had to consider a potential risk of transmission of the undetermined disease to humans. It was therefore decided to act on the danger exposure of at-risk human populations, instead of than on the danger itself (i.e. sanitation of the boar population). Given the apparent low spatial progression of suspicious cases and the supposedly low contagiousness of the disease, risk management rested upon the spatial mapping of the sanitary risk that was derived from the geolocalization of reported cases. The consumption of venison was banned in 29 municipalities in Ardèche, with a continuous revaluation of measures as new scientific data became available.

The temporal dynamics of cases were also useful to make progress in the diagnosis. The temporal dynamics of reported events hinted toward a causative agent that is common to all cases and that is persistent in the environment. However, this epidemiological pattern must be considered with caution since it depends both on the actual disease dynamics and on the dynamics of carcass discovery. In order to control the discovery bias, the approximate date of death was estimated for each carcass. The spatial distribution of events highlighted two distinct hotspots centered on Vals-les-Bains ($n = 28$ events) and Saint-Sauveur de Montagut ($n = 8$) and no specific spatial spread. This particular step in the SAGIR procedure would be significantly optimized with the use of automated tools that allow to monitor the spatiotemporal dynamics of suspicious cases.

After a persistent causative agent was suspected, following analyses focused on toxins that are produced by germs such as *Escherichia coli*. Such pathogens can persist in the environment and have been previously identified in domestic swine, but never in wild boars. They can be responsible for the so-called edema disease, which features clinical signs similar to those observed in the reported cases.

Step 4: Definitive etiological diagnosis and risk management

As previously mentioned, the evaluation of the sanitary risk is based on etiological diagnoses. Therefore, the last step in the diagnostic process was to confirm the presence of *E. coli* in the fresh (< 24-h) carcasses available. Similar to the routine diagnosis process in pig farming, bacteriological and histological investigations were combined on mesenteric lymph nodes. Bacteriological cultures on lymph node samples and digestive content did reveal the presence of *E. coli* and confirm the hypothesis for edema disease.

To our knowledge, this is the first detection of edema disease in free-ranging wild boars. The edema disease was first described by Shanks [SHA 38] in intensive pig farming and it is now re-emerging. Shiga-toxin-producing *E. coli* (STEC) colonize the small intestine and produce verotoxin that damages small arteries and arterioles. This ultimately causes edema, sudden deaths and occasional neurologic signs in pigs due to the swelling of the brain. The ban on venison consumption was ended after the definite diagnosis of edema disease, since both *E. coli* and the verotoxin are eliminated by cooking.

Conclusion

In the case of the edema disease outbreak in wild boars, 5 months were necessary to establish a definitive diagnosis. This delay is both long – given the pressing expectations from the local population – and short – given the absence of data on the disease in wild boars. Dealing with an undetermined sanitary problem and its related concerns requires tools for the real-time management and analysis of data. Computer tools offer the opportunity to be more reactive, efficient and reliable in the analysis of data. Here, for instance, the automated centralization of data would have helped the crisis committee to monitor the situation at standardized time steps.

Box 9.1. *The case of the 2013 edema disease outbreak in wild boars (according to Decors et al. [DEC 15a])*

9.2.3.2. *Rapid confirmation*

By allowing the comparison of lesions across sampled carcasses, necropsy constitutes an additional step toward the rapid confirmation of a common health problem. At this stage, it is possible to document the emergence of a common disease, to refine hypotheses about the ongoing pathological process and to identify potential sanitary concerns.

More importantly, necropsy data are fundamental to establish the clinical and lesion features of suspicious cases. A clear definition of suspicious cases is necessary to guide following sampling efforts and monitor the spatial and temporal spread of the emerging disease. However, pathogens can feature lesions that are highly polymorphic. This can hinder efforts to characterize common rules for the definition of suspicious cases, before the definitive identification of pathogens is confirmed in the sampled carcasses (i.e. etiological diagnosis).

9.2.4. Limits of current approaches

9.2.4.1. Detection bias

The discovery of wildlife carcasses is highly variable in time and space since it is subject to a number of factors including search protocols [WAR 06], the spatial density of carcasses [MIN 88], the phenotype of wildlife species (e.g. size and color) and habitat type [MÖR 02]. It is also dependent of the persistence of carcasses in an open environment (see, for example, Ward *et al.* [WAR 06]) where they are exposed to both scavengers and altering meteorological conditions.

Moreover, generalist event-based surveillance is not standardized and depends on observation efforts that can vary through time and space. The number of observers and the time they spend surveying wildlife in the field is neither quantified nor homogenous across time and geographic areas.

Finally, the eligibility of a given case to be reported and enter the SAGIR process is determined by the observer themself and depends on a number of factors, including the level of interest for the reported species and the observer's awareness of the SAGIR network.

As a result, it is hard to determine whether the observed fluctuations of indicators used in syndromic surveillance result from actual disease emergences, from changes in observation efforts across geographic areas or from changes in the target population that are independent from any disease effect. Local variations in mortality rates can still be interpreted as an indicator of epidemiological events.

9.2.4.2. Sensitivity of human-induced alarms

Local field correspondents are the first members of the SAGIR network to analyze mortality/morbidity events. Although local knowledge is a valuable asset to interpret a rise in mortality/morbidity within a specific area and/or a given time period, perception bias can hinder the detection of epidemiological events of a great spatial and/or temporal spread. In other words, the relevance of mortality events may be diminished to observers at the local scale, although such events can be part of an actual epidemiological event happening at a greater spatial scale.

9.2.4.3. Heterogeneous terminology

Once abnormal mortality/morbidity events are identified, necropsy data are gathered to characterize the clinical features of a putative common health problem among suspicious cases. However, the terms used to describe necropsy data until 2013 are highly heterogeneous, thus preventing the rapid comparison of suspicious cases.

To compensate these limits and optimize the rapid detection of epidemiological events in wildlife, the SAGIR network implemented several tools and procedures that are described in the following sections of this chapter.

9.3. The Epifaune database and computing interface

This section develops the contribution of the Epifaune database and interface to enhance the collection and management of data within the functioning of the SAGIR network.

9.3.1. Accessible tools

Members of the SAGIR network ought to benefit from technical tools that are highly accessible to collect and share data. With the view to enhance data centralization, the ONCFS implemented the Epifaune database under the Microsoft® SQL Server. The dedicated Epifaune computing interface allows members of wildlife surveillance networks to input, edit, validate, browse, analyze, extract and share wildlife health data (Table 9.1). Local field correspondents input descriptive data about the mortality event. Veterinary laboratories supply data including (1) the main observed lesions, (2) the results of complementary analyses', and (3) a conclusion associated with a confidence level. Printed necropsy reports are made available to local field correspondents and are scanned and attached to the dematerialized data to ensure that complete cases are archived. The Epifaune database was brought into operation in January 2016 and is currently being supplied with retrospective data from years 2014–2015.

Field data	Syndromic data	Etiologic data
Date and location - Species - Circumstances - External clinical signs - Individual parameters (age, sex, physiological condition)	Summary of four to five major lesions contributing to the ongoing pathological process	- Results of complementary investigations - Global medical interpretation

Table 9.1. *Data content of the Epifaune database*

9.3.2. *Fast data centralization*

The dematerialization of data enables the SAGIR network to be more responsive. Furthermore, connected tools to collect data appear essential to optimize rapid data centralization and enable "real-time" data exploitation. Fast data sharing is an asset to notify suspicious cases, to follow the spatial and temporal spread of mortality/morbidity events and to enable prompt management procedures if an epidemiological event is confirmed. In 2010, the median period between event discovery and data centralization was 25 days. This delay might stem from the requirement to access the Epifaune database through a PC. The Epifaune computing interface was first accessible through a web browser and is now available as a self-standing application. Future development efforts will be directed toward the conception of a mobile application that can be used by members of the SAGIR network to input and share wildlife health data at any time and from anywhere, directly from their mobile phones.

9.3.3. *Standardized procedures and terminology*

The standardization of collected data is a fundamental prerequisite for the rapid analysis and comparison of suspicious cases. The SAGIR network implemented the use of printed data forms as a first step toward standardized data collection on the field. More recently, the SAGIR network established a list of standardized terminology for veterinary laboratories to produce homogeneous and comparable necropsy data that can be used in epidemiological statistics. A multidisciplinary working group, led by the ONCFS and the French Association of Veterinary Laboratory Executives (*Association française des Directeurs et cadres de Laboratoires Vétérinaires publics d'Analyses* (ADILVA)) elaborated a reference document that contains standardized medical terms to describe disease history, lesions, organs, pathogens, methods and measurements. Such standardized terms are to be input in the Epifaune database through drop-down boxes to ensure maximal compliance to the standardized terminology and to avoid multiple denominations for the same content.

9.3.4. *Data reliability*

Direct data input from local field correspondents and laboratory executives prevents interpretation or transcription mistakes from third parties. As previously mentioned, the Epifaune computing interface is configured with pre-established terms that are identical for all members of the SAGIR network, thus limiting interpretation bias. Moreover, the Epifaune computing interface enables users to attach media (i.e. pictures of a lesion) in order to verify and confirm input data. The core idea is to benefit from factual data devoid of any interpretation that can be analyzed in retrospect, for instance to shed new light on unresolved cases.

9.3.5. *Shareable and interoperable data*

Although data are centralized by a national authority, it must be made available to collaborating entities and members of the SAGIR network to permit the actual networking of wildlife health surveillance. More specifically, in order to optimize the interoperability between the SAGIR database and other French wildlife surveillance networks, the structure of necropsy data was modified to match the following standardized pattern:

Organ/Analyte/Method,

where "Organ" refers to the type (e.g. blood, liver, etc.) that is being analyzed; "Analyte" is defined as a physical, chemical or biological entity that constitutes the lesion/pathogen of interest; and "Method" refers to the analytical procedure that is performed to investigate a given analyte in a given organ.

Moreover, Laboratory Information Management System (LIMS) editors are currently addressing the Electronic Data Interchange (EDI) between the Epifaune database and particular laboratory databases (see Figure 9.3).

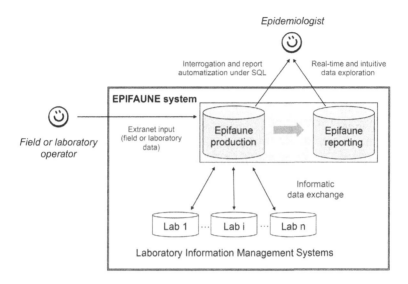

Figure 9.3. *Structure of the Epifaune information system*

While real-time data management constitutes a first step toward the main objectives of the SAGIR network, near real-time analysis remains of paramount importance to detect abnormal signs of mortality/morbidity. With this view, automated alarm detection algorithms are being developed to further enhance the effectiveness of the SAGIR network and optimize the sensitivity and specificity of alarms.

9.4. Automated alarm detection

Today, the alerts for an abnormal increase in mortality events (i.e. the earliest indicator of an epizootic disease) mainly come from field correspondents. In order to supplement the expertise of field correspondents, statistical methods are tested to automatically and regularly detect abnormal mortality signals.

9.4.1. *General principles*

Algorithms allowing the detection of epizooties are studied, in particular, for the detection of:

1) outbreaks (i.e. sharp increases of the total number of events at the national scale), which requires a temporal approach;

2) spatiotemporal clusters (i.e. sudden and located onsets of mortality events), which requires a spatiotemporal approach.

The preconditions for detecting an abnormal signal of mortality are to define a standard threshold and to choose criteria to identify the overrun of the latter. For each approach (i.e. temporal and spatiotemporal), a reference model draws on historical data to define the expected number of events either at a given time or at a given time and a given location. These models are then calibrated with computer simulations in order to determine the better compromise between specificity and sensitivity.

9.4.2. *Retained methods*

To detect outbreaks (i.e. temporal approach), the cumulative sum (CUSUM [HOH 08]) is retained. This method relies on the cumulated sum over time of a function of the number of mortality events that occurred during each unit of time. It is usually used to monitor small shifts in the process mean and is largely used in industrial quality control. To detect clusters of mortality events, Kulldorff's spatiotemporal scan approach [KUL 01] is used. This approach first searches the size and duration of the most likely cluster of ongoing events, and then tests for the significance of this cluster.

To our knowledge, such automatic tools are not yet used for early warning toward wildlife diseases and could substantially improve the sensibility of event-based surveillance, in particular for morbid phenomena that are dispersed in time and space. These approaches are still under investigation, but their forthcoming implementation is expected to improve the speed of detection of abnormal mortality events.

9.5. Conclusion

Since 1986, the SAGIR network has been continuously monitoring indicators that hint emerging epidemiological events in wildlife. Although the traditional functioning of the SAGIR network benefits from national coverage, the local expertise of field correspondents and the contribution of a wide range of disciplines in characterizing wildlife pathogens, some flaws hinder the real-time production, management and analysis of data. Some of these flaws relate to the very nature of the task. To name a few, wildlife diseases are still poorly referenced and environmental factors peculiar to wildlife disease surveillance constitute a great limiting factor for the filling of these knowledge gaps.

Other flaws relate to the information system that was used until now to detect and characterize emerging wildlife diseases. By providing a unique computing interface to all members of the SAGIR network, the Epifaune database aims at enhancing the rapid production and centralization of data that is both reliable and based on standardized structure and terminology.

Moreover, statistical algorithms are currently being developed to enhance the specificity and sensitivity of epidemiological event detection. Their forthcoming implementation might supplement the expertise of local field observers by permitting the analysis of mortality and morbidity events across time and space. These computer tools will hopefully improve the detection of wildlife diseases and allow management measures to be triggered early enough to limit the impact of wildlife pathogens on biodiversity, livestock and humans.

9.6. References

[DEC 15a] DECORS A., RICHOMME C., MORVAN H. *et al.*, "Diagnostiquer un problème de santé dans la faune sauvage : exemple de la maladie de l'œdème chez le sanglier sauvage (Sus scrofa) en Ardèche", *Bulletin épidémiologique santé animale – alimentation*, vol. 69, pp. 2–7, 2015.

[DEC 15b] DECORS A., HARS J., FAURE E. *et al.*, "Le réseau SAGIR : un outil de vigilance vis-à-vis des agents pathogènes exotiques", *Bulletin épidémiologique santé animale – alimentation*, Spécial vigilance vis-à-vis des maladies exotiques, vol. 66, pp. 35–39, 2015.

[HAR 10] HARS J., ROSSI S., "Évaluation des risques sanitaires liés à l'augmentation des effectifs de sangliers en France", *Revue ONCFS : faune sauvage*, vol. 288, pp. 23–28, 2010.

[HOH 08] HOHLE M., PAUL M., "Count data regression charts for the monitoring of surveillance time series", *Computational Statistics and Data Analysis*, vol. 52, pp. 4357–4368, 2008.

[KUL 01] KULLDORFF M., "Prospective time periodic geographical disease surveillance using a scan statistic", *Journal of the Royal Statistical Society: Series A*, vol. 164, no. 1, pp. 61–72, 2001.

[MAR 04] MARKINA F.A., SÁEZ-ROYUELA C., DE GARNICA R., "Physical development of wild boar in the Cantabric mountains, Álava, Northern Spain", *Galemys*, vol. 16, pp. 25–34, 2004.

[MAS 15] MASSEI G., KINDBERG J., LICOPPE A. *et al.*, "Wild boar populations up, numbers of hunters down? A review of trends and implications for Europe", *Pest Management Science*, vol. 71, no. 4, pp. 492–500, 2015.

[MIN 88] MINEAU P., COLLINS B.T., "Avian mortality in agro-ecosystems: methods of detection", in GREAVES M.P., GREIG-SMITH P.W., SMITH B.D. (eds), *Field Methods for the Study of Environmental Effects of Pesticides*, British Crop Protection Council Monograph, Croydon, vol. 40, pp. 13–27, 1988.

[MÖR 02] MÖRNER T., OBENDORF D.L., ARTOIS M. *et al.*, "Surveillance and monitoring of wildlife diseases", *Revue Scientifique et Technique OIE*, vol. 21, no. 1, pp. 67–76, 2002.

[SER 11] SERVANTY S., GAILLARD J-M., RONCHI F. *et al.*, "Influence of harvesting pressure on demographic tactics: implications for wildlife management", *Journal of Applied Ecology*, vol. 48, pp. 835–843, 2011.

[SHA 38] SHANKS P.L., "An unusual condition affecting the digestive organs of the pig", *Veterinary Record*, vol. 50, pp. 356–358, 1938.

[WAR 06] WARD M.R., STALLKNECHT D.E., WILLIS J. *et al.*, "Wild bird mortality and West Nile virus surveillance: biases associated with detection, reporting, and carcass persistence", *Journal of Wildlife Disease*, vol. 42, no. 1, pp. 92–106, 2006.

List of Authors

Tassadit AMGHAR
LERIA
University of Angers (UBL)
France

Maude ARRU
Paris-Dauphine University
PSL Research University
LAMSADE
CNRS UMR 7243
Paris
France

Yannick BARDIE
EDEG-MRM-SI
Montpellier University
France

Florence BAURIER
ADILVA
Laboratoire départemental
d'analyses du Cher
Bourges
France

Alain BOUJU
L3i Laboratory
University of La Rochelle
France

Pierpaolo BRENA
Office national de la chasse et de
la faune sauvage, Direction de la
recherche et de l'expertise
Auffargis
France

Olivier CAMP
ESEO-TECH
Angers
France

Jean-Yves CHOLLET
Office national de la chasse et de
la faune sauvage, Direction de la
recherche et de l'expertise
Auffargis
France

Anouk DECORS
Office national de la chasse et de
la faune sauvage, Direction de la
recherche et de l'expertise
Auffargis
France

Frédéric DEJ
Office national de la chasse et de
la faune sauvage, Direction des
systèmes d'information
Birieux
France

Johnny DOUVINET
UMR ESPACE 7300 CNRS
University of Avignon and the
Vaucluse
France

Dominique GAUTHIER
ADILVA
Laboratoire départemental
vétérinaire et d'hygiène
alimentaire des
Hautes-Alpes
Gap
France

Mathieu GOEMINNE
CETIC
Charleroi
Belgium

Nicolas GUTOWSKI
ESEO-TECH
Angers
and
LERIA
University of Angers (UBL)
France

Slimane HAMMOUDI
ESEO-TECH
Angers
France

Antoine HUMEAU
Office national de la chasse et de
la faune sauvage, Direction de la
recherche et de l'expertise
Auffargis
France

Karin LEMBERGER
Faunapath
Lyon
France

Anne-Marie LESAS
MBDS
University of Nice Sophia-
Antipolis
and
LSIS UMR 7296
Aix-Marseille University
France

Thérèse LIBOUREL
UMR ESPACE-DEV
(UM - IRD - UAG - UR)
Montpellier
France

Annick MAJCHROWSKI
CETIC
Charleroi
Belgium

Jamal MALKI
L3i Laboratory
University of La Rochelle
France

Manel MEZGHANI
IRIT
University of Toulouse
CNRS, INPT, UPS, UT1, UT2J
France

Elsa NEGRE
Paris-Dauphine University
PSL Research University
LAMSADE
CNRS UMR 7243
Paris
France

Christophe PONSARD
CETIC
Charleroi
Belgium

Camille ROSENTHAL-SABROUX
Paris-Dauphine University
PSL Research University
LAMSADE
CNRS UMR 7243
Paris
France

Florence SÈDES
IRIT
University of Toulouse
CNRS, INPT, UPS, UT1, UT2J
France

Mahdi WASHHA
IRIT
University of Toulouse
CNRS, INPT, UPS, UT1, UT2J
France

Index

Printed in the United States
By Bookmasters